house

Rachel Whiteread

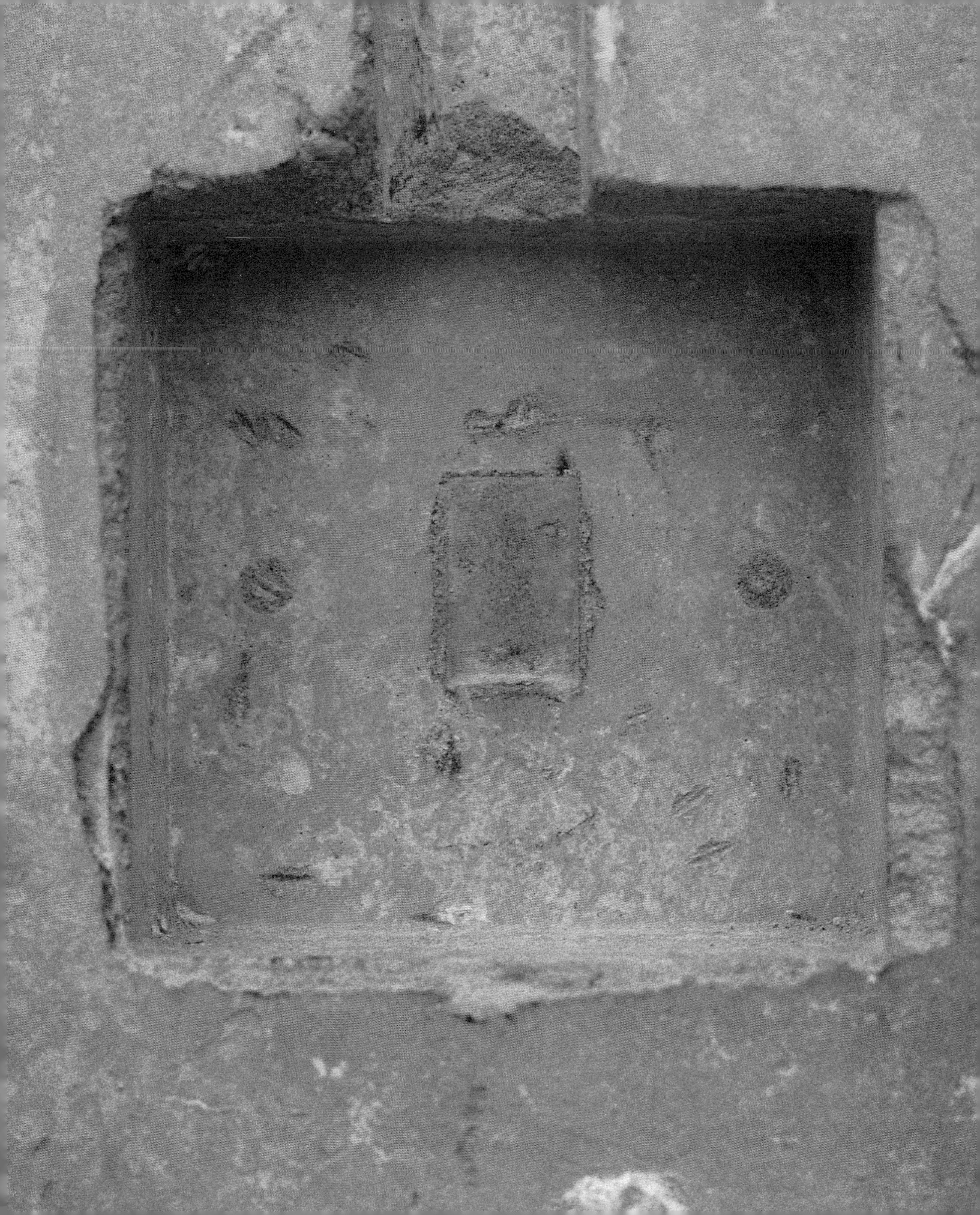

Rachel Whiteread

house

Edited by James Lingwood

Jon Bird ■ Doreen Massey ■ Iain Sinclair ■ Richard Shone ■ Neil Thomas ■ Anthony Vidler ■ Simon Watney

In association with Artangel

Title pages
page 6, Grove Road, August, 1993
page 12-13, Crowds around House, November, 1993
page 34-35, Backview of terrace, Grove Road, 1993
page 50-51, Sophie Dorothea Høyer, death mask, 1809, and marble portrait bust, 1812, Thorvaldsens Museum, Copenhagen
page 62-63, Casting in progress, September 1993
page 96-97, Demolishing House, January, 1994
page 110-111, Graffiti on House, December, 1993
page 126-127, Gunnite spraying, casting in progress, September, 1993

Phaidon Press Limited
Regent's Wharf
All Saints Street
London N1 9PA

First published 1995
Reprinted 2000

ISBN 0 7148 3459 9

A CIP catalogue record for this book is available from the British Library.

Printed in Hong Kong

The development was funded by Rachel Whiteread; Karsten Schubert Gallery, London; Luhring Augustine Gallery, NY; Claire Burrus, Paris; and the Arts Council of England.

Funded by THE ARTS COUNCIL OF ENGLAND

Publisher's Acknowledgements
Thank you to the following for lending reproductions: Artangel, London; AP photos; Bancroft Library, Tower Hamlets, London; Chelsea School of Art Library, London; Hulton Deutsch Collection Limited, London; Jay Jopling, London; Loos-archiv, Albertina; Menil Collection, Houston, Texas; National Portrait Gallery, London; Rijksmuseum, Amsterdam; Saatchi Collection, London; Karsten Schubert, London; Editions d'Art Albert Skira, Geneva; Tate Gallery, London; Thorvaldsens Museum, Copenhagen; Whitchurch Canonicorum, Dorset
Photographers: Marc Atkins, Iain Cochrane, John Davies, D. Grant, Lisa Harty, Lucien Hervé, Sue Ormerod, John Parnell, Barbara Smith, Clare Stent, Bruce Thorndike, Nick Turpin, Stephen White, Karen Whiteread, Rachel Whiteread, Staton Winter, Edward Woodman and Rachel Wyndham

Artist's Acknowledgements
I would like to thank all those who worked so intensively to ensure the successful realization of *House*, and who argued so passionately for it to have a longer life.

From the beginning until the end, and beyond, I have enjoyed the closest collaboration with Artangel and its co-director James Lingwood, with whom I first discussed *House* in 1991. In turn, both of us relied on the tremendous support of everyone at Artangel: Lisa Harty, Melanie Steel and Anna Malyckyj, Co-Director Michael Morris and Chairman Jon Bird as well as Artangel's trustees through that period – Will Alsop, Anne Carlisle, Piers Gough, Nigel Finch, Jeremy King, Sandy Nairne, William Palmer, Phyllida Shaw and Gilane Tawadros. Rachel Wyndham undertook initial research for us in 1992, and Joan Asquith handled press and public relations with considerable calm. Karsten Schubert and Peter Chater of the Karsten Schubert Gallery provided much-needed support throughout.

To turn *House* from a working idea to an actual sculpture, we were indebted to a further large team: to our structural engineers Neil Thomas, Reg Allen and Aran Chadwick of Atelier One who formulated a successful plan of action; to Pat Quarton and Trevor Smart of Tarmac Structural Repairs who supervised and effected the gunnite spraying inside 193 Grove Road and to production manager David Jones; and to all those who laboured on site – Simon Burns, John Guy, Rob King, Michael Landy, Paul Mattocks, Jasone Miranda-Bilbao, Pete, Kevin O'Kane, Val Sutton, David Thomas, Mark Thomas, Matthew Tickle, Tom Wales, Derek Walker and Keith Wilson. The evolution of *House* was carefully documented on video by John Kelly and Helen Silverlock of Hackneyed Productions, and in photographic form by John Davies, Lisa Harty, Susan Ormerod, Stephen White and Edward Woodman.

To obtain permission to make *House*, we needed the support of several councillors of Bow Neighbourhood, notably Giles Gordon, Janet Ludlow and Tricia Webb; many local residents, including Nigel Glendinning, Peter d'Arcy and Joanne Watts, and Jonathan Watkins and Rachel Lichtenstein of the nearby Chisenhale Gallery. We were also grateful for the advice and assistance of Clive Jacotine, Mike Baker, Simon Dunn-Lewin and Bernard Saltmarsh of Tower Hamlets Council.

House was commissioned by Artangel with Beck's, and was further sponsored by Tarmac Structural Repairs. The project received significant support from The Arts Council of Great Britain, London Arts Board and The Henry Moore Foundation as well as Artangel's individual patrons. Whilst the controversy around *House* was at its most vociferous, Channel 4, Beck's, Karsten Schubert and some anonymous donors stepped in to secure the site from Bow Neighbourhood Council for an additional month. We were, and are, extremely grateful to all these individuals and organizations for their support, as well as to Anthony Fawcett and Caroline Hines of Anthony Fawcett Consultants who worked on behalf of Beck's. The sponsorship of Tarmac Structural Repairs was an awards winner under the Business Sponsorship Incentive Scheme, which has subsequently helped us to produce this book.

The concept of this book was developed by James Lingwood and myself during the making and reception of *House*. To commission the writings, and to ensure we had the fullest possible photographic record, we benefited from additional help from The Arts Council of England and the Karsten Schubert Gallery. Again many people helped bring the idea to fruition; Rachel Wyndham, Rachel Inman, and Lucy Reynolds; Iwona Blazwick, commissioning editor for contemporary art at Phaidon and her colleagues Gilda Williams, Clare Stent and Karl Shanahan.

A big thank you to the 5,000 people, including many local school children, who petitioned Bow Council, as well as everyone who visited, debated, enthused and wrote about *House*; to Michael Jopling MP, Hugh Bayley MP and Mildred Gordon, MP for Tower Hamlets, who tabled the early day motion in the House of Commons. And finally a special thank you to my family and friends, and to Marcus Taylor, who supported me throughout the gestation, realization and demolition of *House*.

Rachel Whiteread
February 1995

James Lingwood

introduction

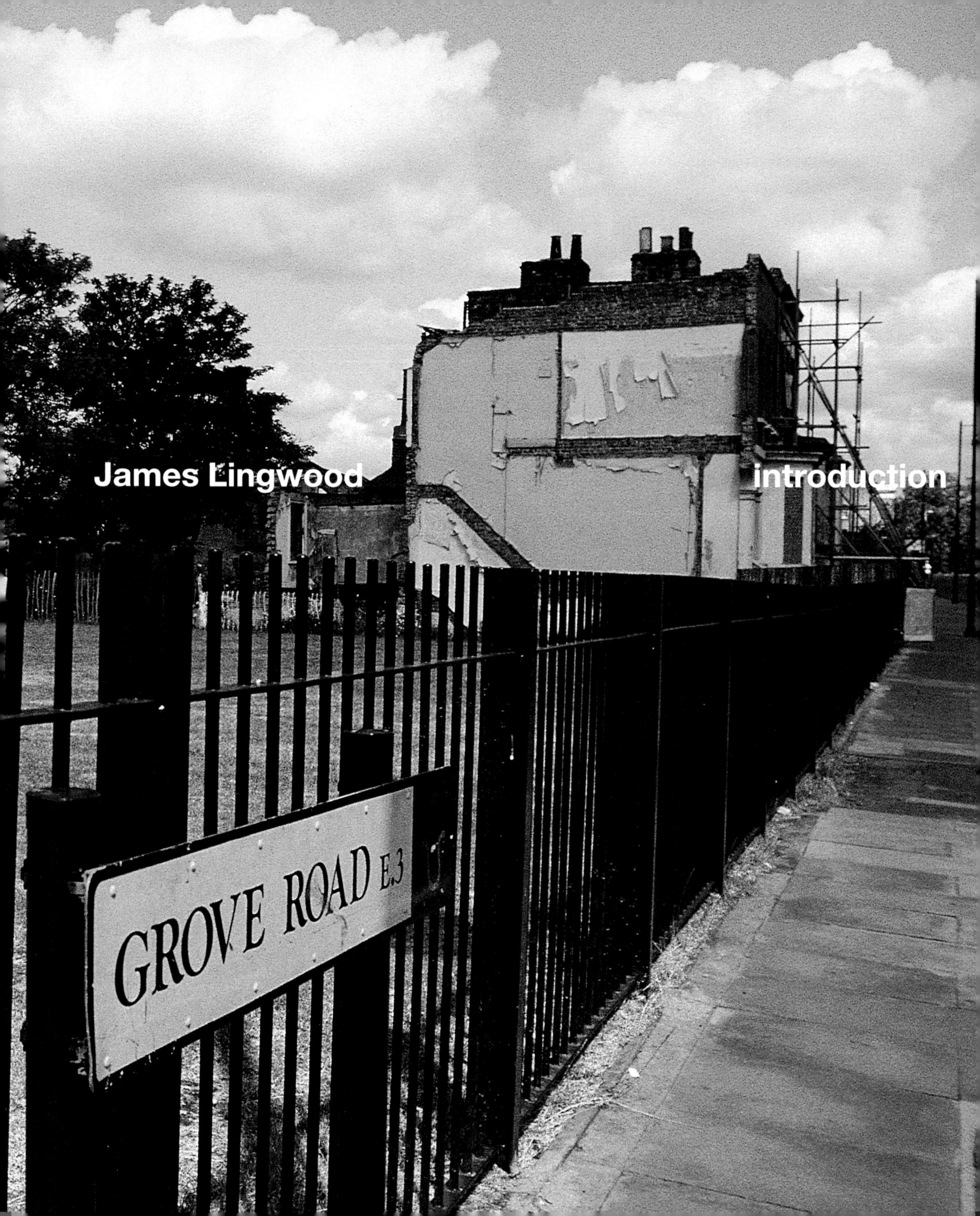

It began, an idea without a name, in the quiet of Rachel Whiteread's studio in East London. And it ended several years later, a sculpture called *House*, demolished in the full glare of the world's media. *House* always had the potential to be a contentious work of art. But in my first conversations with Rachel Whiteread in the summer of 1991, it was impossible to imagine that it would be quite as exposed, quite as contentious as things turned out; and that its transition from private projection to public phenomenon would be so dramatic and so quick.

House could have been made elsewhere, in a different place, at a different time; perhaps with another cast list and chorus. Indeed, Whiteread and I had looked at several other terraced houses in North and East London through 1992 without success. At one stage, a condemned house in Islington seemed possible, but the right permissions failed to materialize. Another in Hackney was knocked down before we could make a proposal to the owner. Finally, after months of private persuasion and occasional public meetings, the councillors of Bow Neighbourhood voted by a small majority to give a temporary lease on 193 Grove Road, one of the few remaining houses in what had once been a Victorian terrace. After several months' more waiting, Whiteread took possession and the physical making of the work began in August 1993. From that moment, *House* was of a specific place and a particular time. And it was this configuration of time and place, with its attendant contingencies of local and national politics and the added spice of the 1993 Turner Prize which, as much as the physical appearance of the sculpture, created the meaning of *House* and determined the course of its short life.

House was completed on October 25 1993. There had deliberately been almost no press until one day before. Slowly at first and then more quickly, interest and comment began to grow in the locality and beyond; in the pages of the national press and on television news. Newspaper leaders and letters, columns and cartoons appeared and multiplied. Visitors grew day by day. On November 23 two decisions were made simultaneously in different parts of London. A group of jurors at the Tate Gallery decided that Whiteread had won the 1993 Turner Prize, and a gathering of Bow Neighbourhood Councillors voted that *House* should be demolished with immediate effect. It was an incendiary combination.

From that moment, the debate which swirled around *House* became increasingly adversarial; in the press, on television and, in a more good-

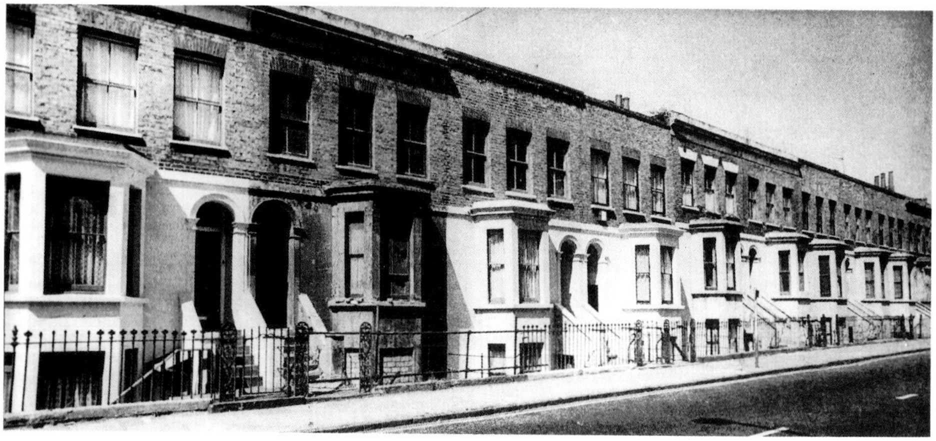

1

1 Grove Road, 1983

humoured way, in front of the sculpture itself. Seasoned campaigners dusted down familiar battle formations from past controversies such as the Tate Gallery's acquisition of Carl Andre's infamous 'bricks'; or, for those few who cared to add an international dimension, the notorious case of Richard Serra's *Tilted Arc*. Others invoked the English taste for iconoclasm which had generated campaigns against public sculptures by Jacob Epstein and Eric Gill earlier in the century. But perhaps the most salient and certainly the most encouraging aspect of the controversy around *House* was the way in which it exposed the inadequacies of these old charts to describe the complexities and the particular contours of this controversy. Local against national, the art world against the real world, grass roots realities against disconnected dilettantes... Such binary oppositions could neither explain nor contain the multiple shades of opinion and sentiment which *House* engendered.

There were passionately different responses, of course. But the differences of opinion were always located *within* any identifiable community or constituency, and not *between* them. There was no consensus amongst the inhabitants of the block of houses opposite, on the street or in the neighbourhood, nor in the letter pages of local and national newspapers. There was no consensus amongst the local councillors. Even the fateful decision not to grant an extension to *House* was taken only on the casting vote of the Chairman after the councillors were equally divided. There was no consensus even within the Gale family whom the Council had moved out of the home which eventually became *House*. *House* did not seek to manufacture some confectionary consensus, as many public works of art are compelled to do. Indeed it laid bare the limits of language and expectation which afflict the contentious arena of public art.

House was literally rooted to its spot, but the meaning of Whiteread' s work was inherently unstable. Unlike the heroic models of triumphal arches and declamatory statues, it was by no means clear what values it sought to promote. It did not seek to predetermine the ways in which people could respond to it. Rather, like notable predecessors of a similarly sombre kind such as Lutyens' Cenotaph in Whitehall, (originally planned as a temporary memorial) or Maya Lin's Vietnam War Memorial in Washington D.C., *House* was both a closed architectural form and an open memorial; at one and the same time hermetic and implacable, but also able to absorb into its body all those individual thoughts, feelings and memories projected onto it.

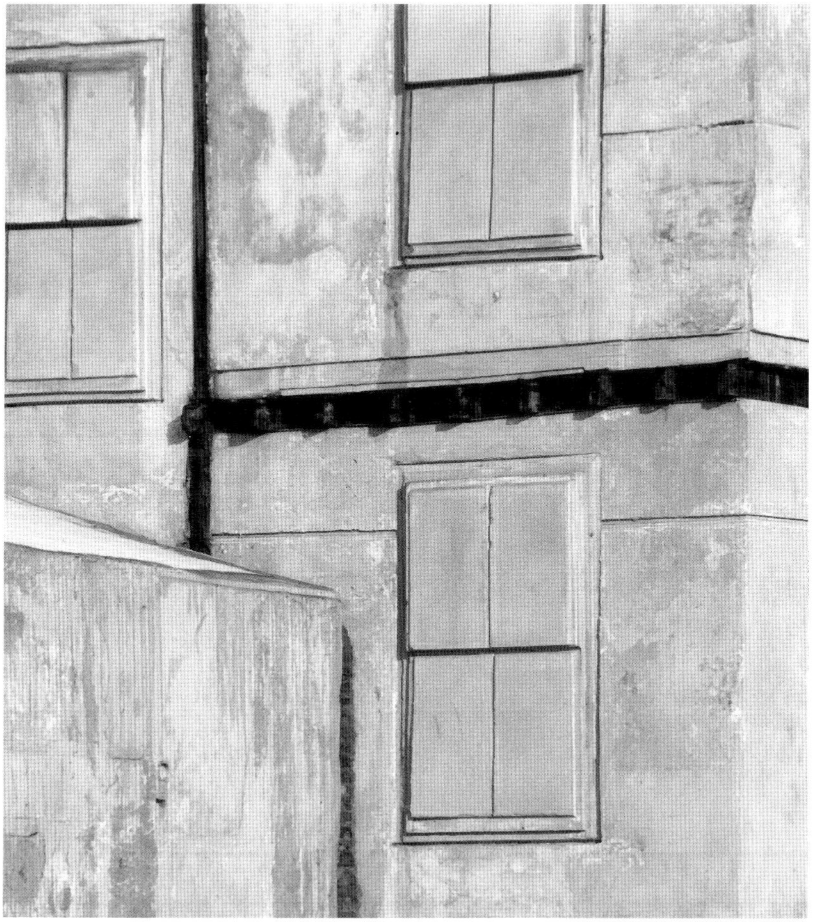

The way in which opinion swirled around it echoed another way in which *House* was constantly changing. It was impossible not to view the whole of the sculpture without also seeing a part of its immediate environment. Close to the textures of the cast, the indentations of domestic details invited contemplation of the interior life the house once had. But from further away, the sculpture gradually became implicated in a mute dialogue with the various architectural forms which surrounded it. Across the road, within a hundred yards of each other were three different churches; Baptist, Jehovah's Witness and Church of England. These modest temples of organized religion contrasted tellingly with the image of Home which in Victorian times had displaced God as the main organizing agent of social stability. Looking from north to south, the view was dominated by Canary Wharf, the tallest building in England and symbol of the transformations which had been wrought upon the East End through the 1980s. And, from far away across the expanse of unused park which had until the Second World War been filled with row upon row of terraced housing, *House* began to appear very small and vulnerable. Towering over it, beyond the section of Grove Road with its churches and refurbished flats, loomed three concrete high-rises, emblems of more recent

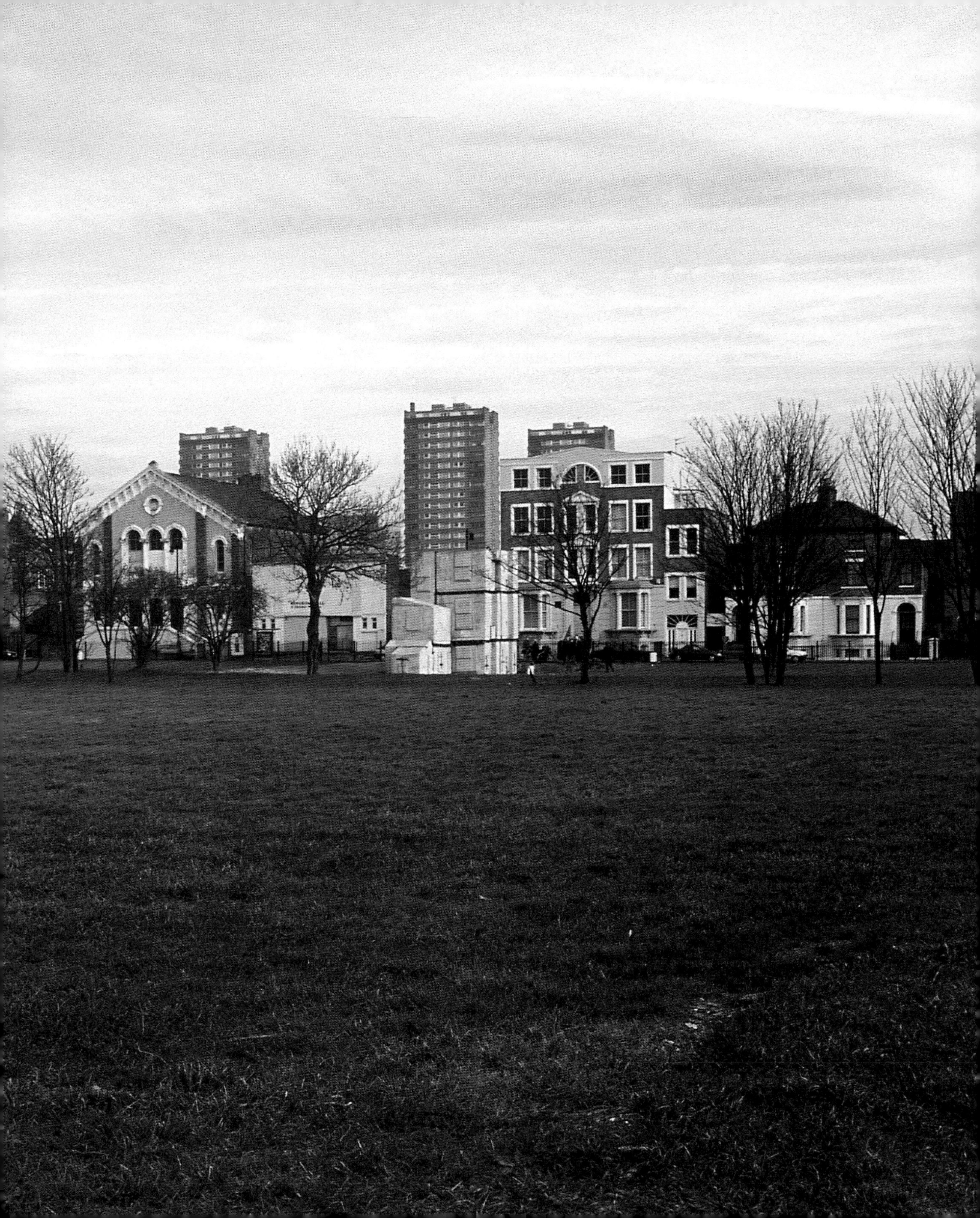

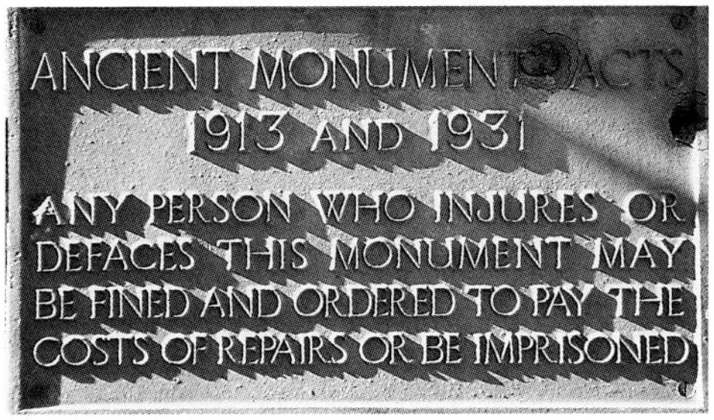

2

2 Plaque found on Grove Road, 1993

ideals of social housing which had at one time supplanted the model of the Victorian terrace. It was not possible to separate *House* from its place, or the place from *House*.

A little way down Grove Road, only a few hundred yards from the place where *House* was made, some wooden sculptures are sited in an adjacent stretch of empty parkland. Carved from trees blown down in the Great Storm of 1987, they stand in a forlorn arrangement. All the time I spent in Grove Road meeting with Whiteread, with local councillors and residents, contractors and sponsors, helpers, students and journalists, I never once saw anyone looking at the wooden sculptures. It seems as if, moments after the commemorative plaque had been unveiled, meaning had evaporated from them as quickly as the local dignitaries had drifted from the opening ceremony.

In his observations on the urban environment of the early 20th century, Robert Musil wrote that 'the most striking feature of monuments is that you do not notice them. There is nothing in the world as invisible as a monument ... Like a drop of water on an oilskin, attention runs down them without stopping for a moment'. The wooden sculptures had acquired that instant invisibility of which Musil wrote; an invisibility which is the precondition of the vast proportion of contemporary civic art, the prerequisite for their commissioning and their survival. *House*, always envisaged as temporary, could not aspire to that condition. In time, over decades, it might have become invisible too. But time was the one thing Whiteread's work did not have.

As I write this, a campaign for a new monument – 'The London Memorial' – is being orchestrated by London's evening newspaper, the *Evening Standard* (who were far from being one of *House*'s most enthusiastic advocates in the autumn of 1993). The London Memorial is planned to commemorate the experience of London and its people during the Second World War before it passes beyond living memory; the people who served, those who died, were bombed out or displaced or survived. And, by some strange irony, a particular street in East London was one of the first places put forward – the place where the first flying bomb fell – none other than Grove Road in Bow. I don't suppose that the connection will be made by the *Evening Standard* – but perhaps their London Memorial has already been and gone.

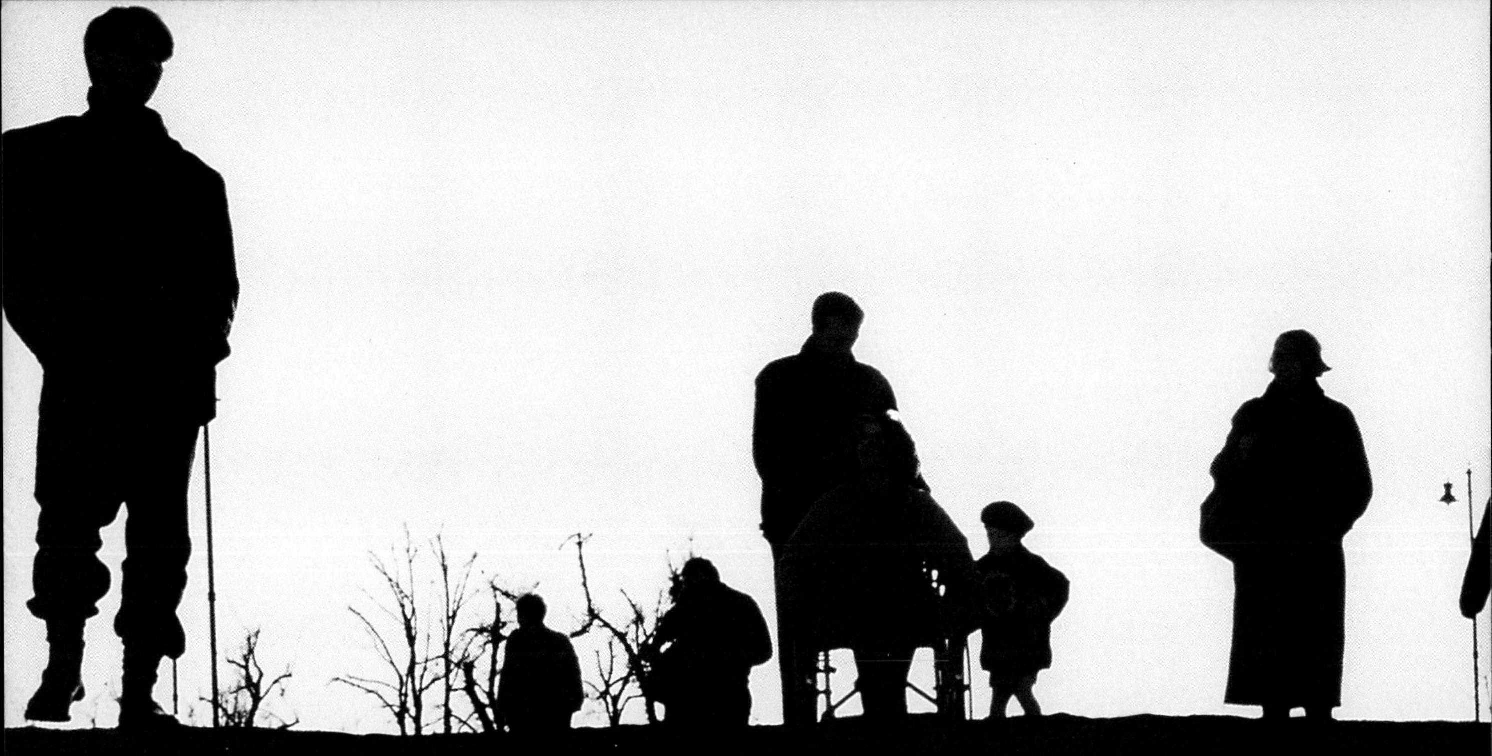

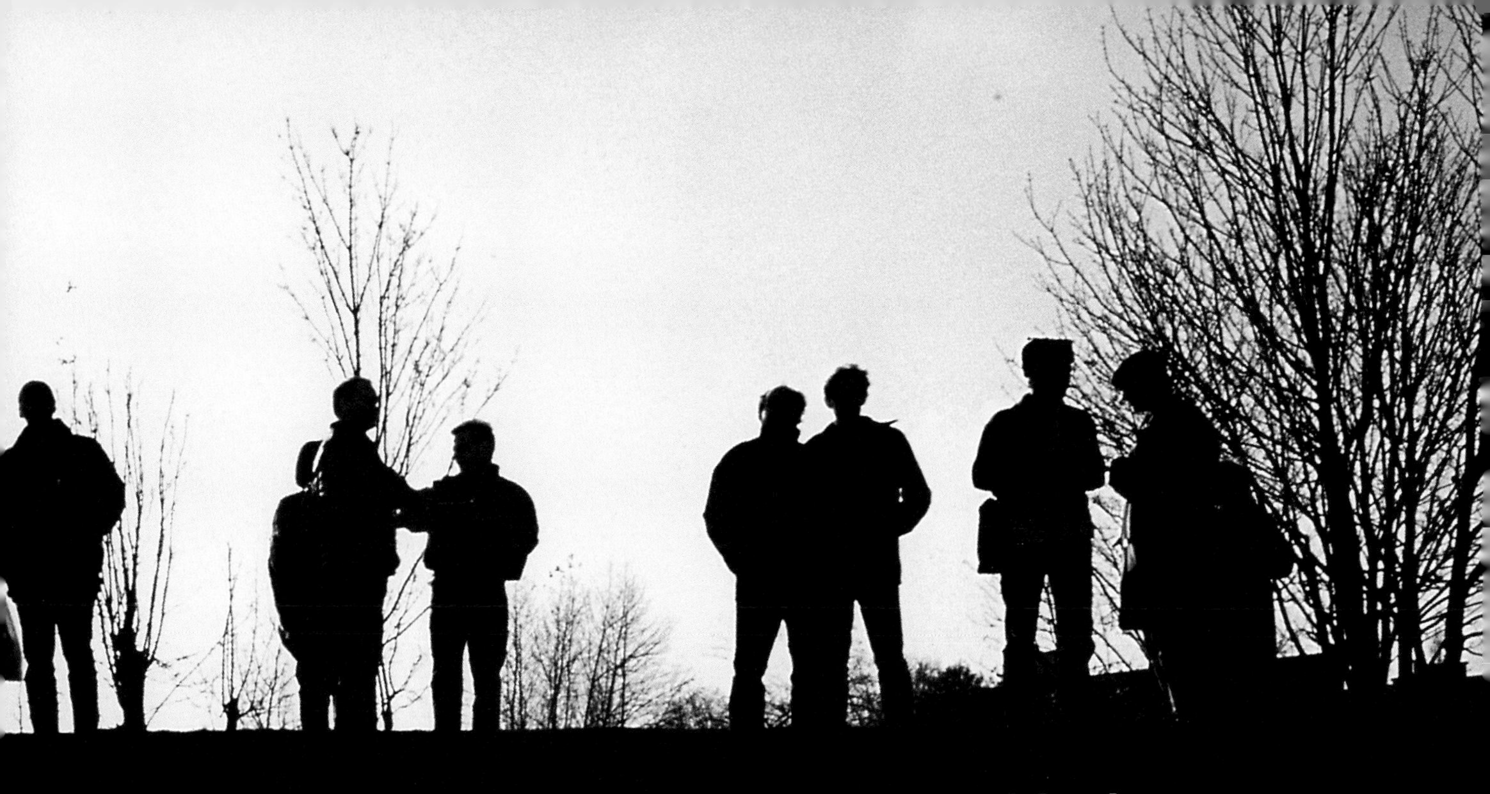

the house in the park: a psychogeographical response

'What did *your* street look like in the past?' One of the more useful ephemerals of the heritage industry is the Godfrey Edition of Old Ordnance Survey Maps: a largely Victorian patchwork intended for those 'who wish to explore London and its history'. A canny piece of merchandizing to set alongside the repair and enlargement, in authentic sepia, of retrieved family photographs (not necessarily your own family); a painless method of acquiring a fraudulent pedigree, of airbrushing the warts of history and providing the hard evidence of a past that never existed. The folded scarlet repro featuring Bethnal Green & Bow (1894) nominates, as its cover illustration, a postcard of the Royal Hotel, Grove Road. (A slightly odd choice given that the hotel is in South Hackney and barely ducks under the cut-off line at the top of the map.) The district on display is a jigsaw of impacted terraces, burial grounds, canals and railways, short on remembered Imperial glory. The chosen image is a frame of film, made over, about to flicker into life (like the honky-tonk interlude in *Butch Cassidy and the Sundance Kid*). A stroller in a straw boater pauses at the kerbside. A horsedrawn cart trundles past, loaded with beer barrels: a sorry precursor of the brass and leather heritage version. A flag flutters above the pediment. There are other nostalgic features, lost but not forgotten, such as a functioning public convenience (Gentlemen only).

It must delight the Parks and Amenities Committee of the Tower Hamlets Council to know that the Royal Hotel survives, freshly painted, hung with flower baskets, obediently empathetic with the royal blue and gold colour scheme that makes the whole zone appear, to the migrant gunning for docklands, like a travelogue down the flank of an upmarket cigarette packet: railings, ironwork gates with chamberpot crowns and gilded lilies, litter bins, plaques offering soundbites of PC antiquarianism. There are now so many of these plaques that, peeping through the fence, it looks like they've let in a plague of estate agents to sell off Victoria Park in strips. These elegant noticeboards are a convenient way of mixing a self-serving rhetoric with the pieties of historical revisionism: we are informed that the park 'suffered from under-investment and remote management' at the hands of the GLC and the LCC. A multi-million pound restoration programme initiated by Bow Neighbourhood – and funded by a list of private sector benefactors and Euro charities that must have kept the sign-painters busy for a fortnight – made this a fit location in which to parade that most precious of icons, Elizabeth the Queen Mother, on her ninetieth birthday. A photo opportunity that linked the triumphalism of the facelifted park (its fountains and sleeping policemen) with newsreel footage of the old duck's previous excursion to East London at the time of the Blitz. Wartime dereliction was therefore twinned with the blight of postwar socialism, woolly thinking and Stalinist incompetence.

Cruder signboards (lower budget) warn the public that 'guard dogs are in use' and that these 'premises' are protected by Armour Security with their manned '24-hour control room'. Grove Road is an avenue of hanging baskets, dazzling pavements from which the filth is regularly hosed, while the people's park has been fenced off, maintained like a roofless marquee, reserved for the exercise of police horses and the exhibition of restored public statuary. The most notable of these casts are the 'Dogs of Alcibiades', a pair of genitally deformed, sightless albinos who frequently

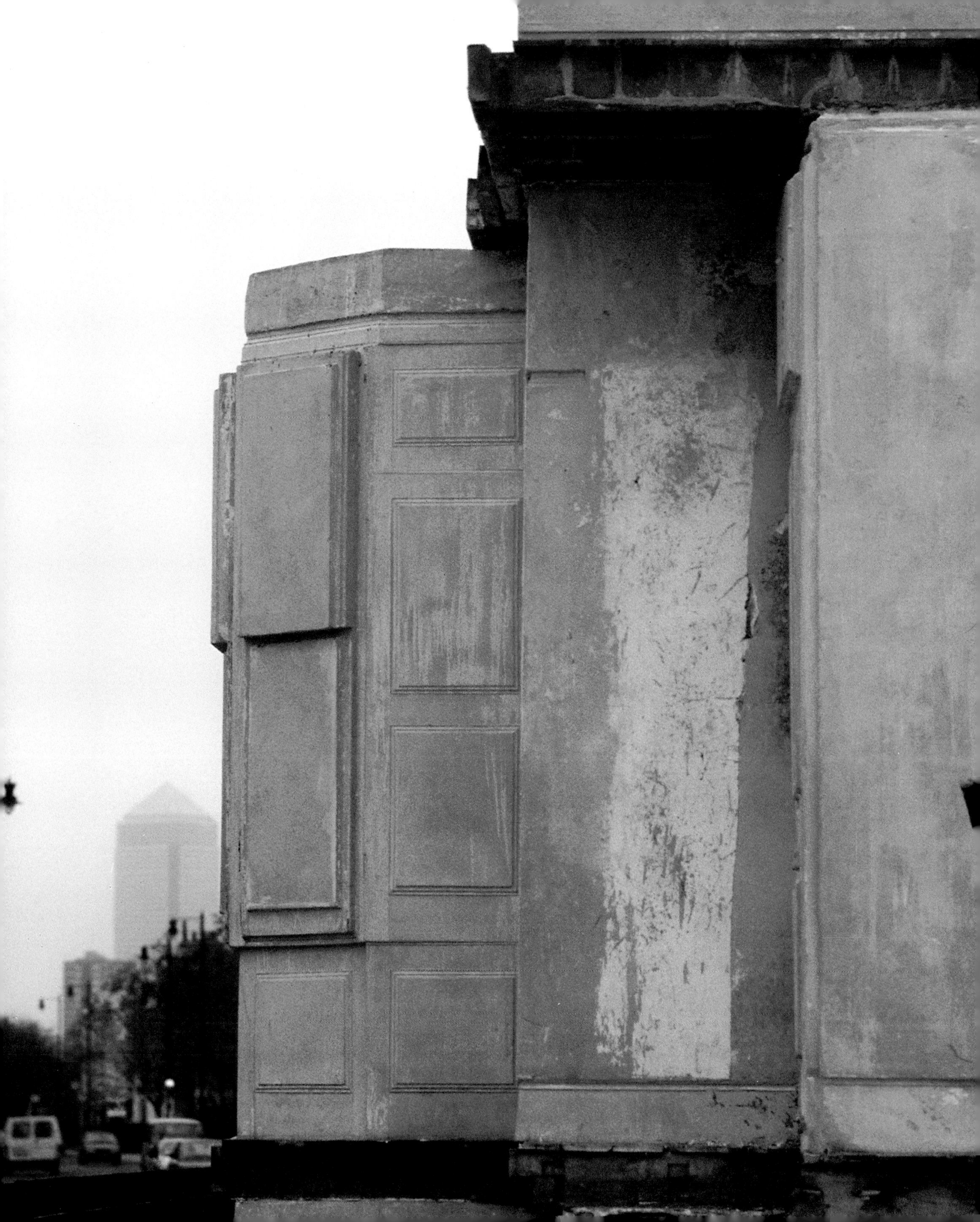

model for the territory's most apposite metaphor: steaming curls of real dogshit placed alongside plaster hounds. Every artefact must align itself with the wacky concept of the 'Bow Heritage Trail', a conceit which it is impossible to imagine anyone actually walking, as it meanders from the dog plinths to the 'Top o' the Morning' public house and its gleeful commemoration of the First Railway Murder.

East End boozers have always followed the market, adopting extreme measures to keep their names in the guidebook: think of the Blind Beggar on Whitechapel Road, obliged to shift its allegiance from the Brothers Kray to the Brothers Roux. A packed conservatory of local businessmen mocks the adjacent Watney Mann brewery, which is no more than a buttressed facade. Even the Royal Hotel got lucky and made it into Duncan Campbell's *The Underworld*. A hitman, having parked a stolen Ford Fiesta on the spot where the Victorian urinal used to stand, took advantage of the walk-through layout, ordered a pint of Foster's, and sauntered across to the table where Jimmy Moody (a face who went all the way back to the affray at Mr Smith's in Catford) was nursing his sundowner. The malign tourist then pulled out a Webley .38 and shot his target four times at point-blank range. As yet there is no plaque to précis the legend – but the 1894 postcard *is* tainted, the crimson border has become a nightmare sky. Hurt can be retrospective. Violent displacements of energy are capable of infecting the membrane of what we call 'the past'. They gift us with memories on which we have no moral claim.

It is tempting for the pedestrian moving south towards Roman Road to close out the civic tidiness of Victoria Park by making treaty with the psychogeographers, paying homage to William Blake's Los who was an earlier pilgrim on this route: 'thro' Hackney ... towards London/Till he came to old Stratford, & thence to Stepney & the Isle/Of Leutha's Dogs ... And saw every minute particular: the jewels of Albion running down/The kennels of the streets & lanes as if they were abhorr'd'. The Hertford Union Canal (itself a failed speculation) is banked by the gutted shells of 'various mills and manufactories'; it waits, in limbo, for investment to catch up with imagination. Developers have to hone their psychic powers, see into the future, ruined husks regenerated, lofts carved into the optimum number of units. Nothing is as it appears. They feed on the predatory instincts of artists who have already surveyed the ground. They follow them into places prepared to yield themselves up to the magic of metamorphosis. They are poets of trespass. They see white gymnasia where the pedants, picking over the heritage maps, locate nothing but serrulated blocks of poverty housing, grey coral packing the space between the Hertford Union Canal to the north, the Regent's Canal to the west, the Great Eastern Railway to the south, the North London Railway to the east. An island of exile known as Old Ford or St Mary Stratford (the 'old Stratford' of Blake). A biopsy of Bow revealing an absence of green spaces, termite ladders parasitical upon the whim of industry. The canals and railways, which carried others through this picaresque desolation, acted as barriers to the indigenous population, snuffing out the fantasy of escape. After Mile End, Grove Road, wide enough to carry a tramline, ceded to a grander highway, named after the charitable Baroness Burdett-Coutts, the privilege of entering Limehouse and 'the narrows of the River's side'.

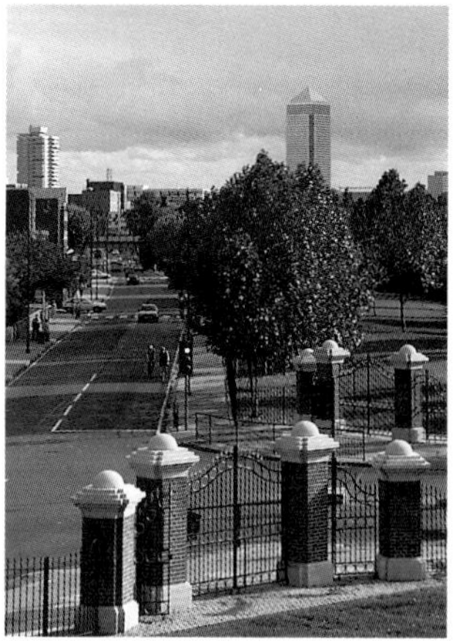
1

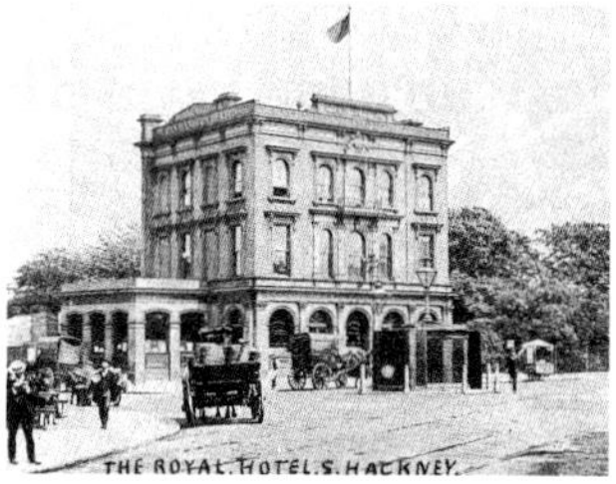

2

1 View from Grove Road to Canary Wharf, Spring 1994 **2** The Royal Hotel, Hackney, cover image from Bethnal Green & Bow Old Ordnance Survey Map, 1894 **3** Bow Heritage Trail plaque

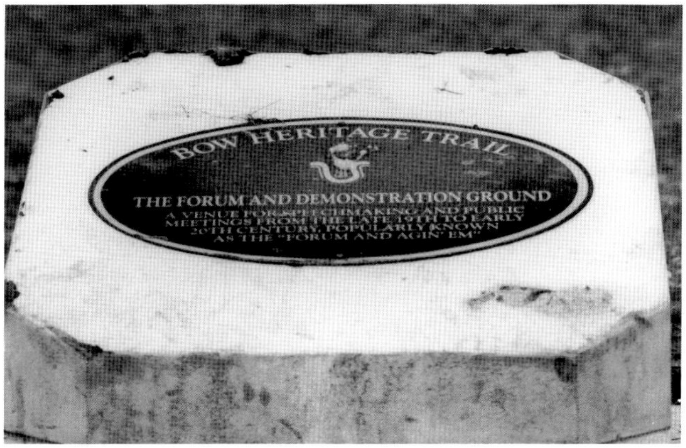

3

The Tower Hamlets planners, to give them their due, were closet visionaries: they conceived the fantastic notion of a Green Corridor to connect all the broken patches of grass between Victoria Park and the Isle of Dogs. They would create a ribbon of urban parkland and sweep away the unsightly clusters of temporary housing. Grass is what they wanted to celebrate: the sickly baize of over-cropped and over-fertilized paddocks. A fenced and locked chain of dog reservations laid to the horizon like regressive pool tables. A Green Corridor that was impossible to walk without constant banishments into the road, the furious traffic runs. Locals rarely bothered to make the attempt. The small parks were left as monuments to their own innate surrealism. They were out of synch with the rest of the borough, *plein air* museums of shadows, humps, hollows, earthed-over streets that threaten to break through the provisional surface.

Wennington Green is the most northerly of these sanctioned essays in the pastoral. The politicians have disguised the lyricism of their modest proposal by talking up the environmental benefits. Councillor Eric Flounders of the ruling Liberal Democrats, unconsciously echoing Le Corbusier, asserted that 'what people who live in tower blocks want is parkland'. An Arcadia for the underclass. Grass hacked to within a centimetre of its life. Wood carvings. Eccentric pathways. Arbours in which lurk strange men and stranger dogs. Rustic camouflage for exiled drinking schools. The whole scheme was a disinterested attempt at municipal aesthetics, paternalistic, bizarre – laying out a mental landscape for a culture of compulsory leisure. Somewhere for the care-of-the-community waifs to kick their heels. Beuys-art interpreted by committee. Green spaces in triplicate. It was appropriate, inevitable, that Wennington Green with its last sorry huddle of housing should be the chosen location for Rachel Whiteread's spectacular cryogenic experiment.

The only entry to Wennington Green on the north side is the inevitable gap in the railings created by fishermen wanting easy access to the canal. Squeezing through, the immediate sensation is troubling: avenues of sycamores trace the faultline where the back gardens of the Grove Road terrace gave way to transitional wilderness. Negotiating moist casts of dog dirt flung up by the rotation of tractor-drawn triples, you approach the badly fitted carpet of replacement turf that delineates the ground where Whiteread's *House* once stood. Wennington Green is otherwise a graveyard without any of the usual prompts, the slabs and angels that list the names and dates of those who solicit remembrance. All the specific provocations of memory have been deleted. This is a field of voluntary amnesia.

It was prescient of Whiteread, after months of careful searches through housing department lists, trawls with James Lingwood of Artangel, inwards through Islington, Hackney and Bow, to arrive at the one site where her project would fuse all the loose wires of potential catastrophe. *House*, seen from across the field, was a giant plug, feeding current into the madness of the city. Grove Road had the lot: a terrace house with three exploitable sides (and a sitting tenant), a hyperactive local politico, anarchist squatters, post-Situationist rock stars looking for the grand gesture, and wild-eyed psychogeographers prophesying war. This terrace was in the wrong documentary. It was an affront to the radiant blankness of the Green Way, an all too human shambles. High art might be a convenient excuse for making the transition, wiping the tape. The intransigence of Sydney Gale (as he was known to the broadsheets), or 'Sid the War Hero' (to the tabloids), was the only thing keeping the ruin upright. 193 Grove Road belonged, through right of long occupation, to Mr Gale and his family. The ex-docker had nothing else to feel so bloody-minded about. Even his surname seemed to allude, punningly, to the night of the Great Storm, the 16th October 1987, an event hijacked by the Parks Committee. The storm was the perfect front for strategic refurbishment, the sealing off of the Victoria Park Lido – as a car park (with no access to the grassland). Mr Gale became the wind of rage incarnate. He was more than ready to busk as a performance artist, to display his own handpainted banner: THIS IS MY HOME, I LIVE HERE. A tautology that was all too soon to be confounded.

Up to this point, before the work began, Artangel and the LibDem caucus, and even Mr Gale, held to their uneasy alliance. Contracts were drawn up. Mr Gale would be rehoused and Whiteread, no stranger to the area, would move in her team, forensically wrapped and masked, to commence the process of mummification. Whiteread's earlier Turner Prize contender, *Ghost*, had been exhibited at the nearby Chisenhale Gallery, a traditional (i.e. ex-industrial) East London space. A functional property with no true function, beyond housing the ghosts of the veneer factory, the voices of the women who turned out Spitfire propellers. These husks are prized for their emptiness, their silence. They make minimalism look good: the least disturbed, the most effective.

Ghost, encountered unexpectedly, was a revelation. Literally so: this cube of retrieved and impacted light illuminated the windowless gallery. The relationship between sculpture and containing space was successfully managed. The piece did not dominate, or deny, the history of the chamber to which it had been brought. A lengthy period of private labour in the original Archway room, casting and reversing, had resulted in this mysterious monobloc. *Ghost* outreached pathos: it was crueller and brighter than that. The allusions are to Egyptian and Babylonian plunder in the British Museum and not to the sentiments of false memory, colonized domestic enclosures. The Archway room was not called upon to surrender the lives it had witnessed, it became an archetype: demotic overwhelmed by hieratic. Set outside, in a sculpture park, a corporate

4 Rachel Whiteread, Ghost, 1990, plaster on steel frame, 270 x 318 x 365 cm

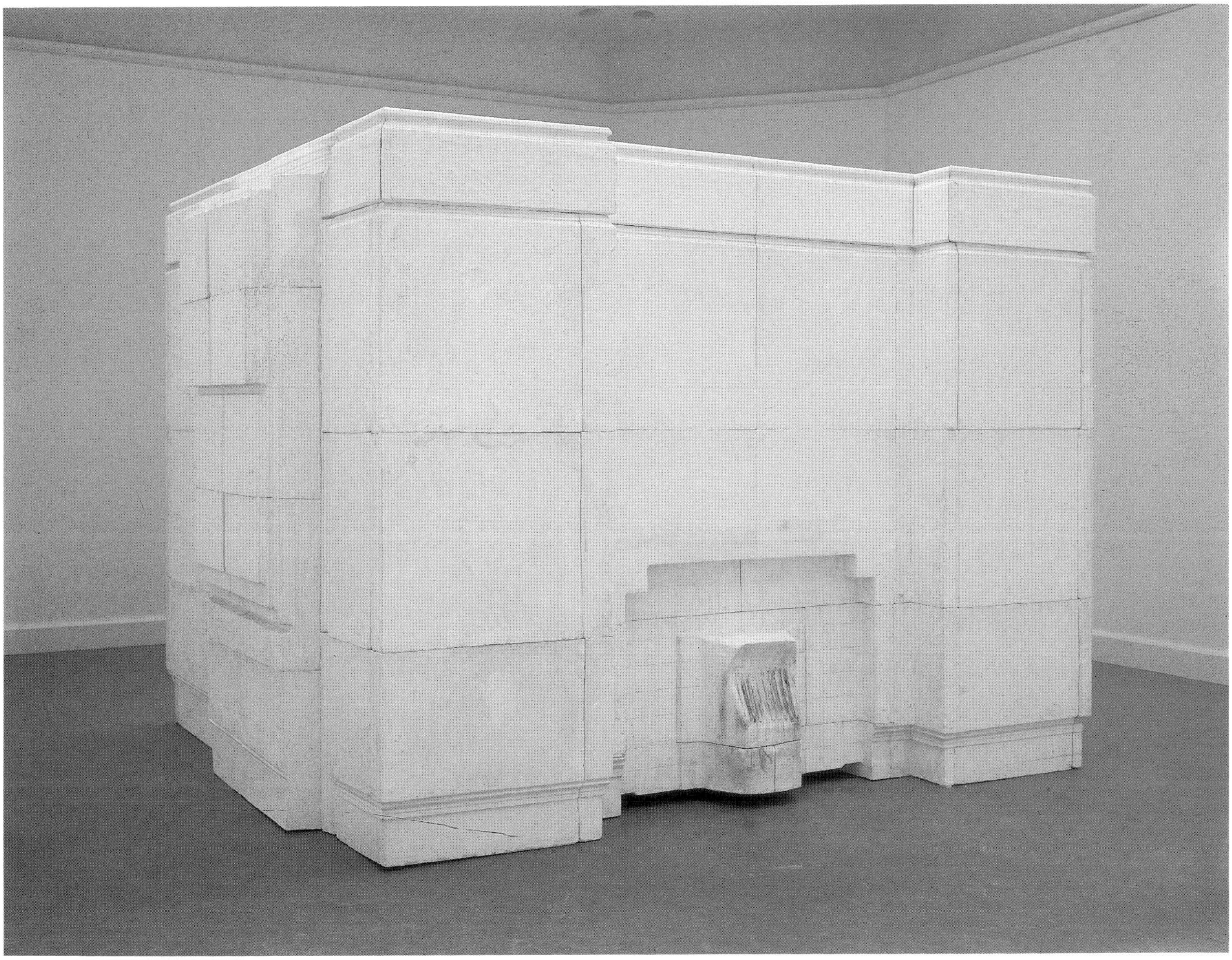

4

watercourt, the venom of *Ghost* would be dissipated. It would be as meaningless as one of those generic 'period' rooms in the Geffrye Museum.

House, a few hundred yards to the west of the Chisenhale Gallery, exposed to the fret of passing traffic, was a trickier proposition from the start. Whiteread, innocent of irony, remarks (in her video diary) how surprised she is that the park will not be secure: 'I hadn't realized the gates would be open the whole time'. She will be watched. The meditative hermeticism of the Archway room will not be possible. *House* is under sentence of death. It will never be brought inside to a controlled environment. It will remain itself: peeled, frozen, laid bare. The bride stripped by her bachelors. *House* is public, front-lawn art – a sponsored bastard. The stakes are high enough to alert every demon in the dictionary: culture vampires, strollers, all those who underwrite any challenge to the torpid energy balance of the Green Corridor.

After their searches through dusty housing records, Whiteread and Artangel were fortunate enough to nominate a vagrant terrace that was under the 'protection' of a spectacularly contrary LibDem cadre. A bunch quite capable of shredding the user-friendly rhetoric of the upriver party spin doctors. An embattled cell of activists who, by loudly championing the 'local', could attempt to promote village values in a panorama of millennial meltdown. Covert racism ('We have produced leaflets with Scotsmen in kilts'), boastful philistinism, and immaculate streets, would be the unspoken manifesto. The slashing of the Arts budget (curtains for the Half Moon Theatre) was therefore twinned with the perverse re-imagination of the rubble of abandoned terraces as sub-Georgian parkland. It wasn't that the neighbourhood bosses disliked art, as such. It was much more that they were themselves artists *manqué*, opponents of the internationalist conspiracy. Under such a regime, the Bow Neighbourhood turned itself into a reservation of pieties, a diverse wedge of well-scrubbed streets lacking any centre, anything worth destroying. The real achievement of Artangel was political: the drawing up of the contract for *House*, the parameters of toleration, while the most effective spokesperson for the philosophy of enlightened prejudice was safely out of the country.

Councillor Eric Flounders descended on the *fait accompli* like an avatar of the Great Storm, a bismuth Cromwell. It wasn't just the name, you couldn't invent Eric: as fiction he was strictly redundant. He had a second life as a flamboyantly drab PR operative for Cunard. The perfect man to produce advance copy for the Titanic brochure, Eric had an instinct for disaster. *House* was a media opportunity not to be squandered, a chance for Flounders to take his grievances upmarket – to defend the eviction of 100 Bangladeshi families, badmouth *Guardian*-reading Hampstead pinkos, and tell art scum sniffling for alms to 'fuck off'. In other words, Eric was a traditionalist, dancing on the grave of concepts that had been buried twenty years ago. You can also admire him: the way he resisted the arm-twisting of the party apparatchiks, the certainty that he was never now going to make it to Westminster, the pressure to avoid yet another LibDem own goal in East London. Flounders stood firm: *House* was 'crap'. 'The more people who want it to stay there', he told the *East London Advertiser,* 'the more resolute I become'.

As is often the case, where aesthetic

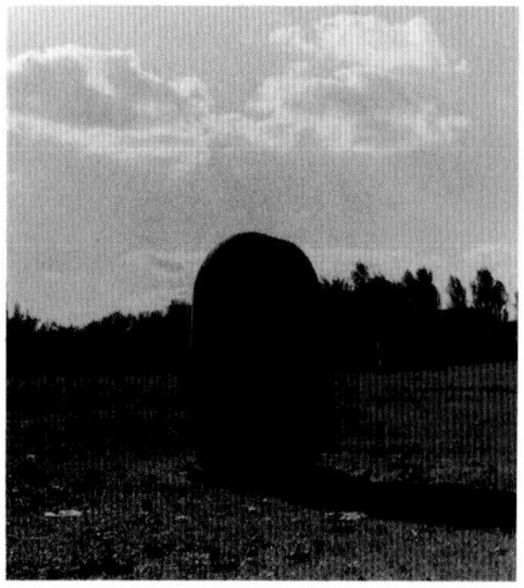

5

5 Acorn sculpture, Haverfield Green

questions are concerned, the most extreme political opponents were in agreement: 'junk'. The disaffiliated class warriors who squatted 199 Grove Road were primed to take an interest in an increasingly volatile situation. Art guerrilla Stewart Home's riposte came in the form of a novel, *Red London,* which joyously deconstructed the event – as it was happening. Which is one of the advantages of the book-a-month school of neo-pulp anarchy. Home's constituents, unaware that they were supposed to be a figment of the author's rancid imagination, were ready to exploit the opportunities offered by a major example of public art being dumped in their lap by outside forces who knew nothing of their existence. Anything short of actually living there: 'Every buddhist Octagon had offered to house in Grove Road turned down the accommodation'. Home, throwing together at speed a wicked cocktail of disinformation, satire, bent gossip, delivered a psychic survey of the climate in which *House* was constructed; a survey more accurate, on every level, than the fact-checked responses of the telephone journalists. Every paranoid excess received its credit: 'The co-op was controlled by a secret committee of monks who'd been co-opted from the Teutonic Order of Buddhist Youth'.

House, standing alone, the solitary representative of all that Grove Road had been, was an affront to the anarchists. It mocked the steady destruction of so much of East London. It should, they felt, be mobilized, like the ghost of some turreted weapon of war (the sawteeth of the absent staircases looked like tank treads), in the battle against the M11 link-road that was being fought in Leytonstone. Solidity should imply solidarity. (Whiteread bumped into a few of the lads who had turned up with sledgehammers and drills to break into the interior of an exhibit that *had* no interior. That was its essence. If they had succeeded they would have reversed time and vanished forever.) This house of memory should receive equal honour with the tree houses occupied by eco-dissidents. And it would command more column inches in the subvertible broadsheets. Having the Turner prizewinner in the frontline would be like having Salman Rushdie walking out to face the bulldozers.

Firm allies of the arboreal squatters, the London Psychogeographical Association, published an editorial, *Housey! Housey!* (Newsletter No.5), which drew attention to a perceived irony in Tarmac sponsoring the delivery of Whiteread's phantom when the trees of George Green were being hacked down by pre-dawn mercenaries to make way for yet more 'motorway madness'. The alignment freaks, sustained by a vision of the city as a living, breathing body, were disturbed by the proximity of *House* to the Greenwich/St Anne's, Limehouse/Meath Gardens axis: a shining path acknowledged, according to Katherine Heron (of Feary+Heron Architects), even by the planners of the London Docklands Development Corporation. 'Surprisingly, the LDDC in its first and only published guide c.1982 chose to keep and accentuate the axis by not permitting any building along its length that would interrupt the view from one place to the other'. A nice theory – which lasted for as long as it took Olympia and York to wave their cheque book. The sighting of Canary Wharf, that misconceived acupuncture needle, induced a new magnetic field. The vulgarity of this false leyline was serviced by the erection of an acorn/omphalos on Haverfield Green

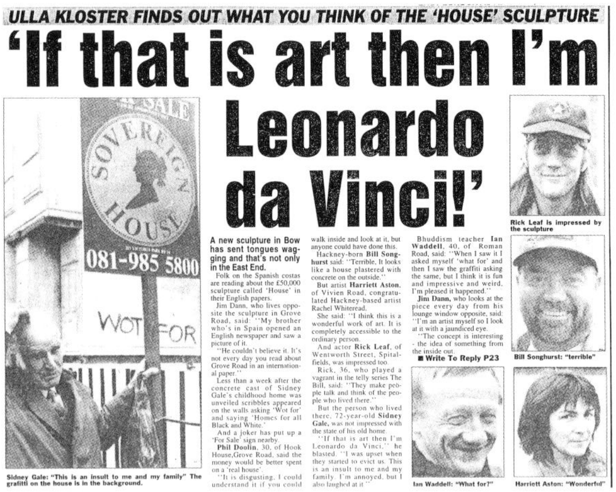

ULLA KLOSTER FINDS OUT WHAT YOU THINK OF THE 'HOUSE' SCULPTURE

'If that is art then I'm Leonardo da Vinci!'

Sidney Gale: "This is an insult to me and my family" The grafitti on the house is in the background.

A new sculpture in Bow has sent tongues wagging and that's not only in the East End.

Folk on the Spanish costas are reading about the £50,000 sculpture called 'House' in their English papers.

Jim Dann, who lives opposite the sculpture in Grove Road, said: "My brother who's in Spain opened an English newspaper and saw a picture of it.

"He couldn't believe it. It's not every day you read about Grove Road in an international paper."

Less than a week after the concrete cast of Sidney Gale's childhood home was unveiled scribbles appeared on the walls asking 'Wot for' and saying 'Homes for all Black and White.'

And a joker has put up a 'For Sale' sign nearby.

Phil Doolin, 30, of Hook House, Grove Road, said the money would be better spent on a 'real house'.

"It is disgusting. I could understand it if you could walk inside and look at it, but anyone could have done this.

Hackney-born **Bill Songhurst** said: "Terrible, It looks like a house plastered with concrete on the outside."

But artist **Harriett Aston**, of Vivien Road, congratulated Hackney-based artist Rachel Whiteread.

She said: "I think this is a wonderful work of art. It is completely accessible to the ordinary person.

And actor **Rick Leaf**, of Wentworth Street, Spitalfields, was impressed too.

Rick, 36, who played a vagrant in the telly series The Bill, said: "They make people talk and think of the people who lived there."

But the person who lived there, 72-year-old **Sidney Gale**, was not impressed with the state of his old home.

"If that is art then I'm Leonardo da Vinci," he blasted. "I was upset when they started to evict us. This is an insult to me and my family. I'm annoyed, but I also laughed at it."

Bhuddism teacher **Ian Waddell**, 40, of Roman Road, said: "When I saw it I asked myself 'what for' and then I saw the graffiti asking the same, but I think it is fun and impressive and weird. I'm pleased it happened."

Jim Dann, who looks at the piece every day from his lounge window opposite, said: "I'm an artist myself so I look at it with a jaundiced eye.

"The concept is interesting - the idea of something from the inside out.

■ **Write To Reply P23**

Rick Leaf is impressed by the sculpture

Bill Songhurst: "terrible"

Ian Waddell: "What for?"

Harriett Aston: "Wonderful"

6

6 'If that is art then I'm Leonardo da Vinci!', *East London Advertiser*, Thursday, November 4, 1993 **7** Housey! Housey!, *London Psychogeographical Association Newsletter*, January, 1994

(the paddock immediately to the south of Wennington Green in the Bow Chain). The acorn was yet another tribute to the Great Storm, part of a series of anonymous windfall carvings, reminiscent of Glynn Williams or Lee Grandjean on a bad day. Bucolic romanticism capable of delighting the shade of Peter Fuller and attracting the attention of freelance aerosol revisionists. Canary Wharf, the wooden acorn, and the Whiteread *House* were in alignment, a shadowline to the true path; debris adding conviction to the geomantic ambitions of the Bow planners.

The psychogeographers were as keen as the tabloid hacks to copyright the indignation of Sydney Gale, the final occupant, in his new and displaced status. The man wouldn't go away. Not required on set, he hung about, polishing his soundbites. 'If that is art then I'm Leonardo da Vinci.' The money was what disturbed him, the figure of £40,000 floated by the press in an uncharacteristically modest understatement. Mr Gale couldn't get his head around the idea that art money is funny money (as the K Foundation, in their confusion, were soon to prove). You don't buy a new flat with this stuff. It's theoretical, an equation that has to be balanced. It's more like a signature or hallmark. Money is the guarantee of seriousness. It proves that the art is kosher. If you're already famous, then it's the material you work with, your medium. If you're unknown and you cop an unexpected bundle from the Saatchis you are promoted directly into the heavy paper surveys. But you can't *spend* this kind of cash. That would be like squeezing the juice from one of Zurbarán's lemons. Contemporary art is about credit: the metamorphosis of money into power. To Mr Gale the Whiteread *House* was simply a haystack of unearned banknotes. The chilling whiteness of the finished sculpture, picked out of the dusk by the headlights of passing cars, reminded him of something in a graveyard; his family home travestied as a Monopoly token.

Whiteread kept a scrupulous video record of the process whereby her concept was brought to life. It's obvious, watching this material as part of the historical record, that the real winners were the industrial contractors, the plant hire boys. *House* was

London Psychogeographical Association
Newsletter
Imbolc 1994 No.5
THIRTY FIVE YEARS 1957 1992 OF NON-EXISTENCE
Published by the East London Section of the London Psychogeographical Association

HOUSEY! HOUSEY!

Two houses in East London gained an international reputation when they faced demolition. One house was the symbol of resistance to motorway madness, the other, sponsored by Tarmac — a company leading the road building lobby — won the Turner art prize.

The latter, Rachel Whiteread's sculpture was finally demolished on January 11th. Whiteread claimed her in-situ work "transforms the space of the private and domestic into the public — a mute memorial to the spaces we have lived in, to everyday existence and the importance of the home." However she is clearly wrong in her claim. It was the council possession order which transformed the private space of Sydney Gale into public space.

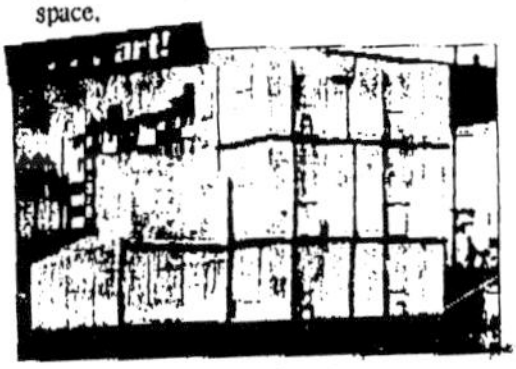

***House*, 1993-4 R.I.P**

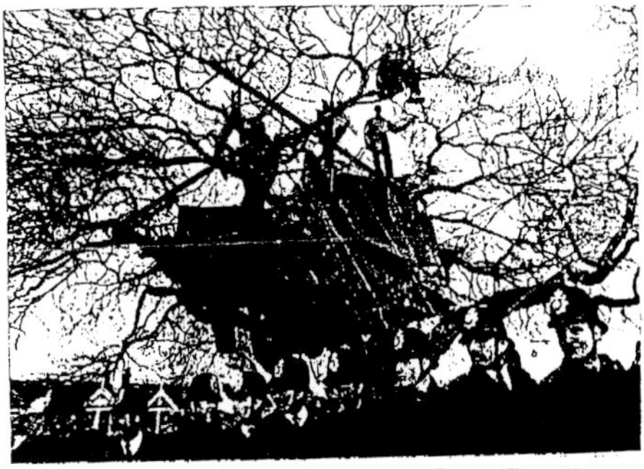

Protestors defy police at the George Green Tree House

Although Mr Gale had lived their since a child the council insisted he move. Mr Gale resisted even when the rest of the houses in the block had been demolished. The last remaining house stood for months, shored up with scaffolding and placards declaring "This is my home, I live here." A cheerful reminder of popular resistance. In her publicity Whiteread made no reference to Mr Gale, even though it was his resistance which lead to there being a single remaining house suitable for casting. When people responded to her work by suggesting the money would have been better spent on providing homes for the homeless, she introduced the topic of homelessness into her rhetoric. This was absent however in her original documentation.

Just as Christian churches were frequently placed on pagan sites in order to incorporate them into the new power structure, so artists take over sites of working class resistance to sanitise them. In a leaflet issued by the Neoist Alliance (BM Senior, London WC1N 3XX) it is pointed out that "In effect *House* robs those who once lived in Grove Road of their own past, replacing it with a supposedly 'higher set of values'. When all is said and done this is imperialism."

In this case Whiteread was sponsored by the notorious Tarmac company. This was the company which sent in thugs to attack the Dongas at Twyford Down in November 1992. They may think that this sponsorship will help give a cultured gloss to their despoilation of the countryside. But actually it exposes the facile level of their understanding.

The demolition of a chestnut tree in George's Green aroused much anger across London and beyond. A tree house had been erected in the tree to delay its destruction. Complete with letter box, this house transformed the tree into a legal dwelling, compelling the Department of Transport to gain a compulsory Purchase Order.

Finally on December 7th, the DoT was ready to move in. Hundreds of people tried to prevent the tree's destruction which could only proceed with the violent intervention of 300 police. 'Protectors' arrived as early as 4am to circle the tree with five rings of people. Many were chained together. In all it took 8 hours for the forces of repression to destroy this tree.

The tree was being demolished in order to make way for the unwanted M11 motorway. Whereas Whiteread transformed someone's home into a featureless concrete block, protesters transformed this tree into a home, gaining a stay of execution for a few days. There is a campaign maintaining squats in condemned houses and organising resistance along the proposed M11 route through Wanstead, Leyton and Leytonstone. They can be contacted on 081 530 5709 or write to PO Box 956, Leystone Delivery Office, 6 Joseph Ray Road, London E11 1AA.

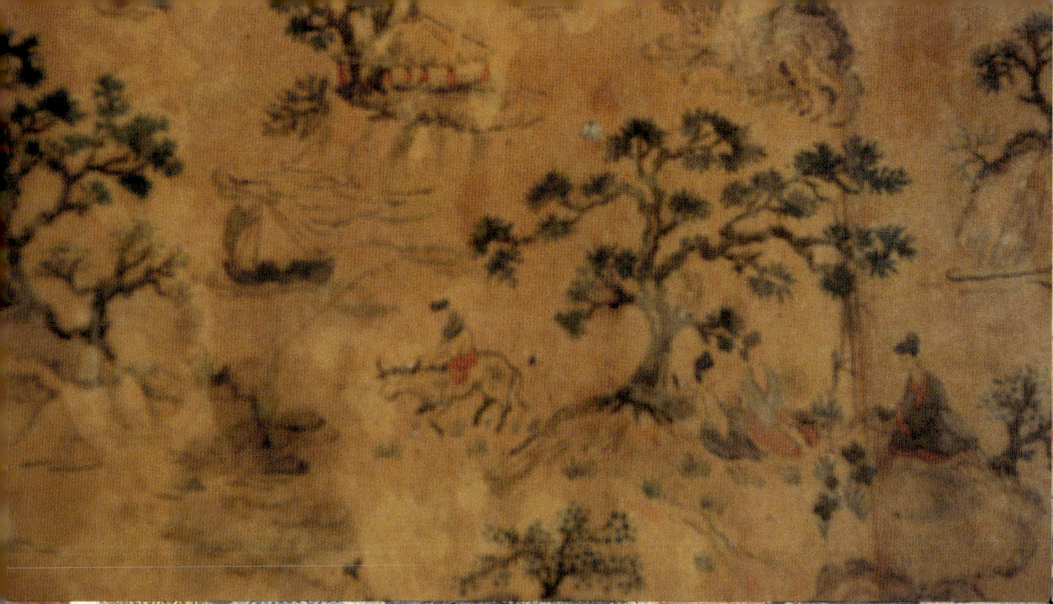
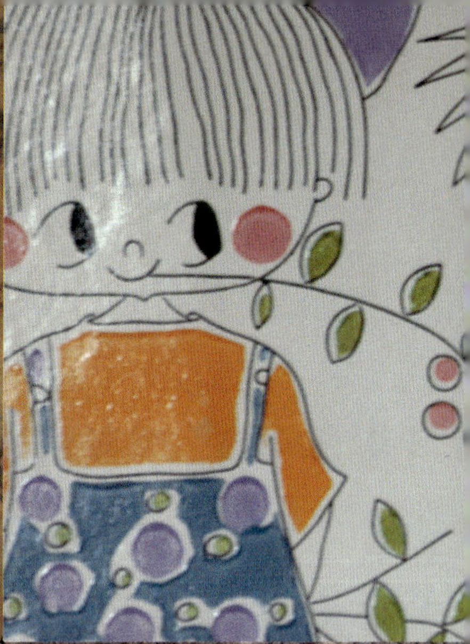
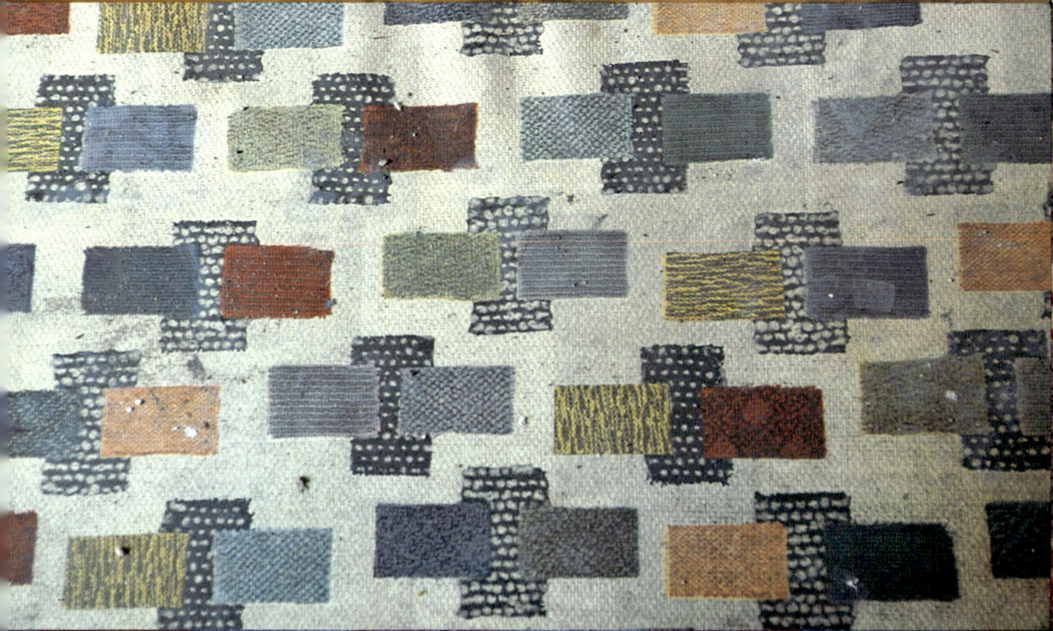
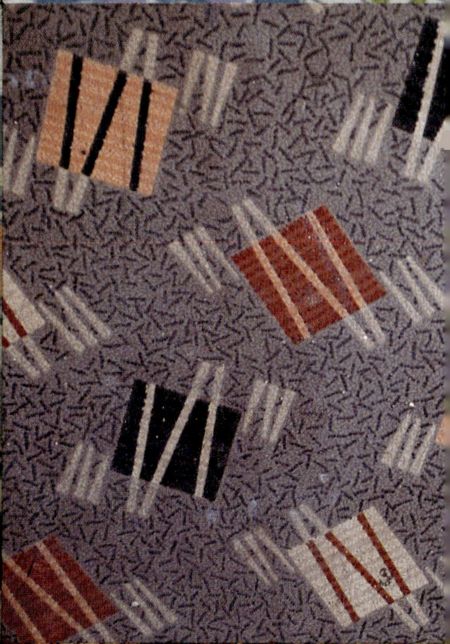
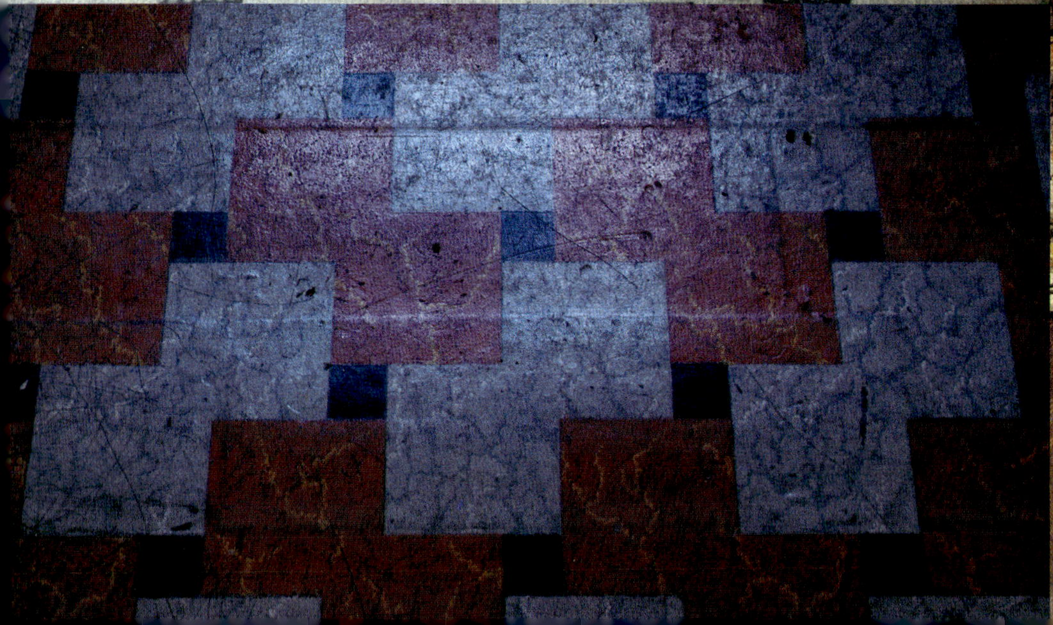
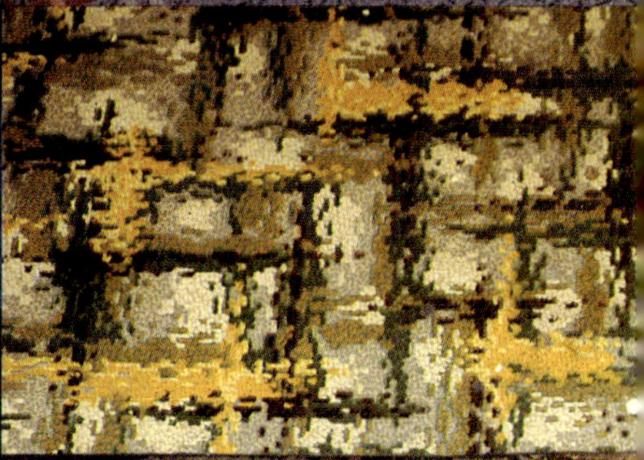
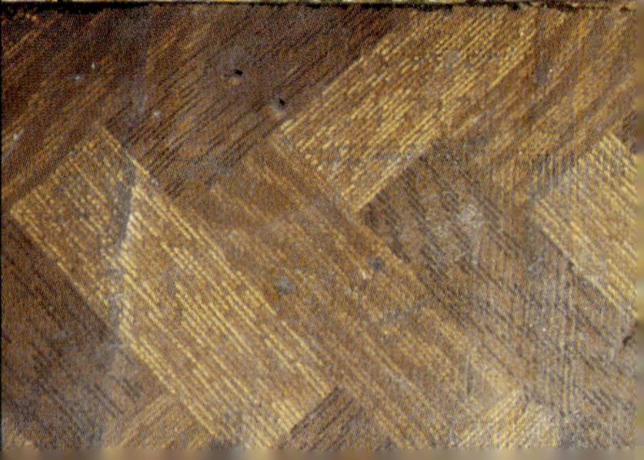

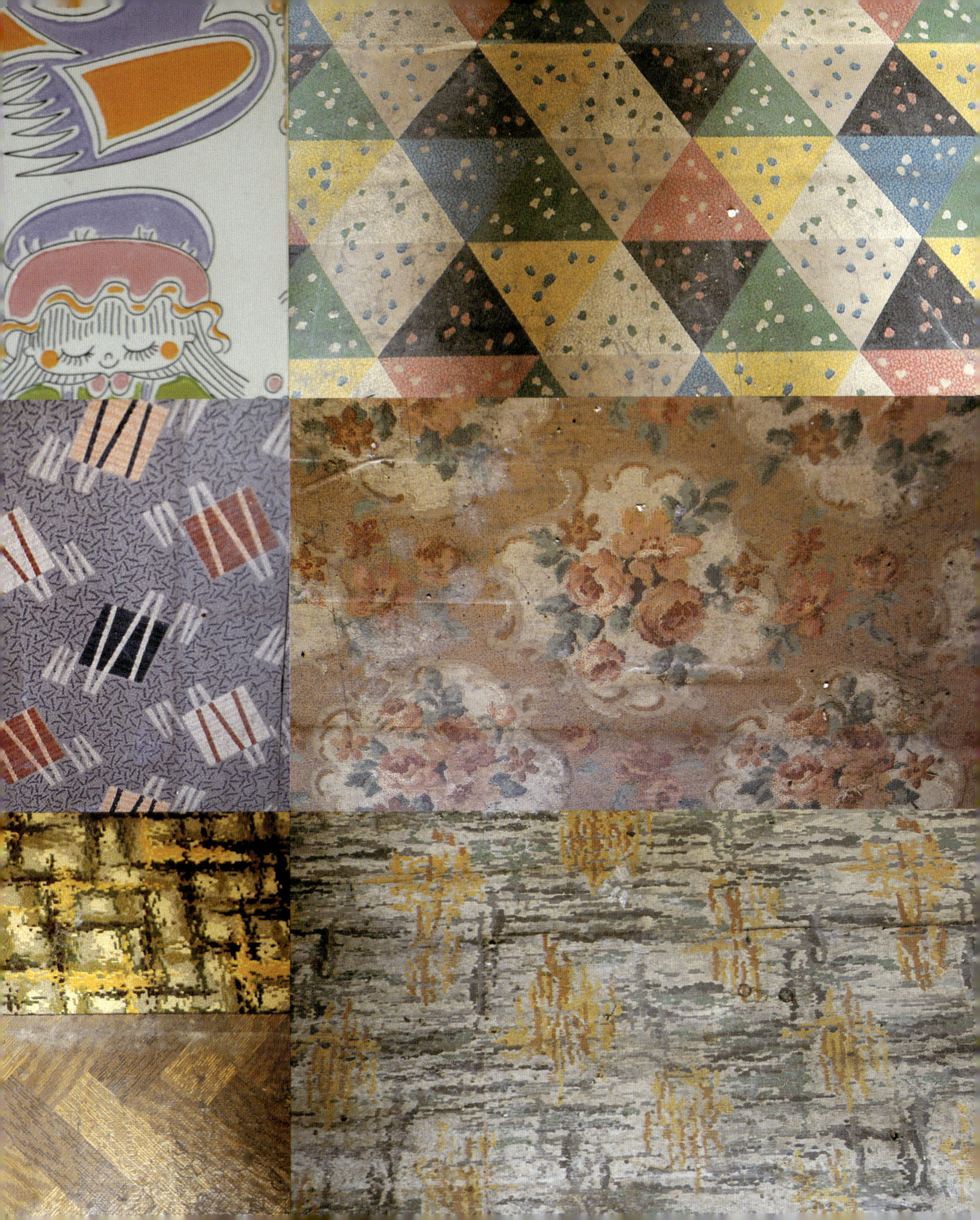

a great deal, a doubleheader, for Stiffell's and the McGrath Brothers: peel off the brickskin, then pop back three months later for a day's work knocking down the most famous sculpture in England (with wall-to-wall TV coverage and high visibility logo).

The early footage in the video is privileged heartbreak: filtered October sunlight exposing the deserted shell to its subtly cruel warmth. Postmortem tableaux of arcane domesticity: contoured floorboards, collisions of insanely assertive wallpaper, gauze curtains of solidified dust. Redundant aspirations. The furniture, the gadgets, the bric-a-brac have been cleared – as if for a death. The house is in limbo. It is tempting to sentimentalize this state, how the soul of the building, the spirit that had evolved between family and place, was still present. A special light, synthesized by Whiteread's camera, varnishes the details by which these people will be defined. It has to be excluded before the next stage of the work can begin, the windows have to be boarded over. Whiteread derives her power from her perception of this transitory place, the temporal entrapment of the unpeopled room. She understands how the exclusion of mundane light converts the room into a recording instrument, a machine for remembering, as well as the memory itself. I am presumptuous enough to assert that this would be the best time, a time of autobiographical reverie, before the collaborators move in – and the rush is triggered.

The pleasures of the chrysalis stage are visceral: brisk technicians spraying Locrete (the stuff they use to patch the cracks in the White Cliffs of Dover) over a gridwork of steel rods. The video allows us to remain inside the shell. The sense of how unpleasant it was to operate in this environment is acute: the wetness of the walls, the morbid fur, the organic weirdness of pod life that is obliterated by the sharp edges of the finished structure. The masked workers in their overalls are like a SWAT team summoned to some tragic address, the suicide of apocalyptic cultists or the cold store of a serial killer. They have been cursed with the task of building a pyramid from the inside, changing fate; starting from what is known and deranging it. The process is forbidden. *House,* as a work in progress, is science fiction – a Tardis regenerating itself from illegitimate evidence. The forensic crew are the exterminators of normalcy.

The dermabrading concluded, *House* stood exposed in a shallow, rubble-strewn declivity. It was now an art object: it had died, its flaws and faults smoothed over with Locrete (plus a splash of cosmetic white to enliven the greyness of the pallor). The virgin walls were an open invitation to the unsponsored care-of-the-community signwriters, the aerosol bandits. WOT FOR?, WHY NOT, and the brushed out subtext, HOMES FOR ALL BLACK + WHITE. The unedited book of the city – railway bridges, canal bridges, doorways – fills with a cacophony of quotations, obscenities, names of lost heroes. Photographed, they outlive their occasion: the innocence of George Davis, the guilt of DC Matthews. WOT FOR? is the riddle in the files of press cuttings.

House, an intrusion in the dim electro-magnetic field, brought disciples running, even those who knew nothing of its history, to Grove Road, to question the nature of interference. The enigmatic object was surrounded, probed, questioned. It was fed by flashbulbs, the tributes of photographers.

Convulsive therapy. The white ghost

8 Previous pages: Wallpaper and lino patterns, 193 Grove Road reversed, seen in negative, printed. Thousands of images. No longer singular: a terrace of reproductions, a city of mirrors. *House*, the paradigm of loss, was multiplied. Loss, carried away, became a general condition, a blight. Professionals, archivists, chemist-shop casuals. In the city twilight, a circle of blue sparks strobe *House*, dividing it into detail and longshot; analyzing and reassembling. The snapshots laid out, side by side, would stretch down Grove Road, repopulating the grass wildernesses, all the way to the point where the first flying bomb fell on London.

Cropped tight (no sky) to banish the dreary park, a formalist shot was deemed suitable for the label of Beck's commemorative beer (best drunk before February 1995). The image has been so starkly edited that it could provoke a prosecution under the Trades Description Act: the park railings, aesthetically incorrect, have been doctored by computer to allow the sculpture to rise directly from the real pavement. No graffiti, no pedestrians. A Mondrian arrangement of rectangles and crossed lines, nicely judged asymmetry in greys and greens.

Moving back, and away, the shape of *House* is much more chaotic: futurist zig-zags, blue smears, the flatness of a septic tank. WARNING HAZART. The night trippers examine this work from the side. Only pedestrians, outside, on the pavement, see anything resembling the Beck's portrait. There aren't many of them. Some of the supplicants have been bussed in, culture punters with serious affiliations. It's like the Mexican Day of the Dead (sponsored by Harvey Nichols) as the Gucci bags, Hermes scarves, leopardskin prints trip across the greensward to pay their respects to Whiteread's sugar-dusted skull. They huddle together to listen to the spiel; fearful of the place and its chill atmosphere, the reek of the canal. Others, energetic anoraks, circumnavigate the perimeter, darting forward to touch the plaster, to admire the vertical coffins of children. There's a favoured distance – about 25 yards back – for prolonged meditation: as if taking up a position at the bottom of the erased garden. Human figures are pegs in the half-dark, black against a powdering of snow on the peppery grass.

In a strange way, part of the strength of *House* was that it repelled those who were most closely associated with it. The achieved work was anonymous, it didn't feel like a 'Rachel Whiteread'. It had developed its own agenda, an urge towards obliteration, forgetfulness. *House,* at the death, was in league with Councillor Flounders and his iconoclasts.

While the friends of Artangel were manoeuvering for time, and the world was camping out to catch a glimpse of the millennial fetish, Whiteread concluded her video diary. Knowing of the structure's death warrant, its fame, the pilgrims had a subdued air. The field was the preview for an execution: winter light. None of this mob would dream of paying a visit to a corrugated-fence terrace marked for demolition. One of those dusty, dangerous amputations with the unsophisticated colour clashes, their dangling wires. *House* gave the curious an excuse to quit their own pinched living spaces, a comfortable way of paying tribute to the spiritual bleakness of this part of London. A final visit to a sickbed, a rehearsed bereavement. They were well-behaved, sombre. They needed floral tributes to occupy their hands, wreaths to leave on the pavement.

There were far too many of them for Whiteread to risk stepping out of her car. She pulled up at a distance, bundled into a heavy jacket, keeping surveillance. If she walked across the grass to *House*, she'd be torn apart. A last roll-up, a whispered confession to the diary: 'If I get out of the car, I'd get swamped by people'. Exiled from her own creation, she was in precisely the situation of Bill Drummond and Jimmy Cauty, the pranksters of the K Foundation, who watched from a jeep parked by the riverside, while their hirelings called Whiteread out of the Tate Gallery beanfeast to face the media scrummage of the booby prize delivery.

Just then, by one of the correspondences by which the whole affair was characterized, an area of grass close to the house Whiteread was moving into in Hackney came under threat. The leaflet on the doormat. This green space also had a history of postwar prefabs, 'temporary' housing that lasted into the 1970s (demolished, finally, to make way for an unfenced rug of grass). Scarcely a park, nor even a public garden, it was nurtured, tended by the more civic-minded of the rate-payers, in the spirit more usually encountered in the dormitory villages of Middle England. Magistrates weeded and planted the borders. Children played on it in the summer evenings, within sight of their homes, and large mixed gatherings (all ages, weights, abilities) churned it to mud in their weekly football rituals. The evident needs and desires of this community were remorselessly ignored by a Labour council as entrenched in its prejudices and petty corruptions as their LibDem brothers across the border. It was decided that a terrace of houses would be shoehorned onto what the square dwellers, signalling their aspirations, liked to call 'The Green'. The Nimbys (who were both surprised and delighted to see Whiteread turn up at their AGM) mounted a prolonged and effective campaign: snippets of local TV, camp-outs, a barrage of documentation, points of order, fighting funds, top of the range legal stationery. Which resulted in a few Gavin Stampist adjustments to the builders' plans and the loss of a prized breathing space in a zone of perceived 'decency' between the termite horrors of Holly Street and the crack barracks that slouched away towards the canal. The energy exchange was almost *too* neat: Wennington Green witnessed the premature abortion of *House* and the reinstatement of ceremonial grassland – while a small corner of green Hackney was built over with houses which, in the limbo of construction, stand white and empty as any work of conceptual sculpture.

Across the canal, and a little to the south of Wennington Green, is another strip of seismically agitated earth now known as Meath Gardens: a site blessed by standing directly on the path of the Greenwich/ Limehouse leyline. Meath Gardens, in an earlier incarnation, was the Victoria Park Cemetery – notorious bonepit, putrid with the multiple occupation of the indigenous underclass. A field of stench and pestilence regularly denounced in the progressive journals, it was the burial place of an Australian Aboriginal cricketer known as 'King Cole', who died in England during the first tour undertaken by a team from the southern hemisphere in 1868. A few years ago, watched by members of a Quantas-sponsored squad, a eucalyptus tree was planted to revive and commemorate this fable; a brass plaque was screwed to a wooden block to record the event. The plaque, along with its legend, disappeared within days of the ceremony. It has not been replaced. Such an act would be

9 Watching the demolition of House, January 11, 1994

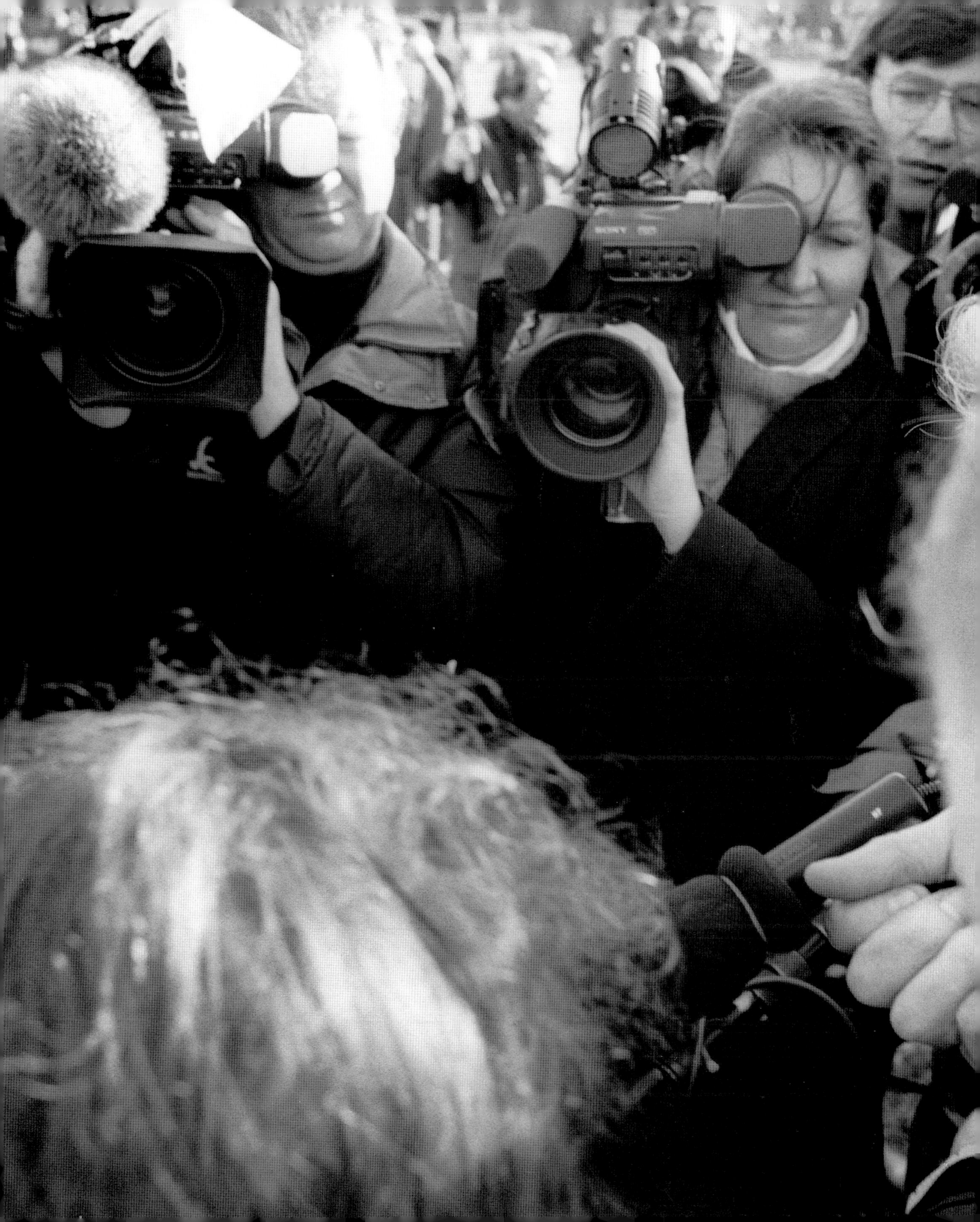

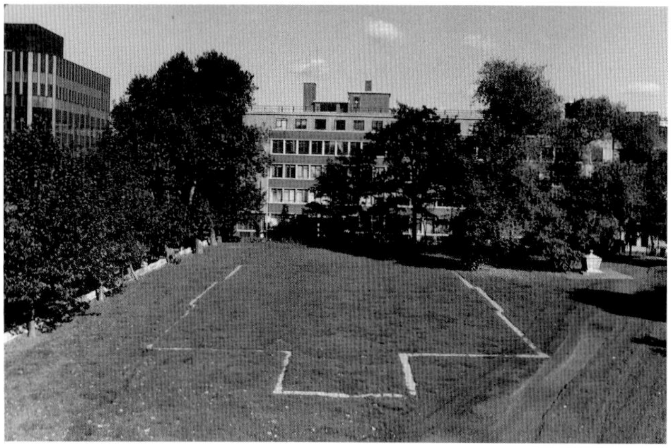

10

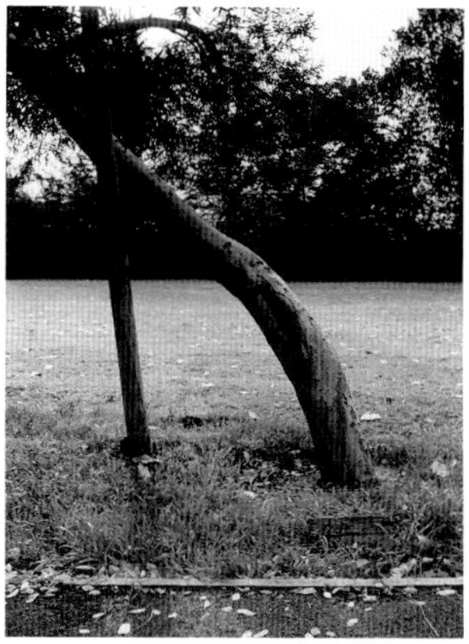

11

10 St. Mary Matfelon, Whitechapel, London E1 **11** Eucalyptus tree 'memorial', Meath Gardens, London E9 **12** Wennington Green, October 25, 1994

redundant. The empty block is useful for scraping off dog dirt. The tree, leaning crazily to the east, supported by a stave, is bent and brutalized. A damaged dreaming. But the validity of the King Cole myth gathers momentum even as the memory-prompts weaken. That is the nature of riparian London with its layers of deletions, resurrections. We are forced to become mediums for the lives and the buildings that have vanished. *House,* through its elimination, joins the company: remembered as an archetype when it is forgotten as an artwork.

House belongs with the invisible church of St Mary Matfelon in Whitechapel, a removed structure from which that district took its name. The church forged its doctrine from misfortune: the Great Tempest of 1362, the fire of 1880 which gutted the building in an hour, the fire-bombs of 1940, the tearing down of the ruin in 1952, the reduction to the status of 'garden' in 1966. All that is left of this dark history is a brick outline in the grass, a psychic barrier that repelled the vagrants who clustered around the solitary sepulchre until the Rowton House (Jack London's 'Monster Doss House') was closed down, to take up its role as a fashionable derelict, a venue for rock promos and performance artists. We can only dowse the history of this location, through worship, plague, war, by contemplating aspects that are resistant to cameras and recording instruments.

A city of parkland phantoms, gravestones cleared to decorate the borders of market gardens. The perpetual metamorphosis of enclosed scraps of ground whose 'story' is scribbled over, re–cut, eternally present: the lost earth of Whitechapel Mount ('considerably higher' than the London Hospital), the synagogues that become Bengali supermarkets, the warehouses that produce and store unseen and unsaleable art. *House* is of this company. The worn squares of turf, like poorly laid cork tiles, that brand a rectangle on Wennington Green, invoke a provisional existence that is close to fiction; true crimes committed by imaginary criminals. Springheeled Jack and Sweeney Todd perverting the fantasies of BNP foot soldiers.

Eavesdropping on the conversations of those who came to debate the nature and essential mystery of the Whiteread *House,* it became clear to me that many felt, or

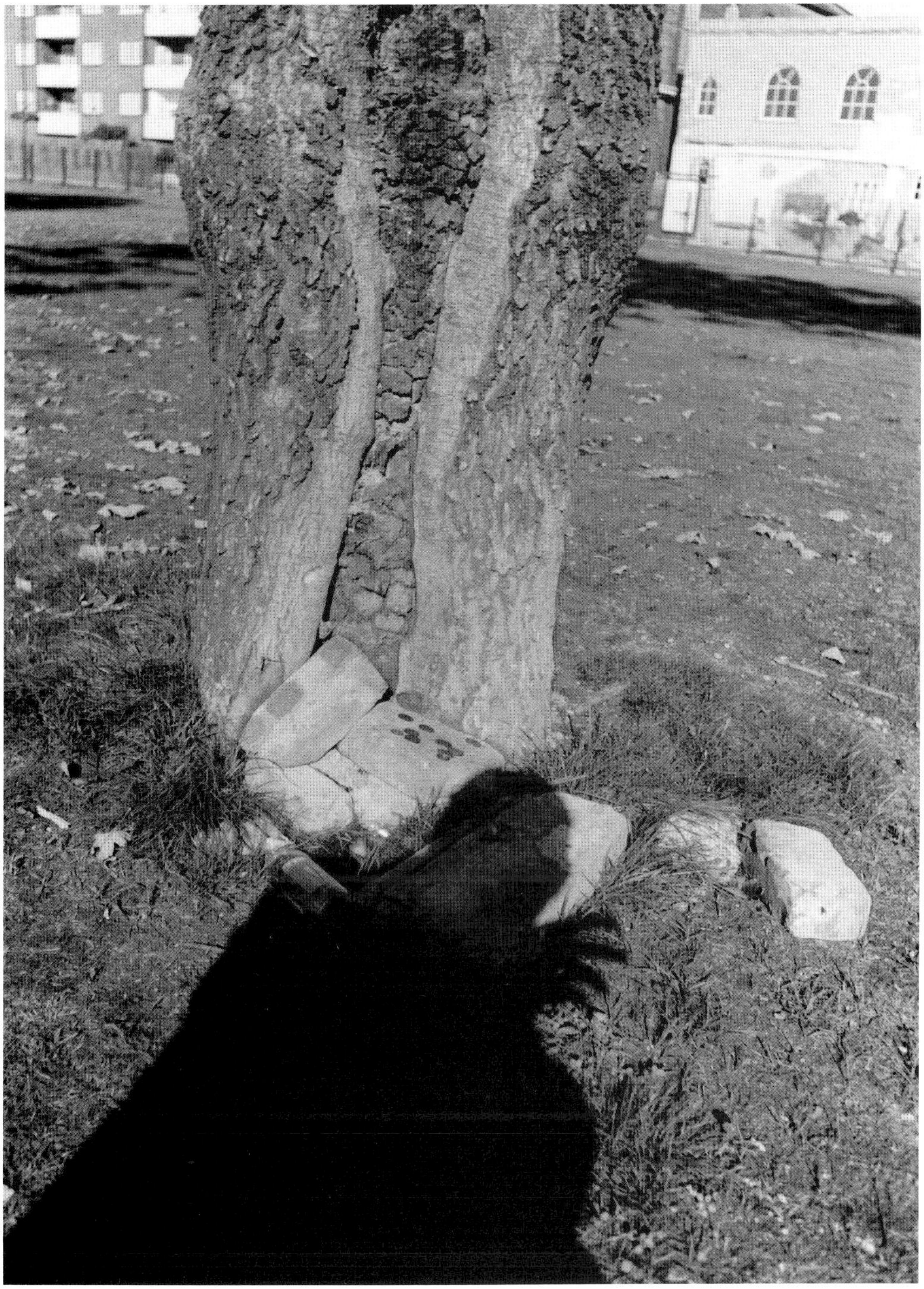

12

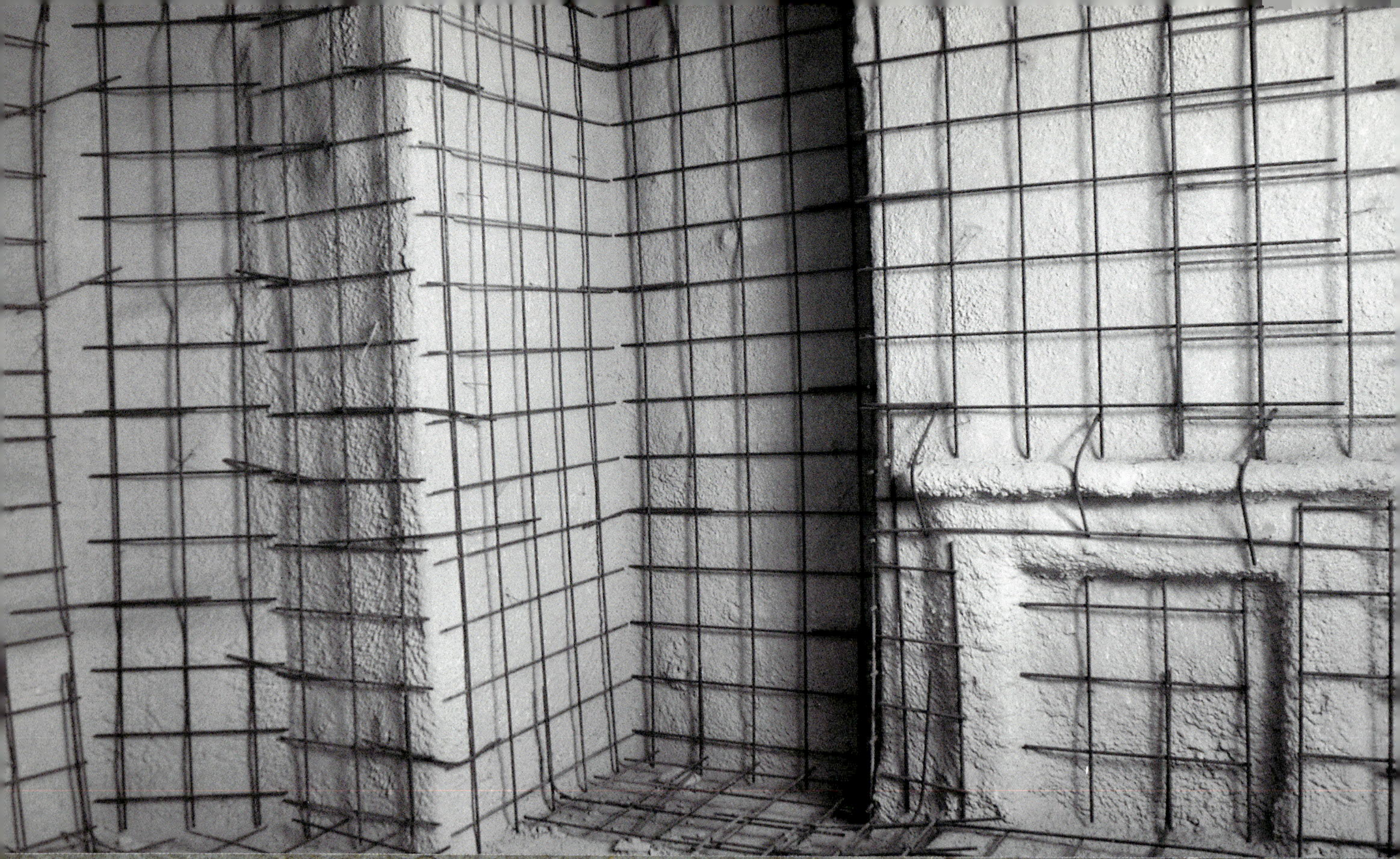

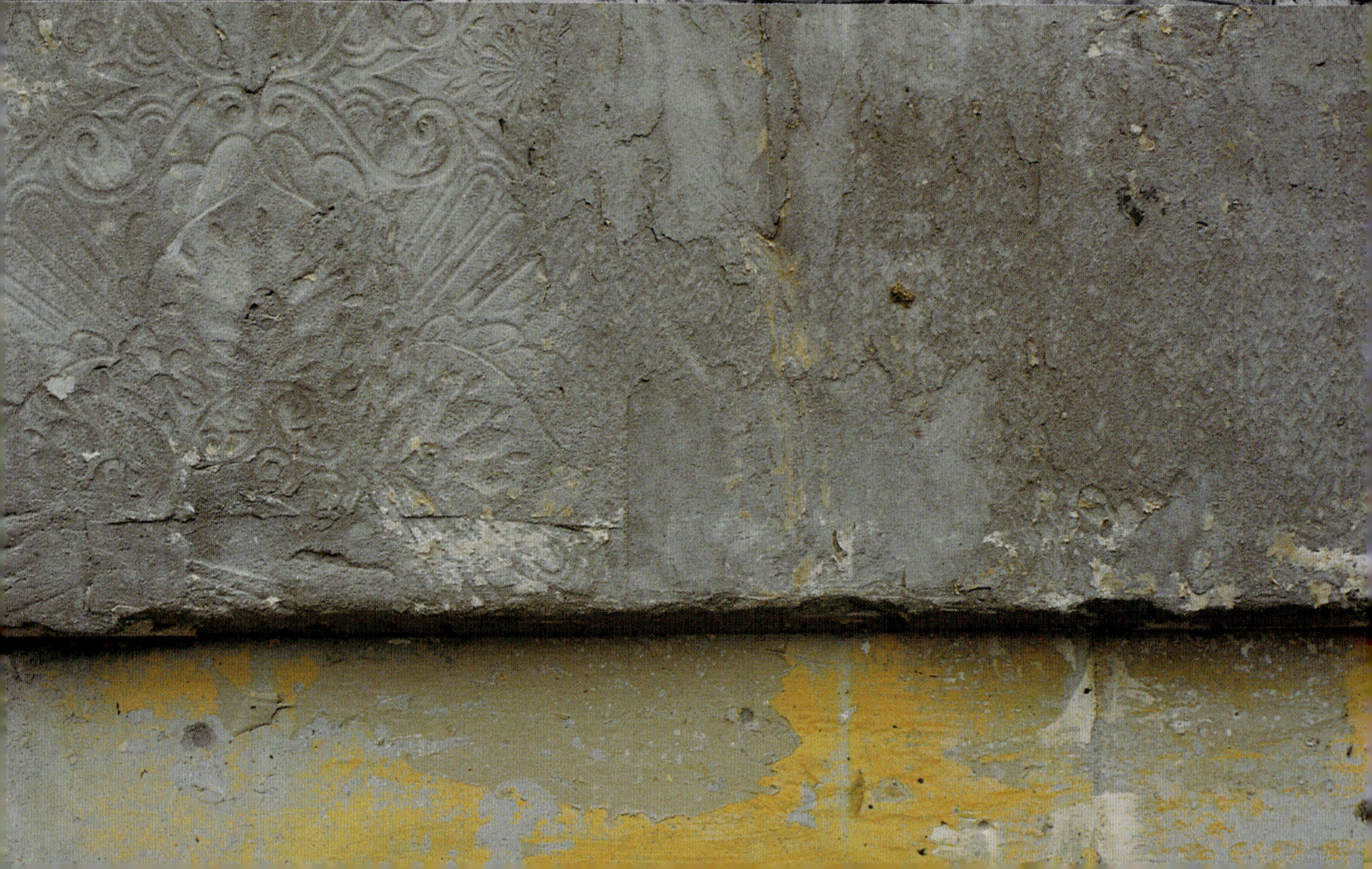

13 Gridwork interior with reinforcing rods, September, 1993 **14** Construction detail, September, 1993 **15** Interior, casting in progress, September, 1993

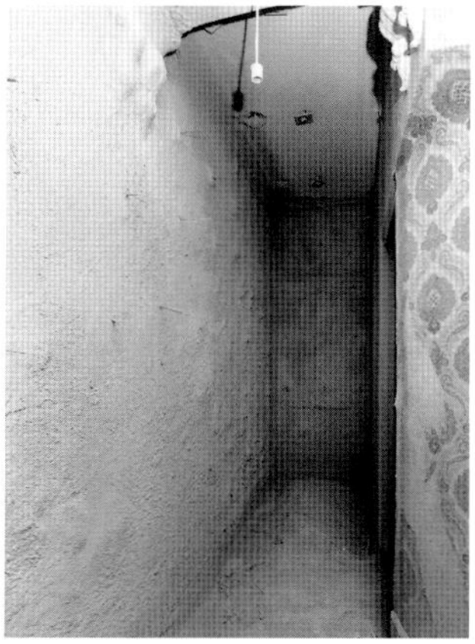

15

wanted to believe, that the Grove Road terrace had been turned inside-out by a feat of gnostic prestidigitation – thereby creating a vacuum in which time itself could be held to ransom. *House* was a vessel packed with mantic darkness, instead of a peeled version of Sydney Gale's family home. They were unwillingly to accept that we were seeing a nest of rooms from outside, with the interference of the bricks: a hologram privilege, a solid X-ray. The process of migration, inside to outside, was limited to the city. Surreptitiously, the tokens and sacred statues from the centre were being banished to the suburbs, so that Temple Bar finds itself marooned in Theobald's Park near Waltham Abbey, and the Euston Arch is broken up and dumped in the River Lea. Monuments were dug out, filched, to add class to Green Belt estates. The centre loses its signifiers as it is colonized by a cult phoney ruralism.

Wennington Green, a year on from the *House* episode, has retreated into a fugue of complacent entropy. The glow of an Indian summer casts a ribcage of charcoal shadows from the surviving trees. The Arcadian conceits of the politicians are justified, for a few hours, by a complicity of light. The palpable absence of *House* validates the grove-like nature of the park. An ash tree confirms the edge of the secret garden. The tree has a deep gash in its bark, revealing a second skin – surgical dressings wadded into a wound. Wasps, tipsy with autumnal liquor, levitate above an offering of glassy white grapes, arranged at the tree's base. They are vile, these grapes, like a tray of artificial eyes offered as sweeteners to the breath. Disguising their presence – in homage to Carl Andre – is a heap of bricks; and on the bricks an obscure collection of copper coins. In the long grass, above thick roots, where the motor-mower couldn't get in, is a broken bottle of Foster's Ice. Random mementoes. Cod sponsorship. Grave goods. There are no other clues from which to uncode this al fresco celebration: no sightings, no culprits. We do not know, or need to know, who came here to honour the anniversary of Whiteread's extinguished vision.

Doreen Massey

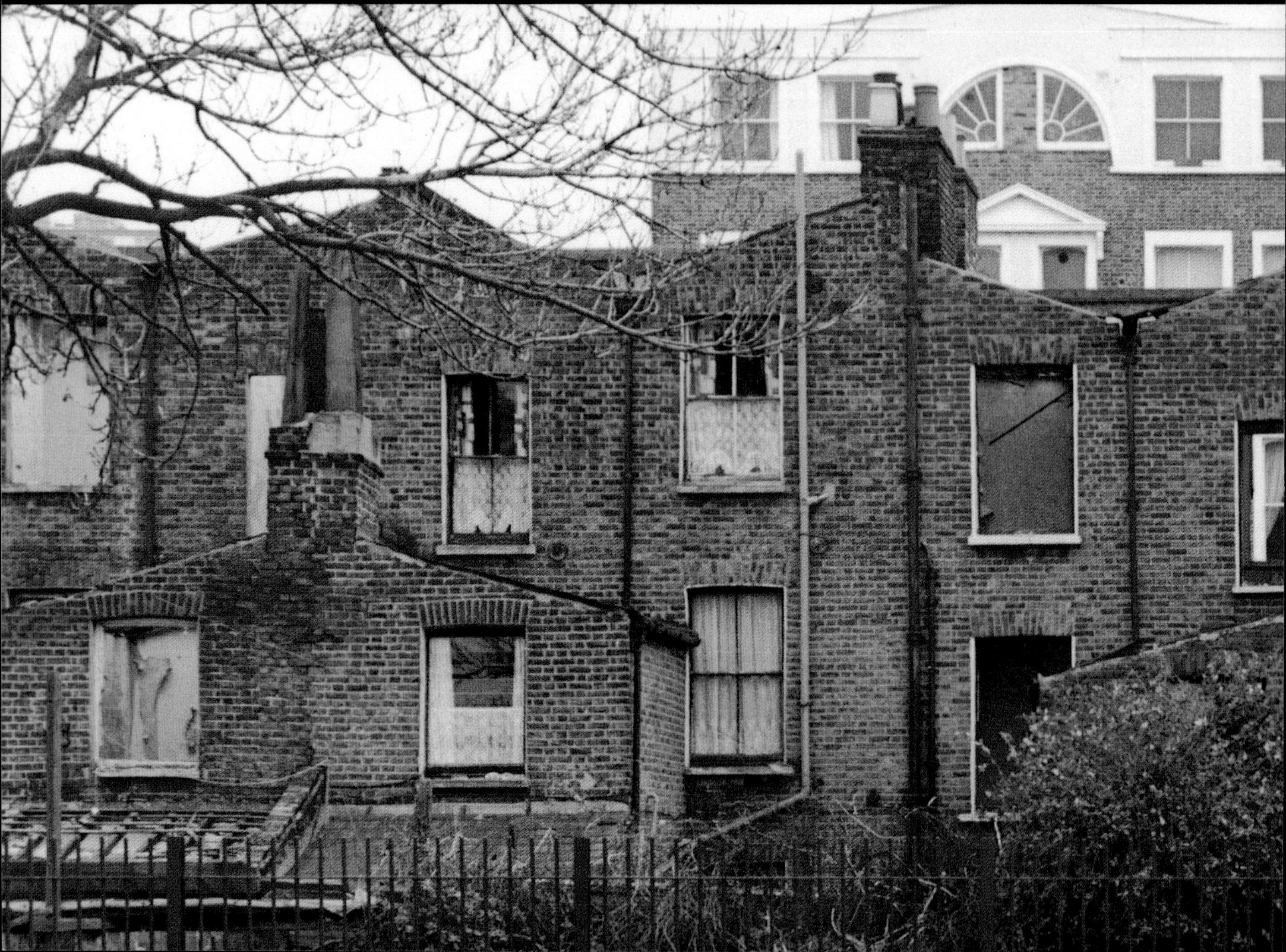

space-time and the politics of location

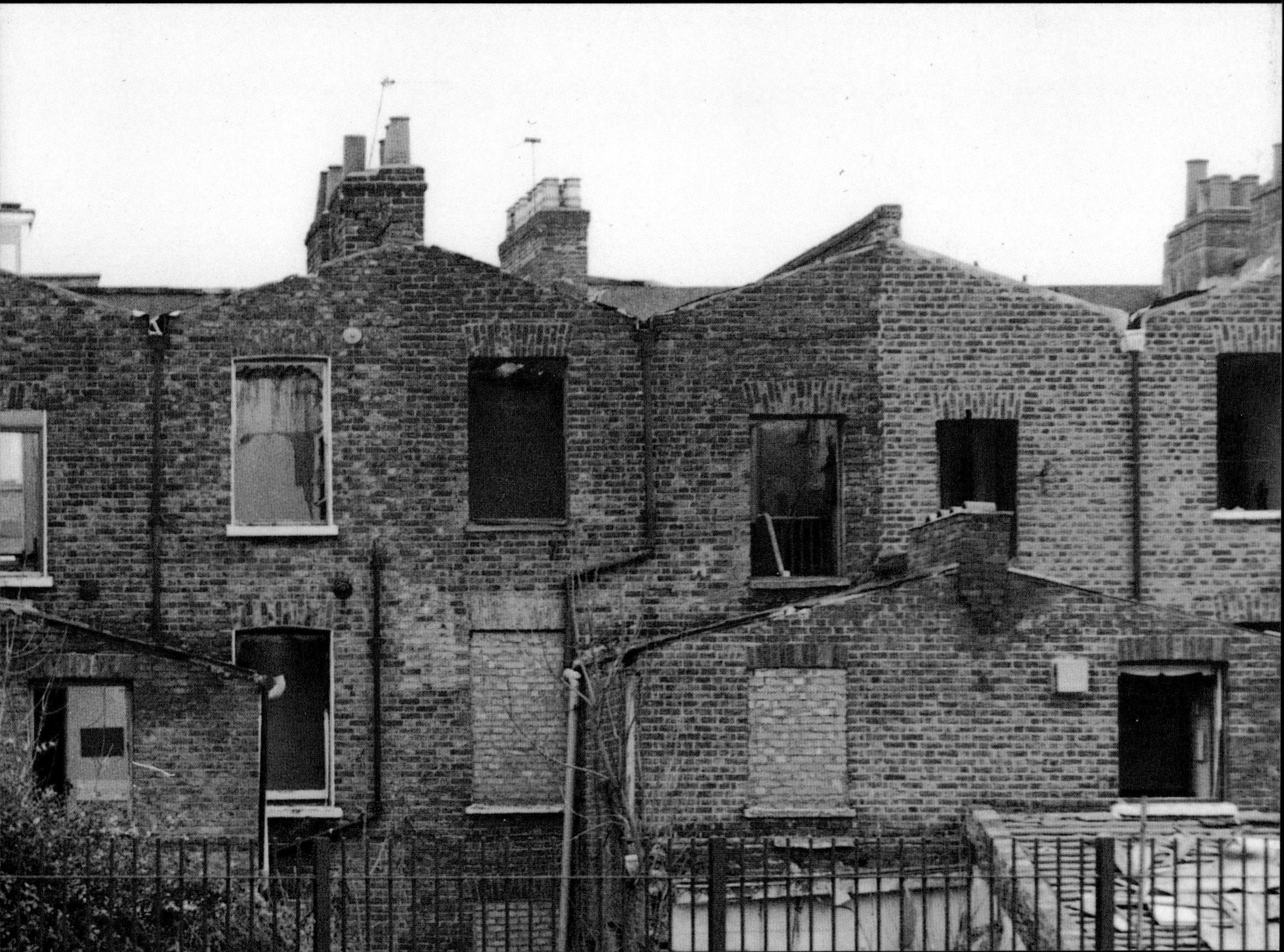

The social spaces through which we live do not only consist of physical things: of bricks and mortar, streets and bridges, mountains and sea-shore, and of what we make of these things. They consist also of those less tangible spaces we construct out of social interaction. The intimate social relations of the kitchen and the interactions from there to the backyard and the living room. The relations with neighbours: talking across the back wall, the more formal hello in the street, the annoyance when they come home noisily and very late, yet again, on a Saturday night. These local spaces are set within, and actively link into, the wider networks of social relations which make up the neighbourhood, the borough, the city. Social space is not an empty arena within which we conduct our lives; rather it is something we construct and which others construct about us. It is this incredible complexity of social interactions and meanings which we constantly build, tear down and negotiate. And it is always mobile, always changing, always open to revision and potentially fragile. We are always creating, in other words, not just a space, a geography of our lives, but a *time*-space for our lives.[1]

Sitting there so solidly, so silently, so implacably, in Grove Road, so physically in just the place it always was, and yet so clearly out of place, *House* worked as a disruption of such social time-spaces. It jumped into and threw awry the 'normal' time-spaces, and the ideas of time-spaces, which we construct in order to live our lives.

It worked this disruption, first and most obviously, in a predominantly temporal sense. It set a familiar past in the space-time of today; it made present something which was absent; it was the space of a house no longer there. Secondly, however, it worked spatially: it turned the space inside out. The private was opened to public view. The little intimacies were exposed: the print of the flex running down the wall to the light switch seeming so personal, so vulnerable now. By this means, the intimate was made monumental and yet retained its intimacy. And this effect of our prying into intimacies was reinforced by the tearing down of the rest of the terrace. Yet further exposure. For neighbouring houses provide protection, enable you to put on only your best face. With them gone we could see what lay behind that solid public frontage. We could see the back-spaces as they fell away in size and somehow in significance, through back bedroom, back extension, scullery, lean-to shed. From public solidity and the front room to the more precarious, personal and informal spaces where most of daily life was lived. Now we could see all of this too.

And third, *House* disrupted our accustomed sense of time-space by apparently solidifying the volume that had once been the interior of the house: the living space, the space of life. Its openness had been filled in. All that was air was turned into solid. In *House*, social time-space was deadened, muted. The movement, the noise, the interchange; these things through which we create the time-spaces of our lives were gone. *House* was emptied of all that, and such a way of asserting what social time-space really is – precisely by so brilliantly emphasizing its absence, its current impossibility – is one of the most

1. For a more detailed discussion, see Doreen Massey, *Space, Place and Gender*, Polity, Cambridge, 1994
2. David Harvey, *The Condition of Postmodernity*, Basil Blackwell, Oxford, 1989
3. Wendy Wheeler, 'Nostalgia Isn't Nasty – the Postmodernising of Parliamenttary Democracy' in Mark Perryman ed. *Altered States: Postmodernism, Politics, Culture*, Lawrence and Wishart, London, 1994

provocative things about this work. Through its very negation it brought home the true meaning of social space.

Given all of this, what is crucial to any assessment of *House* on these dimensions is the way in which the three aspects of space-time disruption work together. Much must turn on the way in which these disruptions functioned in the responses to, and interpretations of, *House*, perhaps especially by local people – people in the East End of London.

Nostalgia

Let us begin this enquiry with the fact of reference to the past – or, better, reference to 'a past', since the point is precisely that there are many versions of this history. Much comment on *House* has focused on memory, on the first – temporal – disruption of space-time which it works. In articles, in interviews, in letters to newspapers, people talk of the sculpture 'bringing back memories', of 'making them (memories) real', of commemorating memory itself, of the evocation of emotional responses of absence/sadness/the transience of things. There is much reference to nostalgia and to nostalgia for a specific place and time.

Now, that kind of nostalgia has been interpreted by many as being a symptomatic, defining, element of the postmodern condition. This, in turn, has been variously explained. On the one hand commentators such as David Harvey see in a nostalgia for place merely a defensive response to the new burst of the globalization of capital, the new and accelerated phase of time-space compression.[2] For them, such a response is a negative evasion of 'the real issues', and nostalgia for place is likely to end up in political 'reaction'. Yet there is another way of understanding this nostalgia which again would see it as a product of the present era but would not condemn it out of hand. Thus Angelika Bammer and Wendy Wheeler interpret it as a symptom emerging from the deprivations of modernity, a response to the too-long-maintained repression of affective desire by Modernism in its various forms. Postmodern nostalgia is the return of Modernism's repressed.[3]

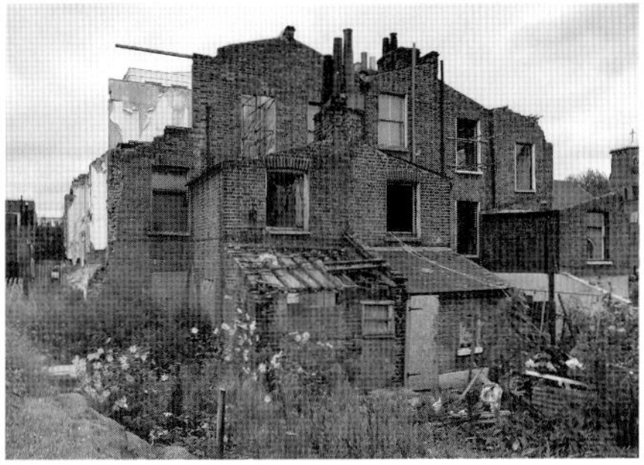

1

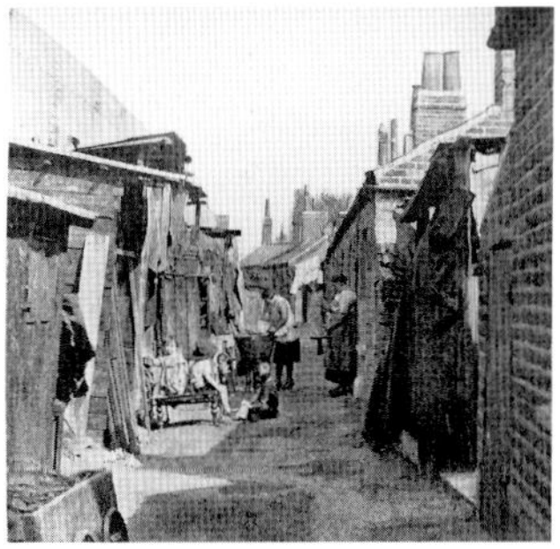

2

1 Backview of terrace, Grove Road, Spring, 1993 **2** Late Victorian slum, London

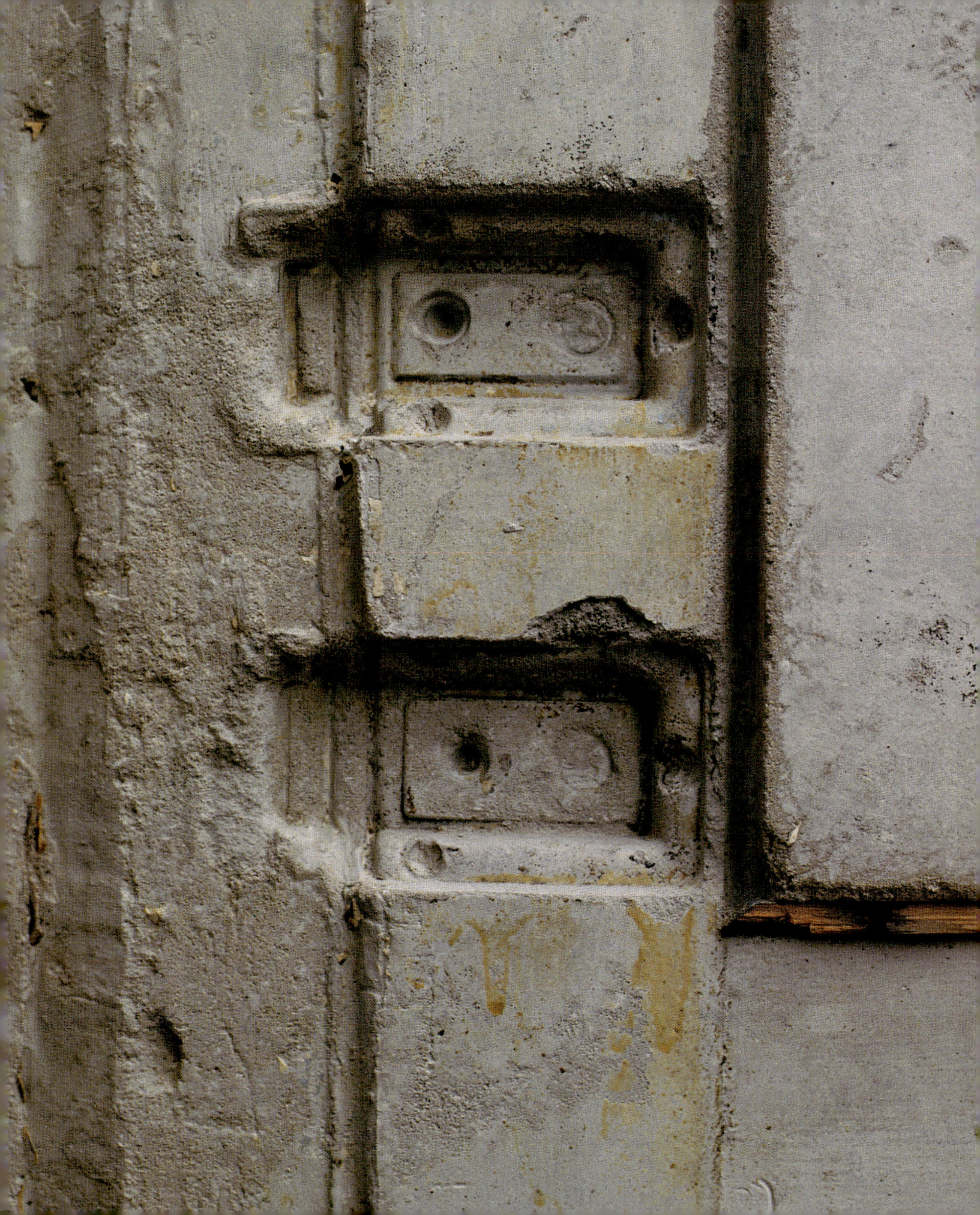

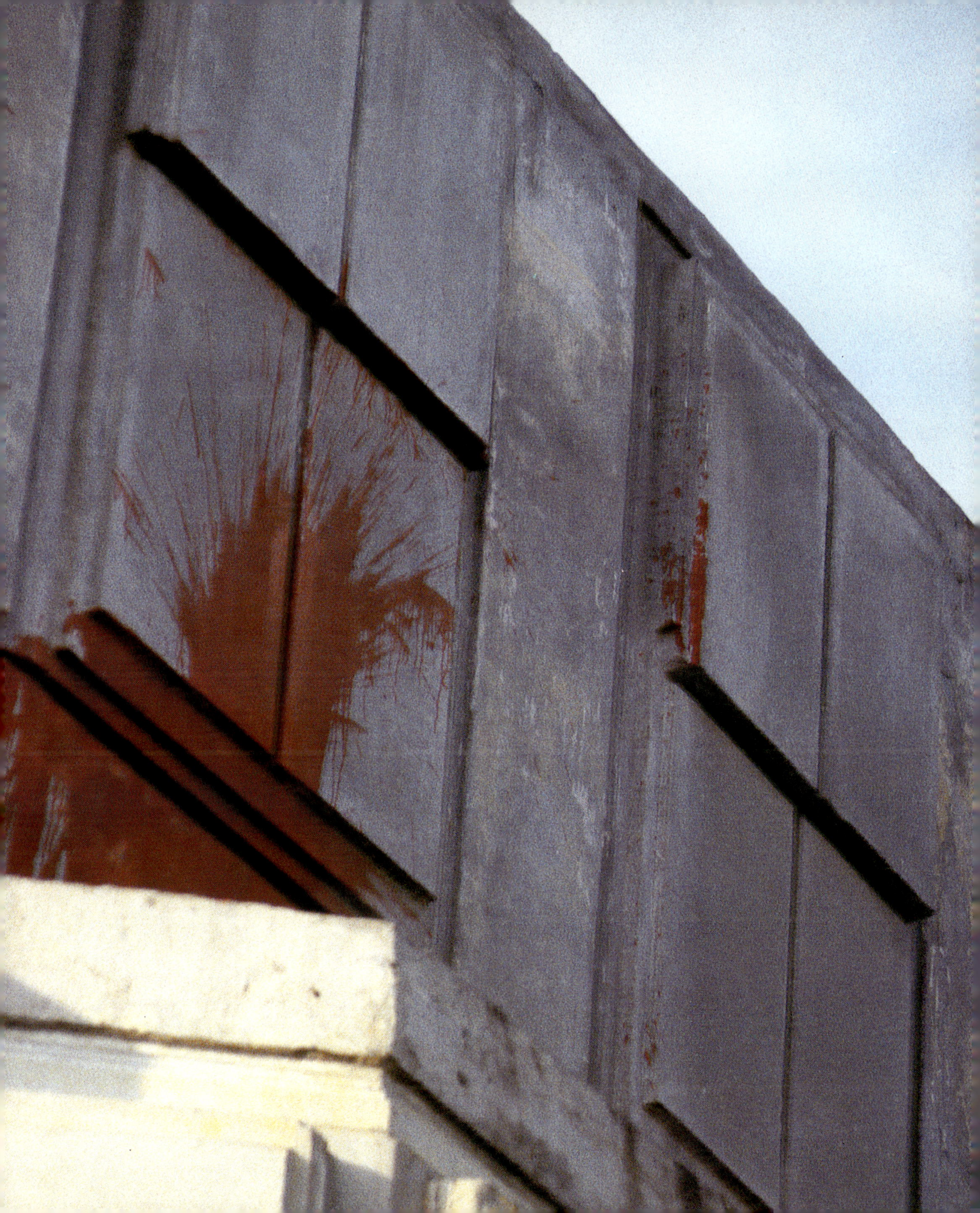

How then is it to be interpreted? Wendy Wheeler, who links this aspect of affect precisely to notions of the uncanny, stresses the element of sharedness which it entails. Postmodern nostalgia she defines as 'the desire for communal identifications'. 'Nostalgia ... turns us towards the idea of the individual as non-alienated, as knowing and being known by others in the commonality of the community which is identified as "home".'[4] It is not necessary to accept that this is the only form of postmodern nostalgia in order to agree that it is an important component. Angelika Bammer, too, addressing the specific issue of 'home', writes of 'fictional constructs, mythic narratives, stories the telling of which have the power to create the "we" who are engaged in telling them. This power to create not only an identity for ourselves as members of a community... , but also the discursive right to a space (a country, a neighbourhood, a place to live) that is due us, is – we then claim, in the name of the we-ness we have just constructed – at the heart of what Anderson describes as "the profound emotional legitimacy" of such concepts as "nation" or "home".'[5]

But if this interpretation, in contrast to that of Harvey, accepts – as it is surely correct to do – the 'emotional legitimacy' of nostalgia for place and home (even if only on grounds of recognizing its inevitability), it is nonetheless the case that such nostalgia can be problematical. For memory and the desire for communal identifications can cut both ways. They can be an aid to reactionary claims for a return (to something which of course never quite was, or which at least is open to dispute). They can erase other memories and other identifications. They can exclude some groups from membership in 'the commonality of the community which is identified as 'home', or they can be a basis for the mobilization of emancipatory political change. Particular evocations of nostalgia must, for that reason, be evaluated individually, in their specificity. Jeffrey Peck, for instance, concludes that in certain times and places (he is writing of Germany at the end of the twentieth century), the particular concept of 'home' is so unavoidably

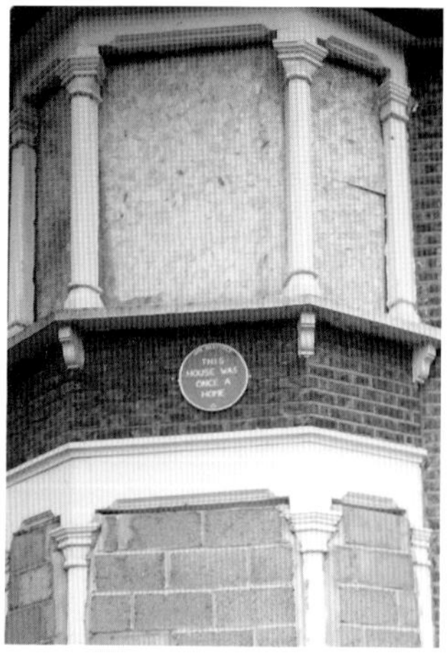

4

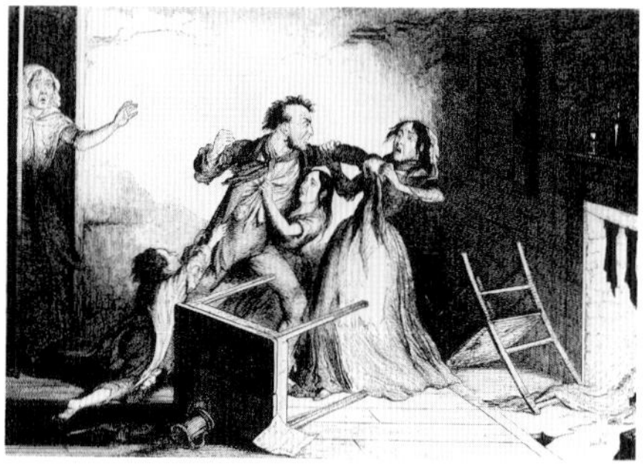

3

3 George Cruickshank, 'The Bottle', 1847, plate V **4** 'This House Was Once a Home', boarded-up house, Leytonstone, London E11 I full of references to exclusion, blood and territory that it is virtually unusable for other, more disruptive emancipatory purposes.[6] Another approach, maybe in other contexts, might be to argue the pressing need for its reformulation. The question is how, in any particular circumstance, a specific form of evocation of memories functions? What effects does it produce? What solidarities (what we-nesses) does it conjure in the imagination? Are its workings those of exclusion or of openness?

House clearly aroused memories and provoked thoughts about nostalgia. Moreover it did so, and quite deliberately, at a specific moment in space-time: a late-nineteenth century house in a once-settled, now partly demolished residential street in the heart of London's East End. How, then, in relation to this question of nostalgia, did *House* work its effects?

The question can be posed at two spatial scales. First, it can be posed at the scale of house and home. Feminists, for instance, have long argued that the resonances once so usually associated with 'home' must be disrupted: that home is not necessarily a place of rest or of respose, that it can be also a place of work, a place of conflict, a place of entrapment. Bammer suggests that 'home, in a sense, has always been *unheimlich*, unhomely; not just the utopian place of safety and shelter for which we supposedly yearn, but also the place of dark secrets, of fear and danger, that we can sometimes only inhabit furtively'.[7]

Second, the question of *House*'s affect/effect can be raised at a broader geographical scale: that of the local area in which it was made. Here what needs to be investigated is its relation to a politics of location. For the sculpture was set in the East End of London and, more specifically, in the borough of Tower Hamlets. And memory and nostalgia are difficult and dangerous things in that area these days. On the one hand is the enormous freight of meaning – and of different meanings – which the very words 'the East End of London' bring with them. On the other hand is the wrenching disruption of this space in the recent past. The docks have closed, their use and meaning is being quite consciously re-worked; to the south Canary Wharf rises on the obliteration of a past which is drawn on only to add a touch of local colour to the new, global developments. And in September 1993, at the very time when *House* was being constructed, the British National Party won a seat on the local borough council.

In this local area, memory and nostalgia are active forces precisely in the constitution of communal identifications and political subjectivities. They are crucial axes around which political constituencies are articulated and individuals interpellated into wider constellations of attitudes. So *House* is an irruption of a past time-space into a present where references to 'the past', and interpretations of the nature of that past and of the relationship between past and present, are key political stakes.

The issue, therefore, is not to attempt to eradicate memory and nostalgia. It is, on the contrary, to ask: how do those other two aspects of the potentially uncanny spatiality of *House* work to subvert what *could* be, given its placing in this time and space, an all-too-*comfortable* nostalgia of home and locality.

4. ibid., p.99
5. Angelika Bammer, 'Editorial: The Question of "Home",' *New Formations*, Lawrence and Wishart, London, no.17, p.xi, 1992
6. Jeffrey M. Peck, 'Rac(e)ing the Nation: Is There a German "Home",' *New Formations*, no.17, pp. 75–84, UK, 1992
7. Bammer, op.cit., p.xi

House and 'home'

What effects, then, do the turning of the space inside out and the solidification of space have when considered at the level of the domestic: at the spatial scale of the home?

One thing to say first is that, of course, this sculpture was not called *Home*; it was called *House*. And this naming, it seems to me, reinforces mightily the impact of all the other challenges to sentimentalized notions of the domestic which it works so well. It immediately distances us, it uses a word somehow from the public sphere to designate a work which is so evidently redolent of what we customarily think of as private, and a word, too, which refers more to the physicality of the walls and roof, which have been removed, which now no longer are, than to the space of social interaction which, in contrast, has now so physically been both exposed and filled in. The very naming, then, gives clues to the spatial disruptions *House* effected.

The first of these two spatial reversions – the turning of the space 'inside out' – works particularly powerfully at this scale of the individual house/home. It is immediately shocking and disruptive. It exposes the private sphere to public view and thereby to questioning. Most importantly, it defamiliarizes house and home. And in achieving that, it challenges us to put our own meanings on them. It exposes the normal, comfortable mythologizing of 'home'. Bammer, following up her argument for the intrinsic double nature of home, suggests that 'Perhaps, in this light, the best we can do about home at this point in time is to bring it, in all its complexity, out into the open'.[8] This, surely, *House* achieves. It is not merely physical space which it turns inside out but the whole burden of meaning and metaphor which this space has so often had to carry (the actual bearing of the burden usually predominantly being done by the women who lived in those spaces). Potentially at least it exposes the complexity of the meaning of 'home'. *House* emphasizes – indeed it throws in our faces – the fact that its meaning always has to be interpreted; that there was never any simple 'authenticity'; that the meaning(s) of home are always open to contestation.

Postmodern nostalgia, it has already been pointed out, has been argued to be the return of the repressed of Modernity. More specifically, it is the return of the repressed in the form of the 'other' sides of all those dualisms which are made to provide the (ultimately oh-so-precarious) foundation for Modernity's assertion of the dominance of unsullied Reason.[9] Among the core set of this bastion of dualisms is that between the famous pair, the private and the public. For Hannah Arendt the distinction between the two is 'between things that should be hidden and things that should be shown'.[10] In *House* the things which should be shown are removed, leaving only their defining shape; while the things which should be hidden are (almost, potentially, in outline) exposed to view. It is a reversal which, certainly, could bear 'the name for everything that ought to have remained... secret and hidden but has come to light'. Moreover, to take a final step along this particular line of thought, Homi Bhabha, drawing on Carole Pateman's work in *The Disorder of Women*, argues that 'By making

5 Big Pit leaflet showing underground tour of coal mine

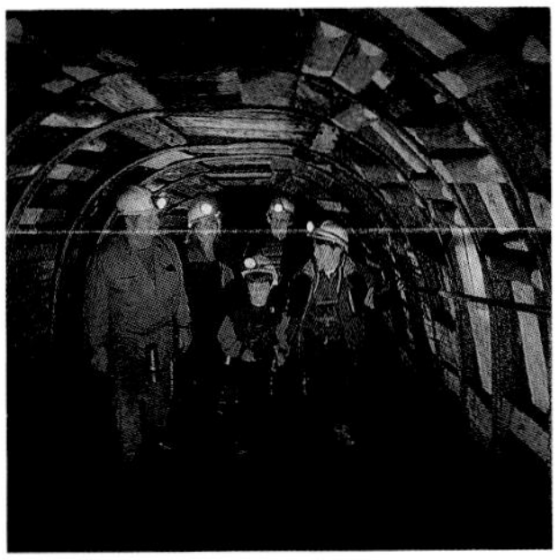

5

visible the forgetting of the "unhomely" moment in civil society, feminism specifies the patriarchal, gendered nature of civil society and disturbs the symmetry of private and public which is now shadowed, or uncannily doubled, by the difference of genders which does not neatly map on to the private and the public, but becomes disturbingly supplementary to them'.[11]

The second spatial reversal worked by *House*, the solidifying of the once-open space (even though it was only an apparent solidification) both further complicates this questioning of the public/private divide and produces other, different effects. For the 'private' sphere (if we continue to use the now-problematized distinction) is of course *not* in fact exposed to view. What used to be a space-time created out of living social relations is by this second reversal made mute and blind and inanimate. On the one hand this forces us, again, to interpret. By defamiliarizing, silencing, the private world now exposed to public view it compels us to do our own work. Mute it stood there, asking us to remember, to think, to question. On the other hand, by evoking so profoundly the absence of that previous life, those now-stilled social relations, by the fact that the house has gone and that the potential for the reconstruction of that social space has been so finally ended by both aspects of this spatial reversal, *House* insists on the impossibility of the recovery of that past. This is crucial; it is potentially, and productively, disturbing. It is a positive, dislocating, evocation of memories. It makes clear that, however you interpret the past, you can't have it back.

It may perhaps seem rather a prosaic comparison to make, but there does seem to be here a glaring – and fascinating – contrast with the way in which the classic 'heritage site' performs its work. In many heritage sites not only are the buildings retained, but within them and around them a version of the social relations of the chosen moment of the past is acted out. A particular reading (sometimes more than one) of those social relations which constituted that particular space-time is preserved, and re-presented. There is frequently a commentary, maybe a written guide explaining things. Such sites, too, can be provocative of nostalgia. As Wheeler says, 'That these are commodified images in no way lessens their effect'.[12] But the effect of this nostalgia is likely to be different from that of *House*. While *House* is a prompt and a disturbance to the memory, the classic heritage site fills in those spaces and restricts the room for interpretation and imagination. Instead of questioning memory and pre-given understandings of the past, the classic heritage site will provide them ready-made. Instead of defamiliarizing the supposedly familiar, it is meant as an aid to further familiarization. It is, by design, an understandable rather than an unsettling space, a comfortable *rapprochement* with another space-time.

The use of such sites in particular localities can also sometimes have the effect of presenting history as continuity, as Tradition in its conventional sense. On this reading, 'tradition' is something which we inevitably lose, as it fades into the past. Such notions of tradition can so easily be congealed into a static essence, as the *real* character of the place: what do we mean when we say 'this is

8. Bammer, op.cit.
9. Wheeler, op.cit.
10. Hannah Arendt, 1958, *The Human Condition*, Chicago University Press, Chicago, p.72, in Homi Bhabha, *The Location of Culture*, Routledge, London, p.10, 1994
11. Bhabha, op.cit.
12. Wheeler, op.cit, p.98

THIS HOUSE
IS A NICE
HOME

the *real* East End'? And what contexts would provoke us to say it?

It has recently been argued by many writers that white British culture and society are undergoing serious anxiety about the nature of Tradition and their relationship to it. Kevin Robins has argued that the burgeoning industry of 'heritage culture' has been in part about attempts to construct, or to respond to the felt need for, 'protective illusions' in the midst of all this anxiety.[13] In one way *House* clearly disallows such protective illusions; the very vulnerability of its inside-outness, for instance, prevents such easy recourse to Tradition in this sense. But there is another aspect to the critique of this concept of local Tradition which raises broader issues. In this critique what is called for is a rejection of the all-too-frequently 'internalist', inward-looking, character of Tradition and a recognition of the past – and the present – as always having been hybrid and open. Homi Bhabha, elaborating the notion of tradition to involve that of cultural translation, argues the need to take on board 'the deep, the profoundly perturbed and perturbing question of our relationship to others – other cultures, other states, other histories, other experiences, traditions, peoples and destinies'.[14] For some this is an issue which has taken on a particular urgency in a Britain which is both in decline and caught up in an accelerated globalization. Thus Robins argues that 'older certainties and hierarchies of British identity have been called into question in a world of dissolving boundaries and disrupted continuities. In a country that is now a container of African and Asian cultures, the sense of what it is to be British can never again have the old confidence and surety'.[15] And Hanif Kureishi insists 'It is the British, the white British, who have to learn that being British isn't what it was. Now it is a more complex thing, involving new elements'.[16] (One might question, as I later shall, whether the issue of British identity was *ever* as simple as both these writers imply; but the complexities currently to be confronted are indisputable.) Robins, moreover, argues that many classic heritage sites (there are exceptions) do little or nothing to confront these responsibilities. Rather,

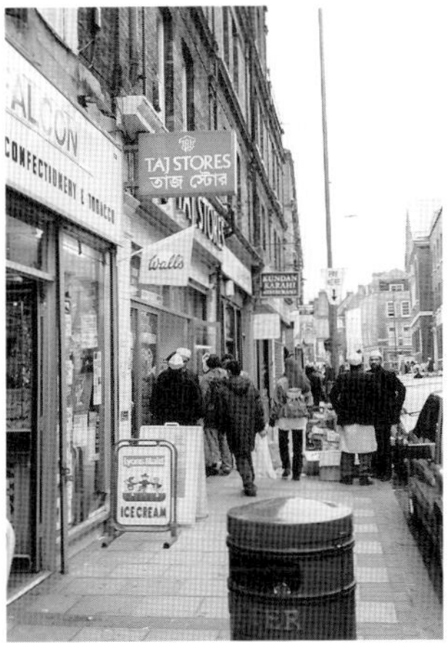

6

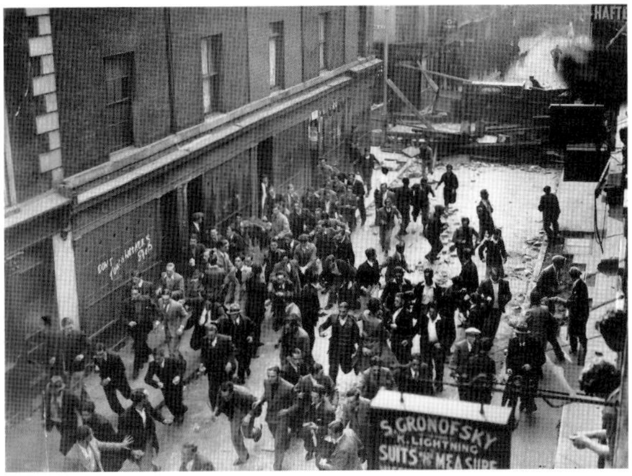

7

6 Brick Lane Market, 1994 **7** Brick Lane riot, 1936

13. Kevin Robins, 'Tradition and Translation: National Culture in its Global Context', in Corner, J. and Harvey, S. (eds), *Enterprise and Heritage*, pp.21–44, Routledge, London, 1991
14. Homi Bhabha, 'Beyond Fundamentalism and Liberalism', *New Statesman and Society*, London, 3 March 1989
15. Robins, op.cit., p.41
16. Hanif Kureishi, 'England, your England', *New Statesman and Society*, 21 July, London, 1989

they present a *protective* strategy of response to global forces 'centred around the conservation, rather than reinterpretation, of identities'.[17] Another question, then, must be: to what extent does *House* problematize these aspects of tradition and identity? It is here that we enter the wider spatial territory of the politics of location.

The Politics of Location

House was conceived and made in the context of the East End of London. And the East End is an area which oozes meaning as a place, both locally and in the national psyche. The meanings are, however, varied and much contested. This is the home both of Alf Garnett and of a constantly-added-to ethnic mix; of the battle of Cable Street, Brick Lane and dockers marching against immigration. It is a locality in which notions of community and of constructing that 'we' of which Angelika Bammer writes, and the communal identifications named by Wendy Wheeler, are at the very heart of politics and of daily life. A reference to 'tradition' in the East End can bring to mind radicalism and ethnic diversity or racism and community closure. In such a context it becomes particularly important to ask how the evocation of memory is working and what effects – social and political – it is producing.

The debates which took place over *House* complicated these issues still further, sometimes productively, at other times troublingly. So-called 'traditionalism' in art crossed swords at times with forms of traditionalism of the locality. The predictable debate as to whether or not this was 'art', although a sterile confrontation in its own terms, threw into relief some other, less expected, alignments. On the one hand, as people from inside and outside the area, indeed from all over the world, flocked to see it, there was an appreciation of the work which was at times undoubtedly elitist. Andrew Graham-Dixon wrote of *House's* critics as 'the myriad dullards ... in all their unutterable boringness ... These people tend not to be actual art critics ... they behave as if the entire history of twentieth-century art had either never happened or had been a terrible aberration'.[18] In giving away the 1993 Turner Prize, Lord Palumbo, then Chairman of the Arts Council, pleaded 'don't let the dunces have their day',[19] and so forth. And in reply came the equally dispiriting jibe from a local councillor that the whole business was 'a little entertainment for the gallery-going classes of Hampstead'.[20] Some highly dubious lines of counterposition were thereby drawn up, between experts and ordinary folk, between I-know-what-I-like traditionalists and an avant-garde which was actually now the establishment, between worthy locals (and local worthies) and elitist outsiders. Thus, one aspect of *House*'s provocation of constituencies looked at first sight pretty dismal.

Yet it was also interestingly contradictory. Thus in one, and only one sense, it was something of a relief that it was, in this public debate, the traditionalists and those who claimed to speak for 'ordinary local people' who so often disliked the work. Had these defenders of all that was so great in those days really loved

17. Robins, op.cit.
18. Andrew Graham-Dixon, "I don't know much about art, but I know what I hate...", *The Independent*, London, 24 November, 1993
19. Deyan Sudjic, 'Art attack', *The Guardian*, London, November 25, 1993
20. *The Independent*, London, January 14, 1994

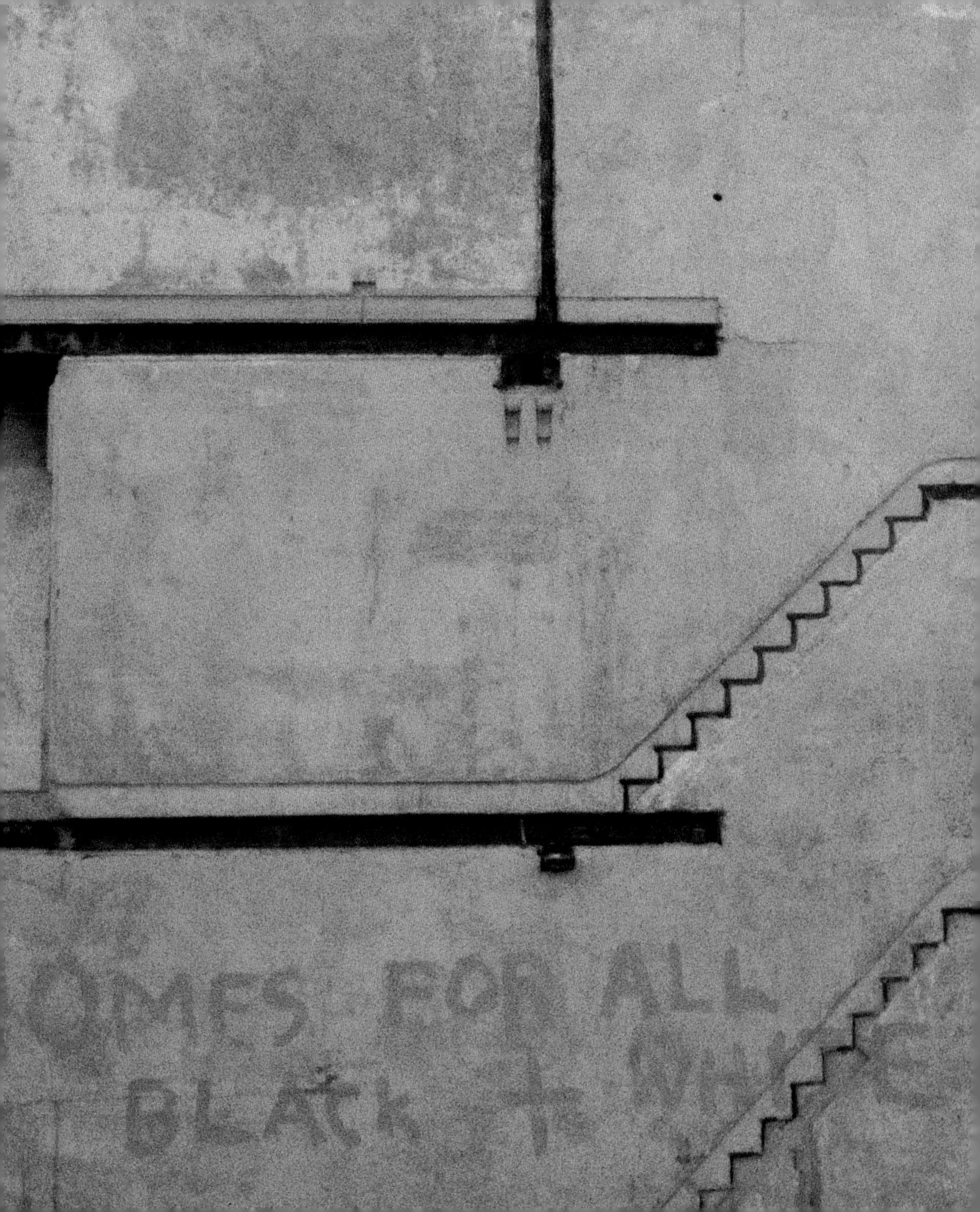
OMES FOR ALL
BLACK +

House, it might have been necessary to question the manner in which it was evoking memory. Had *House* stimulated a positive evocation of the East End for these groups it would probably have fitted into images of good old England and cuddly (white and patriarchal) working-class communities. It says a lot for *House* that it does not seem to have been interpreted in this way directly; that it did not play to that kind of nostalgia, did not stimulate the reinforcement of a backward-looking, reactionary, communal identity. But neither was it rejected by these detractors because it *problematized* that kind of a nostalgia of place. The issue was simply not raised. What these commentators disliked was *House*'s nature as (not) Art, not its representation of the East End.

Matters were equally confusing on the other side of these self-built fences. Although the work was proudly defended by some as modern in artistic terms, some of the evocations of its meaning by the self-consciously artistically adventurous were alarmingly traditional *socially*.

Take the issue of housing, and what it represents socially. John McEwen in *The Daily Telegraph* paraded the classic contrasts: 'grim 1960s high-rises' and 'tarted-up 1980s ones' and 'the twenty-first century megastructure of Canary Wharf'. And, having let us know what he doesn't like, he gives us the alternative: 'the snug 1880s terraced family homes of which *House* is an example'.[21] McEwen's response to *House* did not place him within a 'traditionalist' camp. But when it comes to family-values, domestic bliss and housing, what he appreciates is snug families. Non-traditionalism in art combined with an utterly traditional nostalgia about home. Not only does such a response fail to take on board the potential critique of such forms of domestic organization, but it harks back uncritically to an age which itself has come to have many dubious and debatable political meanings – the Victorian era.

But housing in this area raises other issues too. The iconography of house and home performs a crucial role in the various imagined pasts of this part of London. The far-right election victory in September 1993 was largely orchestrated around battles over housing (of which there is a grotesque shortage), and over the right of 'the locals' to local housing over the rights of others. Housing was at the centre of the battle over who was, and who was not, part of the local community. It was a crucial organizing issue for the increasingly vocal racisms. The British National Party in the East End uses a mythic version of the past of the place as white, as pure English. It refers to a non-existent past 'before immigration'. And Bow, where *House* stood, is, and is seen as, a relatively white enclave within that East End. It was one of the first places where the housing strategy 'for locals' was tried. The fact of the work being a house, and in this precise location, was therefore potentially highly symbolic. What *House* did not do, maybe at the wider spatial scale it could not do, was challenge that kind of construction of home as once pure and now corrupted; that notion of tradition, of traditions of place now lost. While it said that no past is recoverable it didn't problematize, *at the level of the locality*, the memory of what that past was. Although its location was important, *House* did

21. John McEwen, 'The House that Rachel Unbuilt', *Sunday Telegraph*, London, 24 October, 1993.

not say much about the East End as a wider area or about Bow within it: as a place of cohabitation of radicalism and racism, as a meeting-place of immigrants from all over the world and over centuries, as a repository of a bit of English identity, as a site of contradiction between a persistent localism and the context of having been for two centuries and more at the hub of a global Empire. It is often argued, as we have seen, that the current intensified phase of globalization has hybridized all our homes. In fact this is by no means a new phenomenon. Quintessential Englishness is utterly founded and dependent upon relations with elsewhere. And in few places is this clearer than the East End, with its constant flow of new communities and its centuries of contact with the trade routes of the world. The hybridity of a place called home is not new. Could *House* have set in motion forces towards the construction, the reinforcement or the subversion of communal identifications in this place? And what 'discursive right to a space' (Bammer) does that allow such a community to claim? These issues are central to the politics of location in this area. Might the work provoke longings for an imagined past 'pre-immigration'? Or could it help in the construction of a 'we' which is inclusive, and neither defensive nor essentialist? To me, it seemed that *House* did not broach these issues substantively.

This is not to suggest that the work could have addressed these issues directly, and certainly not that it need have answered questions rather than merely raising them. For this is the point. At the level of the internal-domestic, *House* clearly problematized issues. One could not look at it without asking questions. At this level, *House* worked all three disruptions to time-space. It brought back a previous time-space, but it also inverted and apparently solidified it. It thoroughly de-familiarized it. It is less clear at the level of the locality, however, that *House* really posed questions, really *unsettled* in any way the terms of the accepted debate. Could it have de-familiarized the locality too? And while, certainly, it was mute, it was not without content. In its specific location and its evocation of house and home, it might have courted the danger of provoking a nostalgia for a white East End.

And yet it seems not to have had that effect, or not among the reactions which found a wider public. The alignments faced the other way. The British Nationalist Party, by all accounts, were utterly offended by the work. Maybe, ironically, what was active here was *House*'s glorious combination of the evocation of tradition precisely in a non-traditional form of 'art'. If this meant that the history of the locality was not problematized, at least it meant that the work did not become the focus for the celebration of a mythical white past. Indeed, the first graffiti sprayed on *House* read: 'HOMES FOR ALL BLACK + WHITE'.

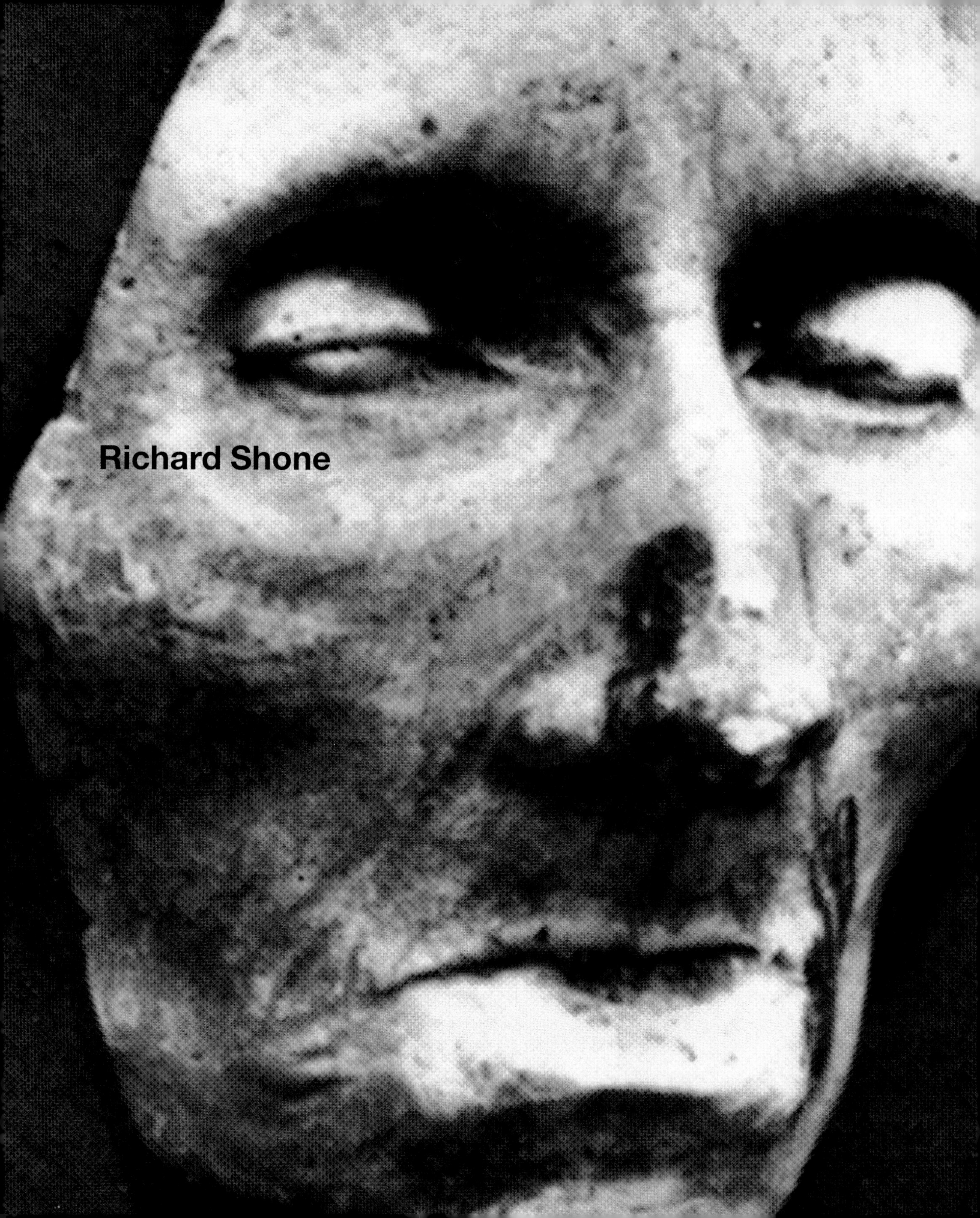
Richard Shone

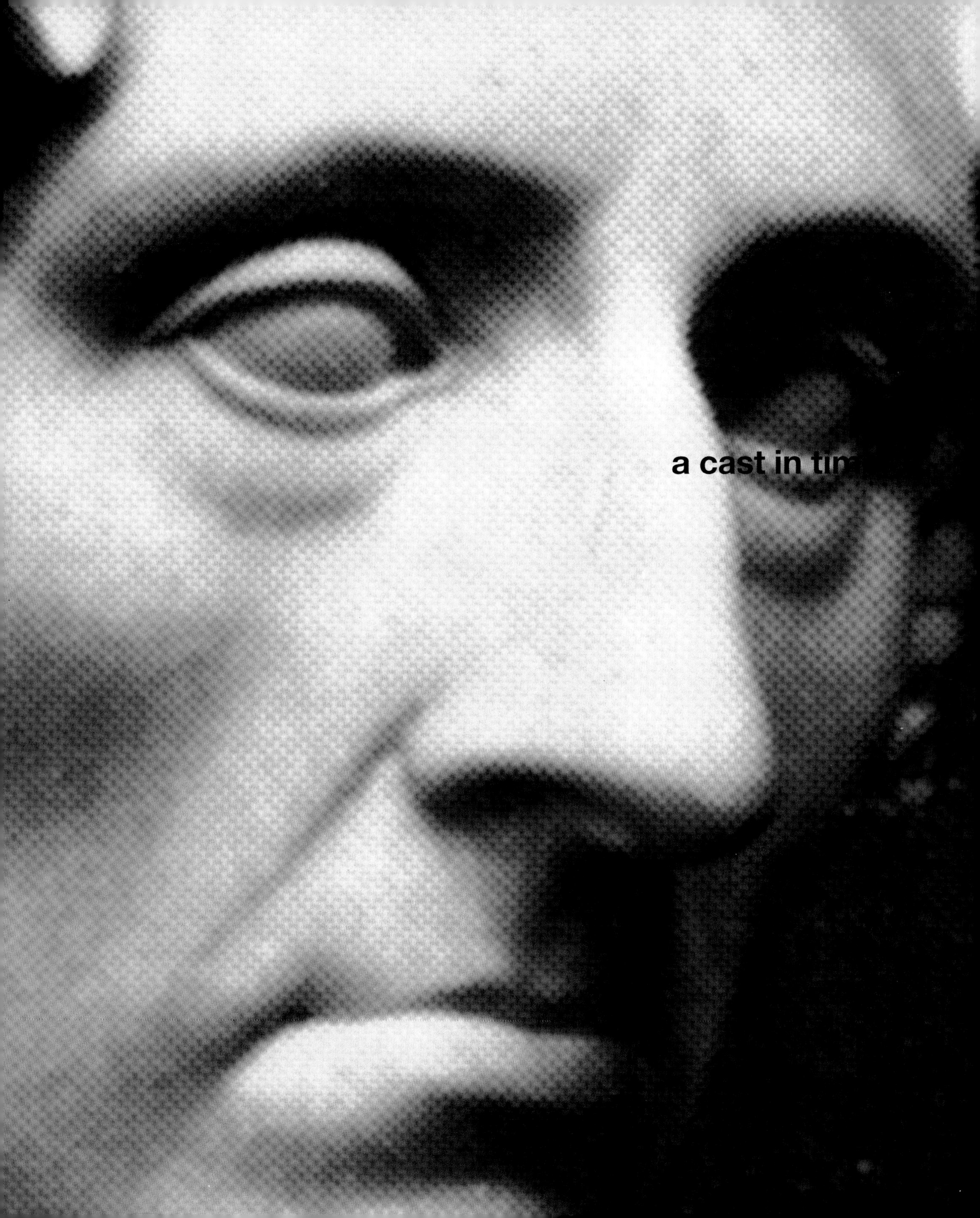
a cast in tim

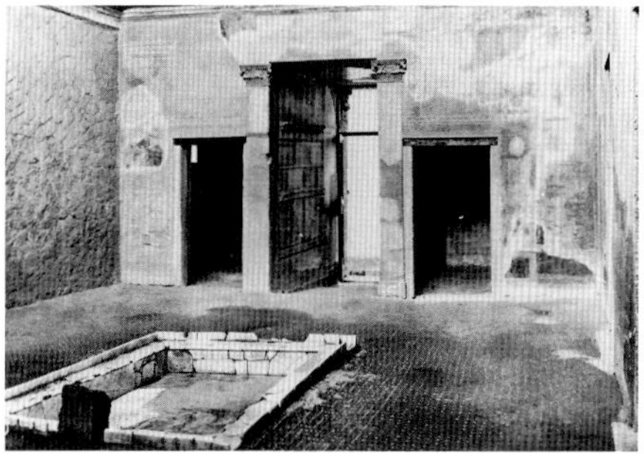

1

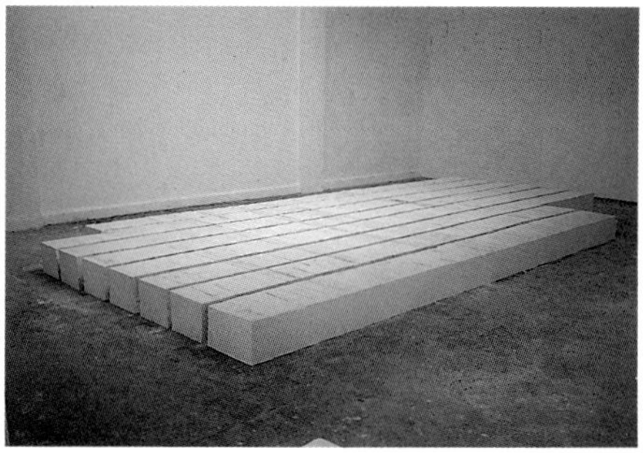

2

1 Atrium of Amnite House, Herculaneum **2** Rachel Whiteread, Untitled (Floor), 1993, plaster, 24 x 281 x 622 cm **3** Rachel Whiteread, Ether, 1990, plaster, 103.2 x 82.8 x 192 cm

A cast of an object traps it in time, eventually displaying two histories – its own past and the past of the object it replicates. The perfect expression of this duality is the death mask. It captures all the physical accretions of the human face soon after that face has completed its living existence and before rigor mortis accelerates it towards disintegration. It remains in the world to remind us of the dead, as both portrait and memorial, a replica and an object in its own right.

House was the death mask of a particular space and a finite period of time. It was the solidification of memory, anonymous history made palpable. The house itself, long awaiting death, had to be demolished before *House* could come into being – and before it too was razed. Now both have been returned to memory. Even at the time, it was difficult to confuse *House* with a building – its surface-appearance denied all such expectations. There was no material differentiation between the imprint of wood or glass, plaster or brick on the concrete from which it was made. Only the dry stains of neighbouring wallpaper held a clue. It was roofless, porchless, its top storey unusually bulky. It seemed, in its flayed geometric pallor, closer to some Pompeian relic than to the Victorian terraced vernacular of its origins. Only because it was quite definitely a sculpture could it brim with a sense of the intimate, continuous life passed there for over a century.

In choosing the process of casting as the predominant medium for her work, Rachel Whiteread extends one of the oldest sculptural practices. The funerary monuments of Roman nobles and citizens often included a death mask to stand above some suitable inscription, 'for the sake of memory and posterity'. Masks of forebears were hoarded by families so that, as Pliny wrote, 'at a funeral the entire clan was present'. In fifteenth-century Florence, casting became a profitable business, particularly of wax casts made from a plaster mould. When Lorenzo de Medici, though wounded, escaped assassination in the Pazzi conspiracy of 1478, his well-wishers demanded the immediate public display of highly realistic images of him as a way of both giving the news of his escape and of 'rendering thanks to God for his preservation'. Wax life masks, realistically painted and adorned with human hair, were raised above appropriately dressed representations of his body. One of these was placed in Santissima Annunziata. This Florentine church was already famous for its huge collection of cast heads, limbs and figures, crowding the floor and closely hanging from the beams – votive offerings commemorating donors both living and dead. Many of these would have

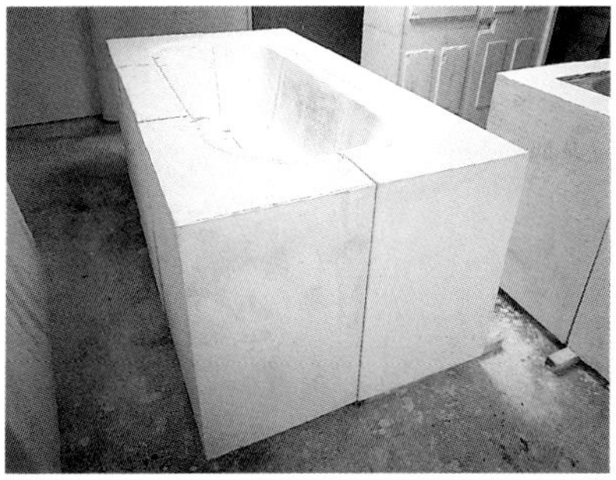

3

been produced by members of the Benintendi family who, working under the guidance of Verrocchio, established a huge workshop for the production of votive figures. Verrocchio's own studio 'specialized in the fabrication of death masks in gesso and stucco' to satisfy the Florentines' sense of piety and an atavistic worship of their ancestors.

Casts became the essential props of an artist's studio – from full-scale copies after the antique to works by admired forebears and contemporaries, from expressive fragments – half a leg of the *Venus de' Medici* or a studio assistant's hand – to small plaster moulds of suitable bases for statues and of thrones and chairs for seated figures. They served as both practical inspiration and as an aesthetic manual. They were a constant reminder of the greatest achievements of the past and as such became a valued property, carefully inventoried and bequeathed. For the sculptor specializing in portraiture, the life mask was an easy way of attaining the 'truth', though it courted derision as being insufficiently aesthetic: in the eighteenth century, Nollekens complained of the numerous wax casts in Westminster Abbey ('I do not mind going to Mrs. Salmon's Wax-work, in Fleet-street [but] Oh, dear! you should not have such rubbish in the Abbey'). But for posthumous portraiture, more commemorative than celebratory, the death mask was invaluable. Nevertheless, a sculptor trod an anxious line between the obvious 'realism' of a cast head and his own creative inclination. In the museum in Copenhagen devoted to Thorvaldsen, there are several comparative examples of sculpted busts based on masks both posthumous and from the life. The ennobling and idealizing superiority of Thorvaldsen's handiwork when set against the too-realistic presence of a death mask is perfectly captured in a letter from one of the sculptor's clients: 'I am sending you the mask of my son – a sad reminder... and ask (you) to try to give life to the clay so that a bust might not call cold death to mind, but depict our loving son just as he lived and lovingly stood before us!' (Letter from Baroness von Dörnberg to Thorvaldsen, 19 July 1824.)

The mechanically authentic properties of the cast became reserved for waxwork museums and curious, private devotions; the aesthetic high ground was occupied by the often bland and enervated presence of the marble bust. In this context, it is interesting to note that some of the complaints directed against *House* centred on its lifelikeness, that the artist had not done enough to relieve the structure of its unsavoury ordinariness. The house she had cast was already 'an eyesore', a shabby survival from a time of good riddance; why perpetuate it as such? Others, however,

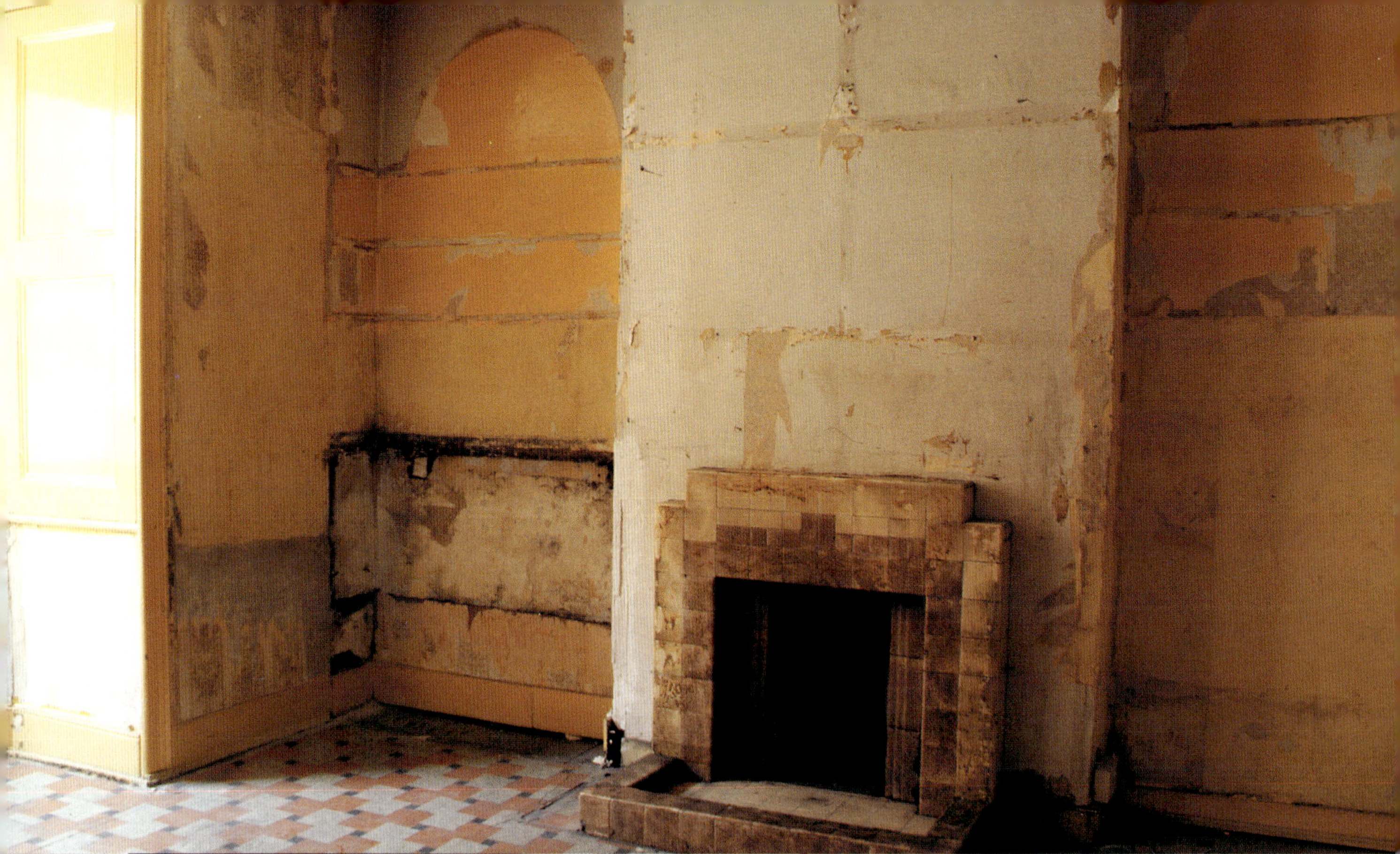

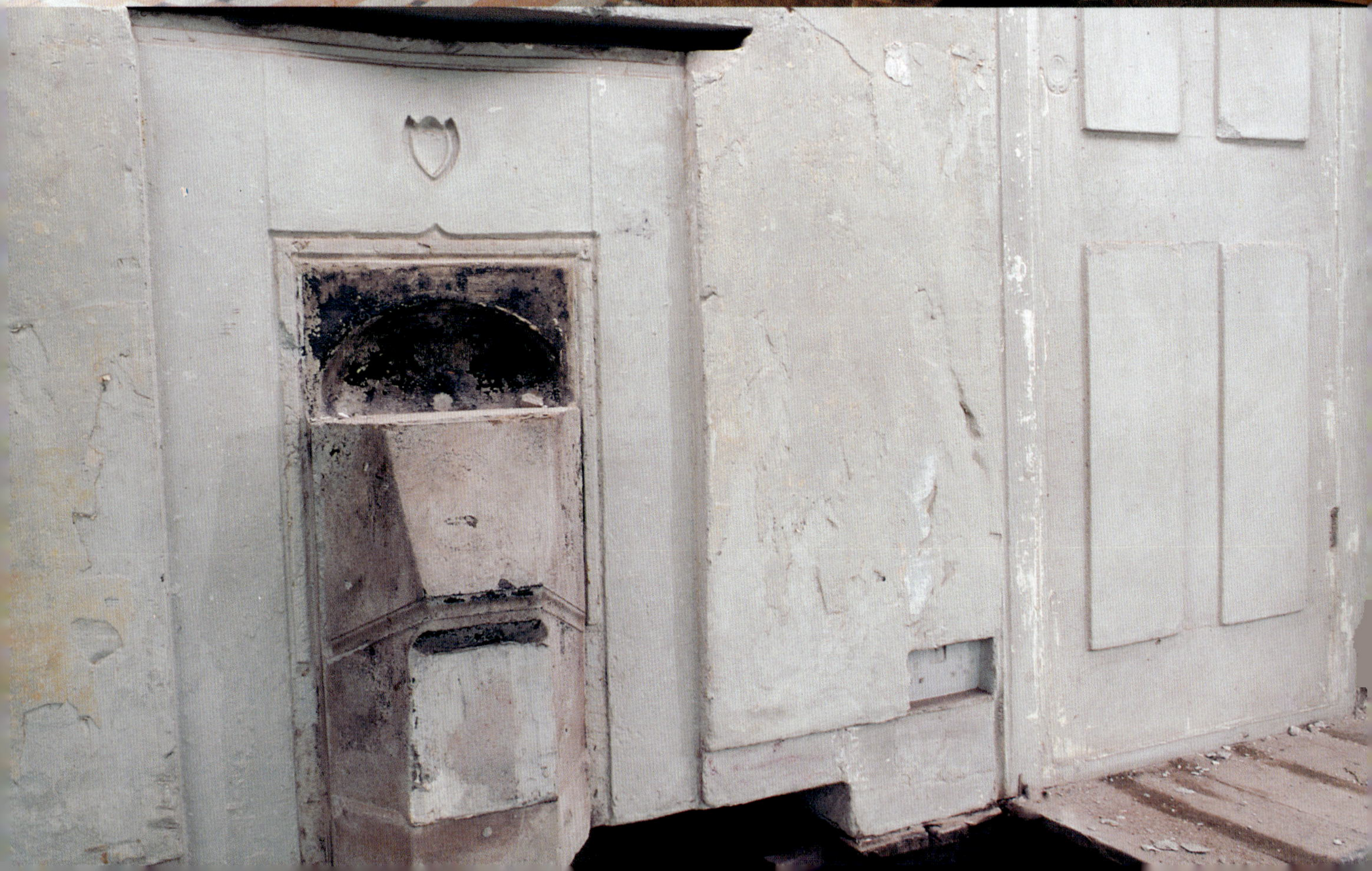

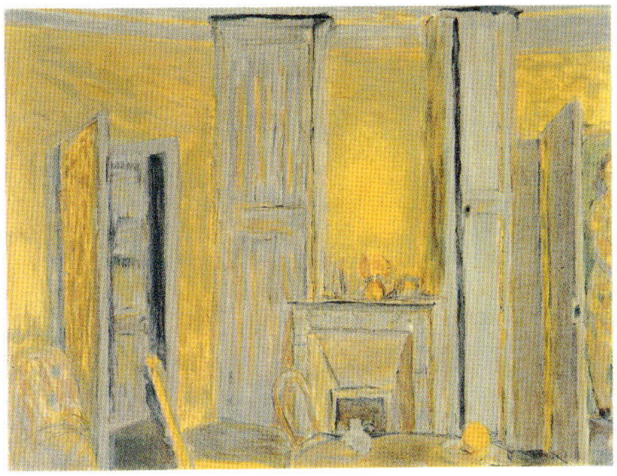
6

4 Interior of 193 Grove Road prior to casting process, September, 1993 5 House, November, 1993 6 Pierre Bonnard, The Yellow Room, 1942-45, lithograph put on stone by J. Villon, 52.5 x 66 cm

found its inside-out reality its most affecting quality. The magical properties ascribed to casts in earlier ages appeared undiminished in the passionately mixed reactions to *House*.

II

In the central section of *To the Lighthouse*, Virginia Woolf pictures the long neglect of the Ramsay family's summer home by the sea. The objects and furniture left within the house take on a life of their own as they submit themselves to the passage of Time. The orderly sense of space containing objects of personal significance – a chair, a chest of drawers, a mirror – is shattered. They no longer maintain their human usefulness. Time re-moulds, decays, transfigures them. They become vessels of memory and touchstones of experience. In order to assume a substantial structure in the mind, they must be divested of their mundane physical presence, as a cast is made by the destruction of its subject.

All of Rachel Whiteread's work, even at its most severely formal, touches this nerve of memory. She casts from basic pieces of furniture and domestic goods – from cupboards and tables to mattresses and sinks. They are the archetypal objects of urgent daily use, nagged and stained by wear and tear. They come to her from wasteland, rubbish tip, street corner and scrapyard. Hers is a lowly repertory in which the humblest examples of their kind are commonly linked by their lack of intricacy or ornament. The space they occupy or conceal is measured by the universal requirements of the human body. Its imprint is everywhere – from the indented, nippled mattress to the rusted bathtub. Sounds and gestures are evoked throughout her work – the splash of water through the sink, a body turning on a bed – with an eloquence entirely dependent on the physical properties of the object. We as viewers provide what narrative we must, read where we will among these blocks and sleepers and concavities, these anxious soundings from a reality we thought we knew. Whiteread's achievement is that, through an almost indifferent application of a logical and age-old process, she produces works that, formally archetypal, are highly particularized in their resonance. She makes not an accurate portrayal of a bed, a room, a house but a convincing representation of them and thus resurrects them with an authority they had never had before.

Rooms take on a pervasive significance in our lives – their shape, size, light, colours, (in)-adequacy, their furnishings (or lack of them). Some remain, for all time, the apple of our eye; others are festooned in our mind with boredom, deterioration and death. There are rooms

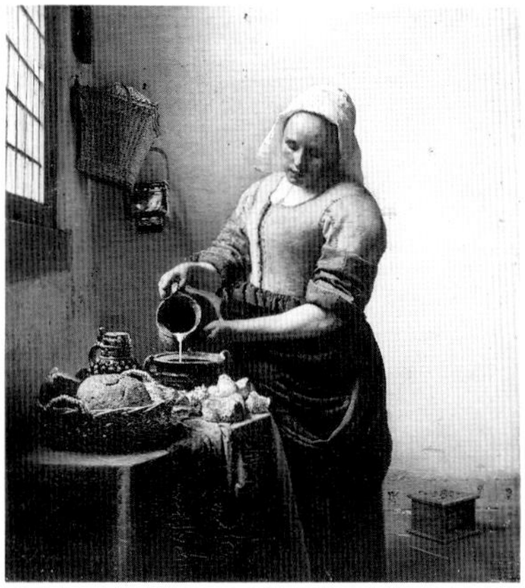

7

remembered for how we viewed ourselves at a certain moment, rooms haunted by other people, etched for us by particular actions or a volley of words, rooms that form rafts of a submerged narrative. We remember how a table was placed just so, a stain was made, how a door wouldn't fully open against a cupboard, how slowly the water drained from a sink, how the bed, once positioned, assumed an authority it held in no other part of the room.

Whiteread suggests all this without resorting to anecdote or blackmailing us with emotional particularity. In this sense, her casts are dumb, her walls bare; we tap round them with our eyes as though with a white stick. Every bump and mark, each soiled underside, each remnant of a human presence becomes collectively significant with the artist's intervention. This concentration on outer materiality guides us to an inner reality, without compromising the formal integrity of the object.

There is a painting by Bonnard of a room in his house, predominantly yellow and a filmy grey. At the far right, through a door that is open towards us, half a figure can be glimpsed; most of the rest of the picture is a representation of woodwork and plaster. Throughout there is a strong vertical emphasis, only interrupted by the central rectangle of a fireplace. Bonnard suggests privacy – for the half-seen figure is a naked woman – with the minimum of means, investing the simple structural features of an 'ordinary' room with the brimming disquiet of the present moment. Yet the room has the look of some part-excavated burial-chamber, as though Mme Bonnard, who had died a few months before the picture was painted, had risen from her sarcophagus-bathtub to hover like a wraith beyond the door.

In another room, dominated by a plaster wall parallel to the picture plane, Vermeer has placed a woman pouring milk. She is clean, comely, capable, and performs her task with care. Pleasure in the immediate moment is suggested as much by her action as by the bread and comestibles on the table and the full morning light from the window. Yet this light reveals a threadbare interior. The wall is pockmarked with nails and nail-holes; the plaster has crumbled above the tiled skirting; damp discolours the wall below the sill. Temporal erosion and the boredom of domestic continuity give tension to this superficially tranquil image of daily life.

In a third room, Henry Wallis has depicted with hallucinatory attention to detail the chamber in which Shakespeare purportedly was born. It is neither rich nor squalid but has a worn plainness suggestive of the mundane origins of the spectacular figure who first saw the light of day

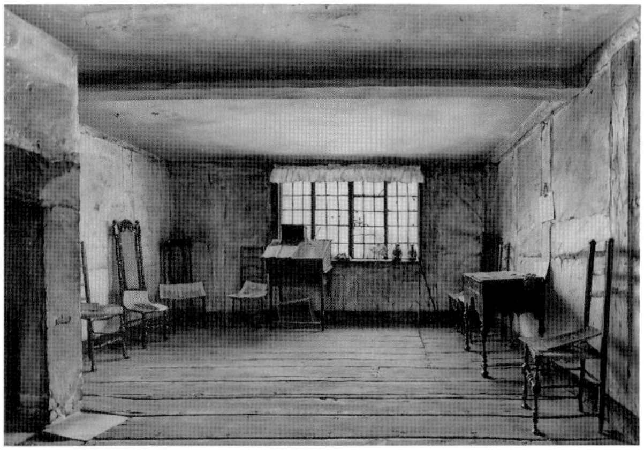

8

7 Johannes Vermeer, Maidservant Pouring Milk, 1660, oil on canvas, 45.4 x 41 cm 8 Henry Wallis, The Room in Which Shakespeare Was Born, 1853, oil on panel, 27.6 x 39.6 cm

there. The furniture, casually displaying books and prints, is pushed to the edges of the room against the graffiti-covered walls. Light rakes the nail-notched floorboards, as if they were the intended focus of our attention. On the window sill are two busts of Shakespeare and, lying face up, a death mask of him, invented by the artist. Pathetic relics on the outskirts of the room allow free play to the symbolic centre, cleared for a public for whom Shakespeare represents a nation and its history. The room, almost empty, becomes both memorial and votive offering, the dead minuteness of its depiction echoed in the mask on the sill.

Each of these works encapsulates the slog of daily life, the tussle between compulsion and habit. *House* conveyed all this – from the mundane outcrop of fireplaces, now become the incinerators of memory, to the isolated structure itself, made almost against all odds and offered as a token of the past.

III

The close inspection that *House* demanded – as though we were potential tenants or purchasers going round it with a checking eye – generated a succession of speculations and memories. They billowed in the mind as the curtains, on a summer's evening, must have ballooned in and out below the window sash thrown up as high as it could go to catch the breeze. Memory hangs on slight threads such as these. If details of the lives of a house's occupants are unobtainable, then the kind of life lived there slides in sepia between the eyes and the house's imperturbable facade. We provide our own sounds, smells, explanations, add our own commentary to the anonymous sequences of a silent newsreel.

To say that 193 Grove Road was in a working-class neighbourhood by no means settles the fine shades of its tenants' social standing, their particular niche through its long history. It lacked amenities, was not especially well-built, it lent no note of individuality to the graceless terrace; yet by its bay window, railed area and steps up to the porch it proclaimed itself a cut above the two-up-two-down houses in some of the adjacent streets, where there was only a front door between privacy and the pavement. There was a rise in the scale of respectability for the first occupants of this stretch of Grove Road when they moved into its brand-new houses in the early 1870s and placed an emblematic vase in the front window. The northern section was the last to be built up and was favoured by being above Roman Road, which was given over to trade, and by its proximity to Victoria Park, the great lung of East London opened in 1847, which the

9 Grove Road, Victoria Park, 1910 **10** Grove Road, 1952

top-end of Grove Road bisected. This stretch remained mixed, with a sprinkling of professional people (a doctor, an architect, a surgeon-dentist) alongside those occupants making a living in the best way they could. Although Grove Road remained essentially residential, small businesses were carried on by those residents with a yard or workshop at the back (all mainly on the east side of the street). Cabinet-making was one of the chief trades of Bethnal Green, and Grove Road made its contribution. For years there was a piano manufacturer at no. 214, a respectable business carried out by Arthur Ferdinando and later by his son Sidney in a workshop bordering the canal which slithered under the road before you turned into the Park. At 180, W. C. Chandler and Son were established as high-class furniture makers for over sixty years. The tallest house in the street, no. 182, was one of Dr Barnardo's Homes for Children until 1911. In the 1920s, Olive Fowler, a dressmaker, was on one floor and J. Lynch, supplier of photographic enlargements, on another. Next door, nearly overwhelmed by the Baptist church, was the Victoria Park Picture Theatre. No one could say the street was left behind the times – especially when the trams came to replace the horse-drawn omnibuses. The 77 was routed through Grove Road on its way between the Docks at Poplar and the Angel, Islington. In good weather, the cars were crammed with people making for Victoria Park.

As with several of the better streets of the district, Grove Road began to deteriorate between the wars. Detached villas across Roman Road became empty and then derelict, their strips of garden full of discarded mattresses and broken goods, fronted by hoardings proclaiming bumptious entertainments. When the bombs began to fall in late summer 1940, the walls of the houses bent and the family in 193 drank tea in the basement. There was a Z Rocket battery in Victoria Park from which a salvo of a hundred rockets at a time could be fired; to hear it was like an express train roaring through the living room. But it kept the spirits up. On the billboard by the Picture Theatre, 'Drink Bovex Before Bed' changed to 'Buy War Bonds'. St Barnabas was shaken and had to have its spire lopped off. The first V1 – the 'doodlebug' – to land on London struck the railway bridge further down Grove Road. There was solemn excitement when King George and Mr Attlee came to look at the ruined houses across Roman Road. Later, the terrace between Bunsen Street and the canal was badly damaged as were the houses in Gardener's Road which ran parallel to Grove Road.

After the war the road became schizophrenic as pockets of the old life alternated with rank

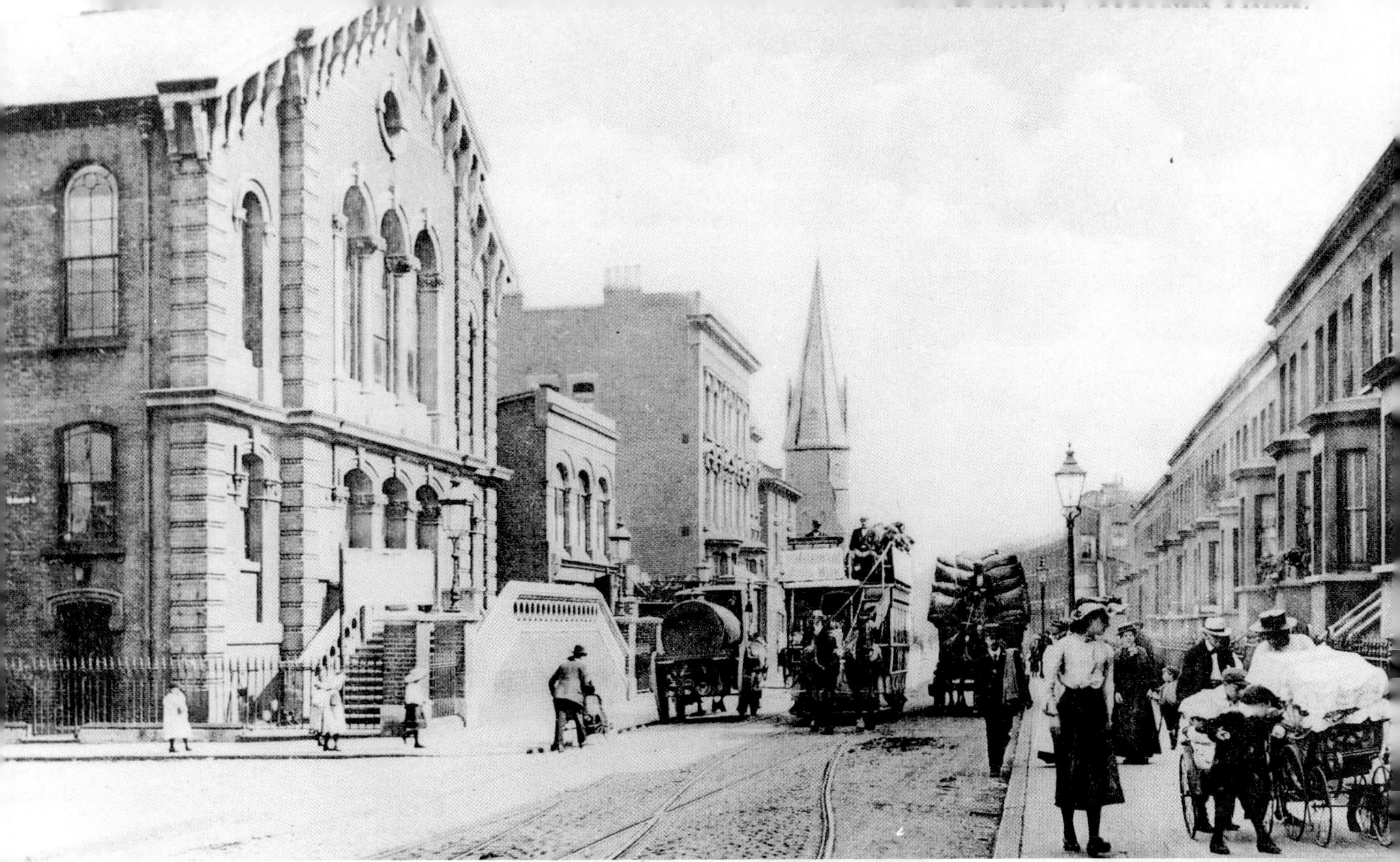

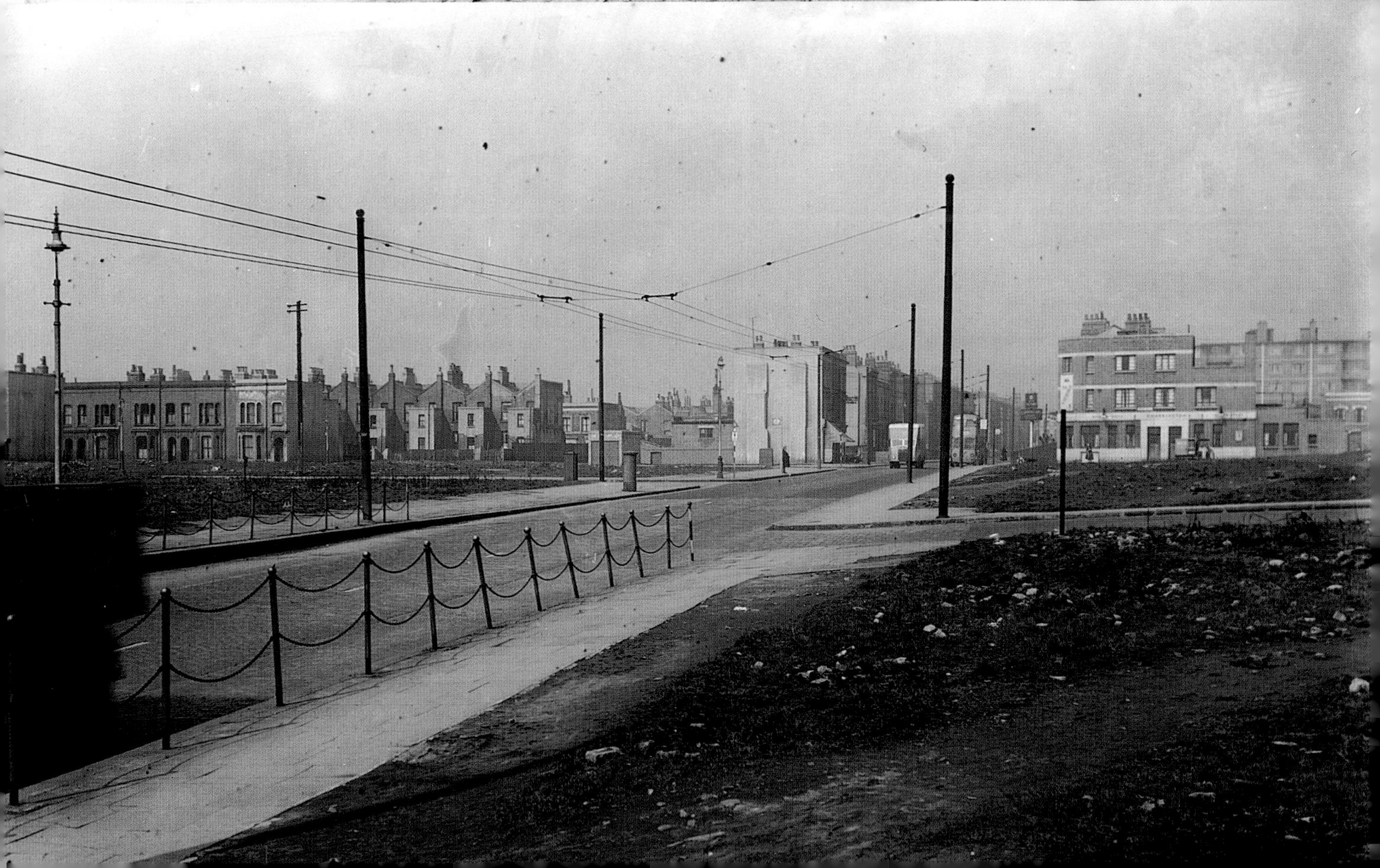

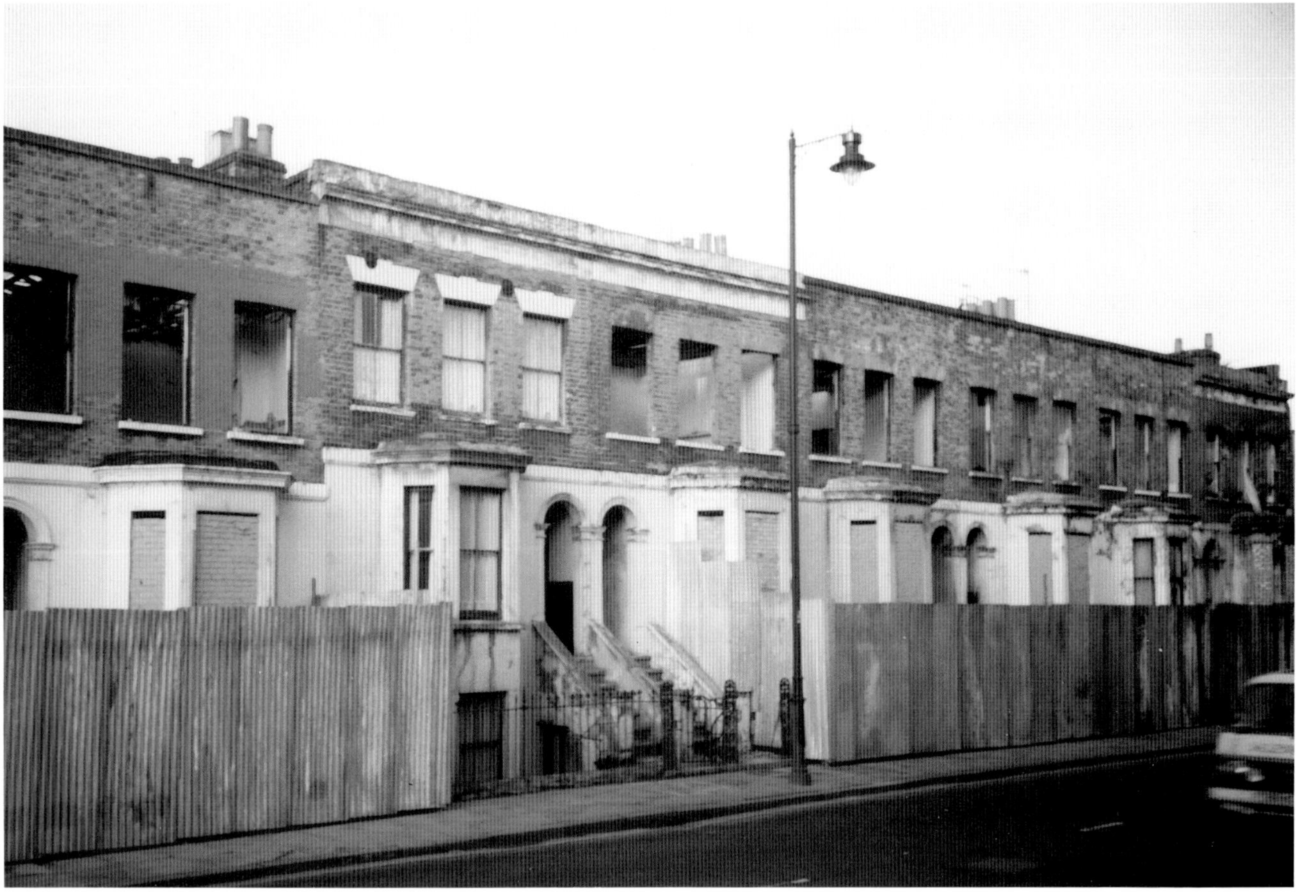

11

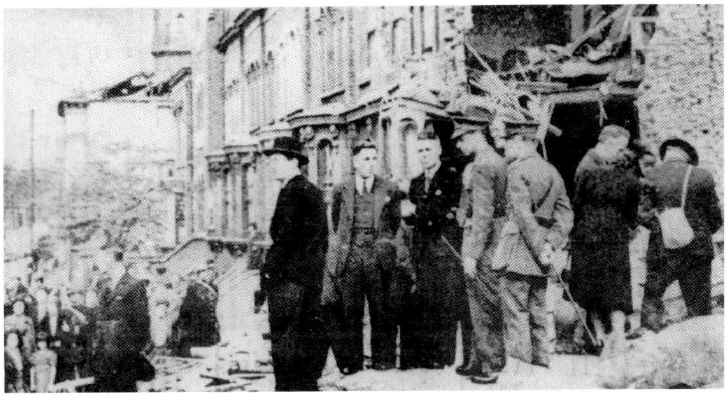

12

11 Grove Road, 1993 **12** King George VI and Prime Minister Clement Attlee visiting bomb-damaged houses on Grove Road, 1940

stretches of bomb-swept rubble; dejected properties along the west side, below Roman Road, faced the new blocks of dwellings on the east. Bunsen House was opened in 1950, its balconied flats in their post-war, pin-bright brick, almost disdainful of the shabby terrace opposite, now like an elderly relative fallen on hard times. The Picture Theatre became a Kingdom Hall of Jehovah's Witnesses; cheap handbags were made at no. 182 where Olive Fowler had had her dress-making business. Pre-fabs came and went in Gardener's Road, their larkspur and lupins and rows of onions the only testament to the market gardens of a century before. Blight and renewal were as intricately interwoven here as in the rest of East London.

In more recent years, the terrace survived but was obviously scheduled for demolition. The intended open space that was to replace it was announced, even while some of the houses were still standing, by 'tasteful' new gates at the Roman Road corner. No. 187 became derelict: buddleia, like a plague cross on a door, seeded itself between the railings and up on the parapet. There was no place for the terrace in Bow's 'Heritage Trail', with its gold-on-blue signs re-drawing another history of the neighbourhood. But a member of the family who had moved in before the war was still resident fifty or more years later at no. 193. This house and those immediately either side of it were the last three to remain.

When *House* was revealed to the public in late 1993, it stood in pale, forlorn dignity against a vivid backdrop of grass and trees. It had the appearance almost of an apparition, flat yet solid, palpable yet not quite believable, the ambiguous centrepiece, hugging the front of stage, of some curious theatrical performance. But how modest it was, how discreet, how little space it occupied, shy of an audience that increased day by day, but unperturbed by the squall of comment that swelled around it. By night, in the streetlight, while still holding fast to its secrets, it seemed to take on an animation denied to it in the wide pallid daylight of East London; the protrusions and indentations of its form became sharper, its loftiness above the pavement more imperious, its colour more subtle and diverse. In a nocturnal setting, stimulus to 'gothic' reverie was intensified as the sculpture's features came to resemble more closely the truth of their origins and transcend them. It began to startle, to take you unawares. Skinned of its precarious physical reality, *House* implanted itself in the mind, an unforgettable image of arrested time.

In the account given here of Grove Road, I have made free use of facts and details found in the archives of the Local History Library, Bancroft Road, Mile End, in the London Telephone and Street Directories of the period, in the book by Young and Willmott cited below and conversations with local residents in the Grove Road neighbourhood.

Bibliography:
M. Young and P. Willmott, *Family and Kinship in East London*, London, 1957
R. Sinclair, *East London*, London, 1950
Bethnal Green. The Official Guide, London 1930 (and sixth edition, 1938)
S.Beckett, *In Living Memory*, Tower Hamlets, London, 1989
A. Warburg, 'Arte del Ritratto e Borghesia Fiorentina' in *La Rinascita del Paganesimo Antico*, ed. G. Bing, Florence, 1966
D. Freedberg, *The Power of Images*, Chicago and London, 1989
D. Helsted, *Life and Death Masks in Thorvaldsen's Collection*, Thorvaldsen Museum, Copenhagen, 1985
M. Pointon, *Hanging the Head*, London & New Haven, 1993

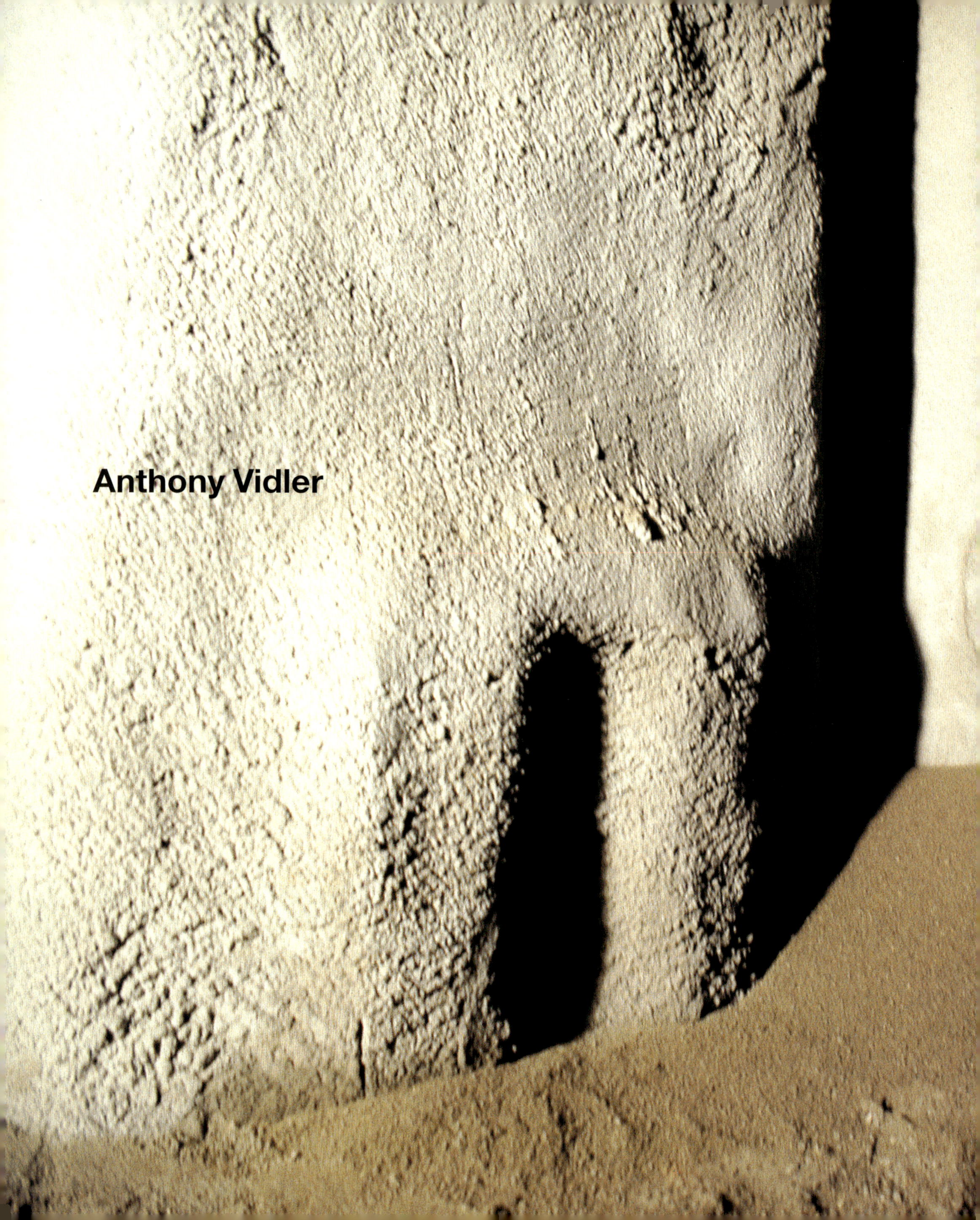

Anthony Vidler

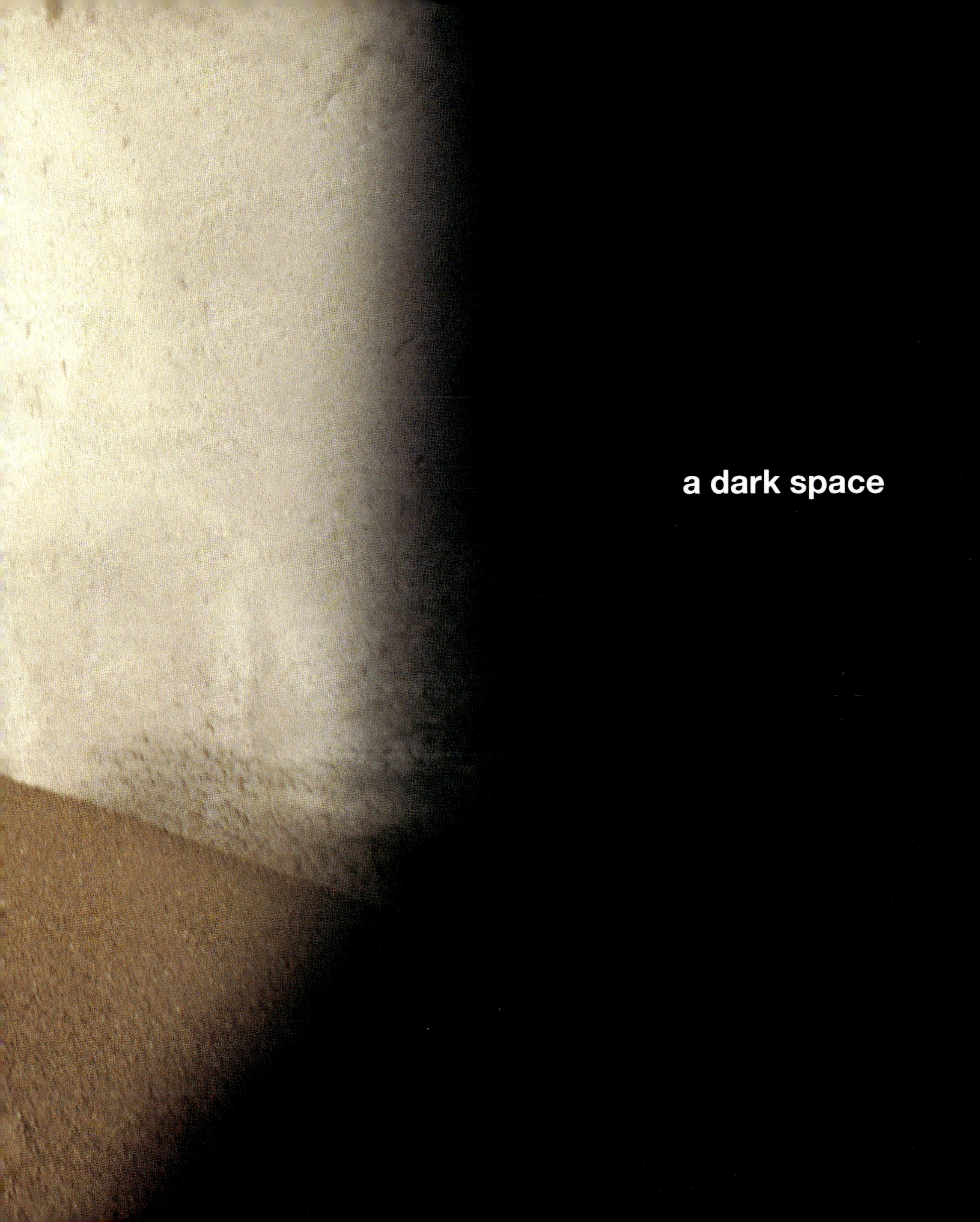

a dark space

The notion of architecture as comprised of 'space', rather than of built elements like walls and columns, is a relatively modern one; it first emerged with any force at the end of the nineteenth century as a result of German psychological theories of *raum* – one thinks of psychologists like Theodor Lipps and Robert Vischer; sociologists of space like Georg Simmel and their art-historical followers, August Schmarsow, Paul Frankl et al. in their attempt to universalize the categories by which historical art was analyzed. Space, together with other formal categories of three-dimensional composition – mass, surface, line, and form – gradually became the key to the study of architecture, an art that in its essence seemed to compose with and through space. As a concept, space was adumbrated as a product of, and experienced through, bodily movement and psychological and optical projection. Space was interior, enveloping, enclosing, ritually sanctioned and structured by the body's motion through it. As such it tended to break down the rigid stylistic categories of architectural history, privileging the internally engendered architectures from Egypt to the Baroque as against the conventional idealization of Greece and the Renaissance.

But, as the spatial histories of historians like Frankl demonstrated, the traditional history of styles, from antiquity to the present, was too entrenched in conventional forms of historicist narrative to be superseded entirely. Space, in this context, simply became another attribute, albeit more abstract, of stylistic and period description; and the historian's task became one of identifying the special nature of, say, Gothic, Renaissance, mannerist, or baroque, space. Inevitably, however, this led to the logical question, taken up by Sigfried Giedion in the 1920s: 'What is special about *modern* space?' And if the baroque was, as most historians agreed, the last identifiable authentic space-making epoch, how might Modernism be seen to construct a new vision of spatial form appropriate for its own era?

Architects, from Adolf Loos to Le Corbusier, Frank Lloyd Wright to Theo van Doesberg, theorized this new space, and quickly associated it to movement, speed, rhythm and above all transparency. Space became one of the watchwords of modernist architecture, rapidly emerging as a primary critical term for the definition of what, indeed, was 'modern'. 'Space', more than even 'function,' became a limit-term for modernity, not least for its connection with 'time' and 'relativity' both before and after Einstein. Space moved; it was fluid, open, filled with air and light; its very presence was a remedy for the impacted environments of the old city: 'space', the modern carrier of the Enlightenment image of hygiene and liberty. 'The plan is the generator' became the battle-cry of this modernity, fine-tuning interior space to the restless movements of the athletic, aerobic body, and exploding its private realms into the public air.

For most modernist architects, space was universal, and was destined to flood both public and private realms equally. Le Corbusier spoke of *l'espace indicible*, which badly translates into 'ineffable space' but which properly denotes an idea of infinity, of interpenetration of the house and the city, of a horizon that is ever-expanding. Space in these terms, at least after the 1920s, was even politically charged. Just before being forced into exile by the German occupation of Austria, the historian Emil Kaufmann argued the virtues of modernist, social-democratic space inherited by Le Corbusier and Richard Neutra from the Enlightenment and Revolution; his historical opponent, Hans Sedlmayr, countered that the French Revolution had destroyed all space in his 'humanist' definition that closely followed the Nazi line; and, after the War, the Italian critic Bruno Levi argued insistently that Wrightian space was synonymous with democratic space, as against a previous and undemocratic 'Fascist' space of false monumentality and display.

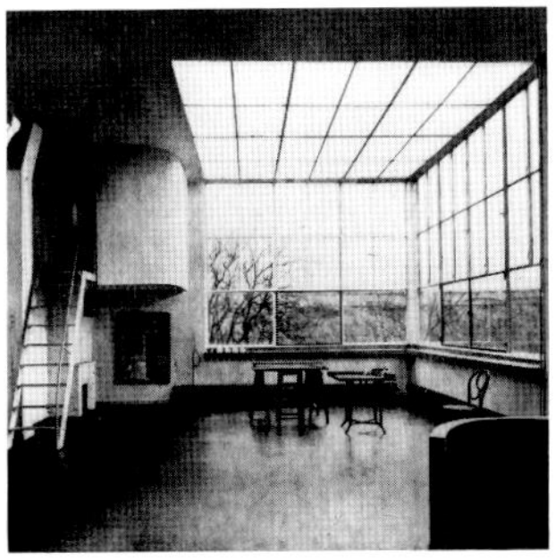

1

1 Le Corbusier, Maison Ozenfant (studio), Paris, 1923

With hindsight, the specific kinds of politics embedded in the idea of modernist space have inevitably become more ambiguous, as the trumpeted beneficence of modern architecture and its attendant 'space' for contemporary living has all-too clearly demonstrated its shortcomings, at the same time as the alliances of modernist architects and unsavoury theorists and patrons in the 1920s have been revealed by historians. More recently, postmodernist critiques of modernist universalism have similarly questioned the values inherent in the open plan and *ville verte*.

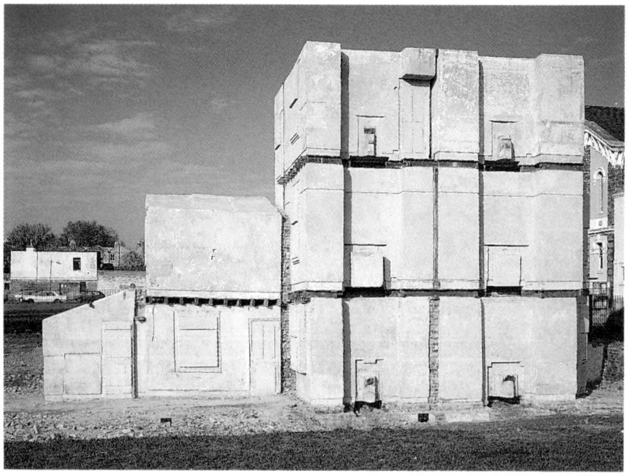

Yet the notion that space is a universally shared good has hardly been erased completely from our mental vocabularies. This might well be a result of what one might call space's historical pedigree. As a product of theories of psychological extension – either of projection or introjection – space naturally and early on took on the characteristics of a propaedeutic to be wielded against the twin phobias of late nineteenth century urbanism – agoraphobia and claustrophobia. To open up the city would, in Le Corbusier's terms, and in much post-CIAM rhetoric, rid it of all closed, dirty, dangerous and unhealthy corners; and, in the absence of dramatic contrast between open and closed spaces, rid metropolitan populations of any spatial anxiety they might have felt in the first wave of urbanization.

Perhaps it is the residue of this attitude that partly accounted for the virulence of the leader of Bow Neighbourhood's attacks on Rachel Whiteread's *House*; attacks that saw it as standing in the way of slum-clearance; of blocking the planting of healthy greenery, of making a monument to an unhealthy and claustrophobic past. When Le Corbusier proposed his celebrated 'Plan Voisin' for Paris in 1925 he was similarly irritated by the intractable masses of existing buildings and suggested the almost complete erasure of the Right Bank from the Louvre to the Bastille, keeping only a few isolated historical reminders of the city fabric. The infinite city projected by Mies van de Rohe's disciple

Ludwig Hilbersheimer for the Great Plains in the 1940s was equally antagonistic to any object that might break into the universal transparency of the environment. Polemically directed against what Le Corbusier and the International Congress of Modern Architecture (CIAM) termed *îlots insalubres*, the notion of unbroken space held within it the moral imperative of a vaccine. And if this were the doxa for the public realm, then the 'open plan' or 'free plan' had already established a parallel role for the open space of the modernist villa. Domestic secrets, psychological interiority, anti-sociability and counter-familial behaviour would disappear, replaced by the roaming of a perpetually nomadic subject through the interior landscape of a 'house' whose interior would no longer be arbitrarily separated from the exterior. On this level, that of the 'house', the simple act of filling in space, of closing what was once open, would naturally counter the received wisdom of a century of planning dogma that *open* is better if not absolutely good.

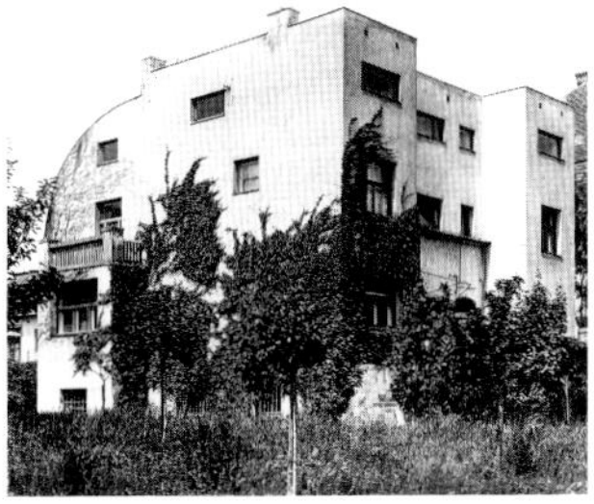
2

2 Adolf Loos, Steiner House, Vienna, 1910

From another viewpoint, however, Whiteread's *House*, far from undermining Modernism's spatial ideology, reinforces it, and further, on its own terms. For, since the development of Gestalt psychology, space has been subject to all the intellectual and experiential reversals involved in the identification of figure and ground, as well as the inevitable ambiguities between the two that were characteristic, as critics from Alois Riegl to Colin Rowe have pointed out, of Modernism itself. Thus many modernists have employed figure/ground reversals to demonstrate the very palpability of space – the Italian architect Luigi Moretti even constructed solid plaster models of interior spaces in the 1950s to illustrate what he saw as the history of different spatial types in architecture. These models were cast as it were as the solids of what in reality were spatial voids; the spaces of compositions such as Hadrian's Villa were illustrated as sequences of solids as if space had suddenly been revealed as dense and impenetrable. Architectural schools from the late 1930s onwards have employed similar methods to teach 'space' – the art of the impalpable – by means of palpable models. By this method, it was thought, all historical architecture might be reduced to the essential characteristics of space, and pernicious 'styles' of historicism might be dissolved in the flux of abstraction.

In these terms, Whiteread's *House* simply takes its place in this tradition, recognizable to architects, if not to artists or the general public, as a didactic illustration of late nineteenth-century domestic 'space'. To an architect, whether trained in Modernism or its 'Brutalist' offshoots, her work takes on the aspect of a full-scale model, a three-dimensional exercise in spatial dynamics and statics. An architect of the generation of Paul Rudolph, for example, would no doubt read her house as an exploration of the traditional domestic interior.

But, more than this, a not entirely accidental side-result of this exercise is the transformation of the nineteenth-century *realist* house into an abstract compostion. Whiteread has effectively built a model of a house that resembles a number of paradigmatic modern houses, from Wright to Loos, from Rudolf Schindler to Peter Eisenman. Here, if one were to read her inside as outside, the concrete shoe simply registers what might be an exercise in three-dimensional composition based on the procedure of cutting away or excavating a solid block for the contingencies of site or use. Le Corbusier, in his paradigmatic illustration of 'Five Compositions' in 1925, already codified such a method of composition side by side with four other 'types' of architectural design, including the open-plan and the prismatic solid. In this sense Whiteread's *House* is modernist to the core, and would naturally arouse the ire of the entire postmodern, neo-traditionalist and heritage movements in Britain and elsewhere, movements dedicated to the notion that 'abstraction' equals 'eyesore'.

But it seems also true that this project touched another nerve entirely, one not dissociated from those we have mentioned, but more generally shared outside the architectural and artistic community, and deeply embedded in the 'domestic' character of the intervention. Whiteread touched, and according to some commentators, mutilated, the house, by necessity the archetypal space of homeliness. Article after article referred to the silencing of the past life of the house, the traces of former patterns of life now rendered dead but preserved, as it were, in concrete if not in aspic. To a cultural historian, this commentary, pro and con, was strangely reminiscent of the accounts of the discovery, excavation

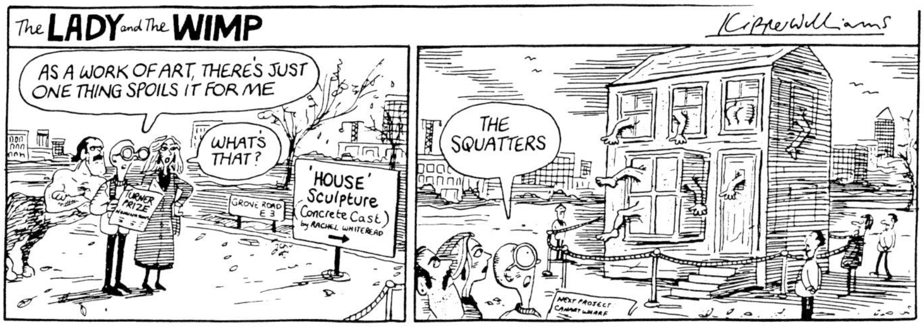

4

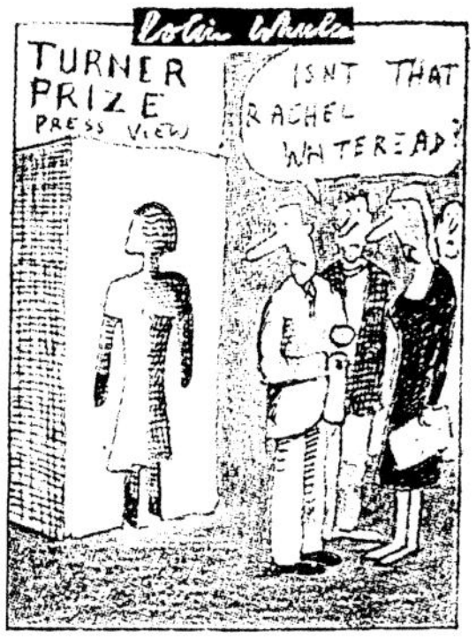

3

3 Colin Wheeler, cartoon, *The Independent*, November 3, 1993 **4** Kipper Williams, The Lady and the Wimp, cartoon, *Time Out*, November 3-10, 1993

and subsequent exhibiting, of Herculaneum and Pompeii.

These disintered cities, that had been preserved precisely because they had been filled up like moulds by lava and ashes, seemed when excavated to have been alive only shortly before, their inhabitants caught by the disaster in grotesque postures of surprise as they went about their daily work. Much travel and fantasy-literature of the nineteenth century circled around this point; the life-in-suspension represented by mummified traces of everyday existence. A cartoon of the Whiteread *House* by Kipper Williams fed on just this fear, that of being trapped inside a space filled so violently, the space and air evacuated around a still-living body.

Nineteenth and twentieth century writers and literary critics, from E.T.A. Hoffmann to Henry James, subsumed this horror of domestic interment/disinterment in the popular genre and theory of the uncanny, a genre that was often evoked in the discussion of Whiteread's project. This characterization would have it that the very traces of life extinguished, of death stalking through the centre of life, of the 'unhomeliness' of filled space contrasted with the former 'homeliness' of lived space (to use the terminology of the phenomenologist and psychologist Eugène Minkowski), raised the spectre of demonistic or magic forces, at the very least inspiring speculation as to the permanence of architecture, at most threatening all cherished ideals of domestic

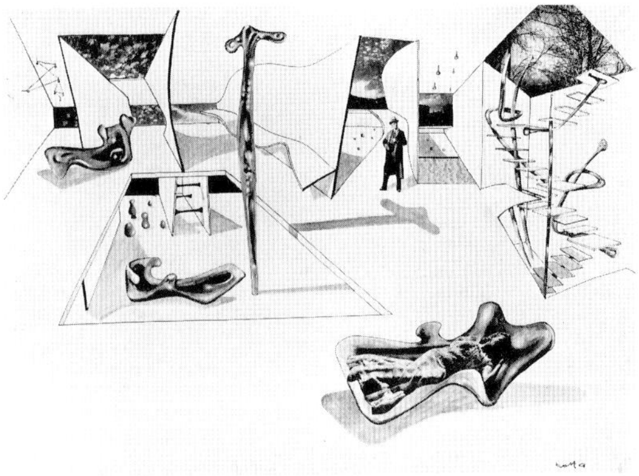

5

5 Matta, Projet-maquette d'appartement, 1938

harmony – the 'children who once played on the doorstep' variety of nostalgia so prevalent among Whiteread's critics. Colin Wheeler's cartoon of the impression of Rachel Whiteread's 'cast' body in the wall of the Turner Prize exhibit echoes this sensibility; unwittingly it stems from a line of observations on the uncanny effects of impressions of body parts beginning with Chateaubriand's horrified vision of the volcanically 'cast' breast of a young woman at Pompeii: 'Death, like a sculptor, has moulded his victim', he noted.

Added to, many writers have noted what they saw as the disturbing qualities of the 'blank' windows in *House*; this might be traced back to romantic tropes of blocked vision, the evil eye, and the uncanny effect of mirrors that cease to reflect the self; E.T.A. Hoffmann and Victor Hugo, in particular, delighted in stories of boarded-up houses whose secrets might only be imagined. The abandoned hulk of Whiteread's *House* holds much in common with that empty house on Guernsey, so compelling for Hugo's fantasies of secret history in *Les travailleurs de la mer*. It is perhaps not accidental that the use of the word 'uncanny' to denote supernatural power cited by the Oxford English Dictionary is that of the transcendental Ralph Waldo Emerson, who quoted on the 'uncanny stones' of Stonehenge, an especially hermetic grouping of solids that refuses to give up its secrets easily.

Psychoanalysis, however, and especially since the publication of

Freud's celebrated article on 'The Uncanny' in 1919, has complicated such romantic reactions by linking the uncanny to the more complex and hidden forces of sexual drives, death wishes and Oedipal fantasies. Taking off from the difficult formulation hazarded by Schelling in the 1830s that the uncanny was 'something that ought to have remained secret and hidden but which has come to light', Freud linked this sensation to experiences of a primal type – such as the primal scene witnessed by Little Hans – that had been suppressed only to show themselves unexpectedly in other moments and guises. Joined to such primary reactions, the causes of uncanny feelings included, for Freud, the nostalgia that was tied to the impossible desire to return to the womb, the fear of dead things coming alive, the fragmentation of things that seemed all too like bodies for comfort. Here, we might recognize themes that arose in some of the responses to *House*, among which the literal impossibility of entering into the house itself, as well as the possibility that its closed form held unaccounted secrets and horrors.

In psychoanalytical terms, then, Whiteread's project seems to follow the lead of Dada and Surrealism in their exploration of 'unhomely' houses precisely for their sexual and mental shock-effect: the 'interuterine' houses imagined by Tristan Tzara, the soluble habitations delineated by Dalí, the 'soft' houses of Matta offer ready examples. As critics have noted, Whiteread's notion of 'art' as temporary act or event similarly takes its cue from Dada precedents. But against these types of interiority, themselves pitched as conscious critiques of Corbusian Modernism, Whiteread's *House* turns Dadaist and Surrealist tactics against themselves once more. For in its post-avant-garde terms the *House* seems to pose itself as a decidly *non*-uterine space, a *non*-soft environment. Where Tzara was eager to counter transparency and universality with womb-like examples – the *yurt*, the igloo, the cave – that would receive their inhabitants as if in perpetual wombs; or where Matta conceived of a psychologically reactive house that would respond to touch and movement as well as vision – a haptic house with soft columns, rubber and cork surfaces – Whiteread seems to deny any nostalgic return to the womb, to refuse all access to domestic familiarity.

Freud's analysis of the sources of the uncanny, however, has always seemed wanting precisely when confronted with terms that imply a non-object based uncanny – an uncanny generated by space rather than its contents. Despite a late recognition that space might be less universal than Kant had claimed, Freud remained singularly impervious to spatial questions and it was left to phenomenologists from Minkowski to Binswanger to recognize that space itself might be psychologically determined and thereby to be read as a symptom, if not an instrument, of trauma and neurosis. Tellingly, Minkowski writes of 'black' or 'dark' space, that space which, despite all loss of vision – in the dark or blindfolded – a subject might still palpably feel: the space of bodily and sensorial, if not intellectual, existence. It is such a space that Whiteread constructed, a blindingly suffocating space that, rather than receiving its contents with comfort, expelled them like a breath.

And it is this final reversal that seems in retrospect to have been most pointed. For what was the modern house, if not the cherished retreat from agoraphobia – that 'housewive's disease' of the 1950s so common in suburban development and council estate from Levittown to Milton Keynes, and so gendered as feminine from its first conception in the 1870s? Thrust so unceremoniously into the void, the domestic subject no longer finds a shell, clinging, as if to Géricault's raft, to the external surface of an uninhabitable and absolute claustrophobic object, forced to circulate around the edges of a once womb-like space. Nostalgia, noted Freud, was always to be connected to that impossible primal desire to return to the origin, the womb itself. Therein lay an origin of the uncanny feelings that arose when such desires, long repressed, suddenly re-emerged in unexpected forms. In Whiteread's world, where even the illusion of return 'home' is refused, the uncanny itself is banished. No longer can the fundamental terrors of exclusion and banishment, of homelessness and alienation, be ameliorated by their aestheticization in horror stories and psychoanalytic family romances; with all doors to the *unheimlich* firmly closed, the domestic subject is finally out in the cold forever.

John Davies

a photographic essay

August 1993-March 1994

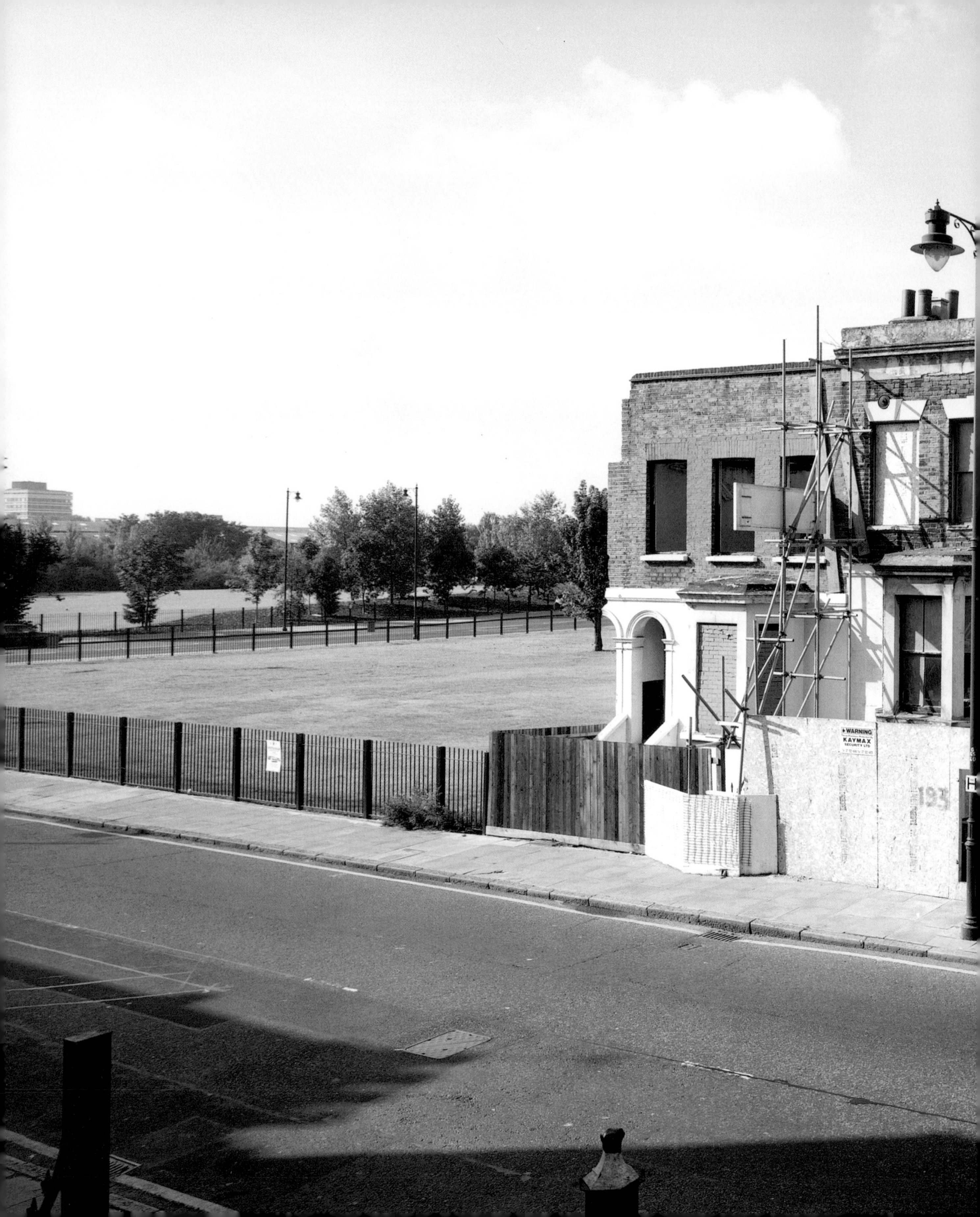
WARNING
KAYMAX
SECURITY LTD
193

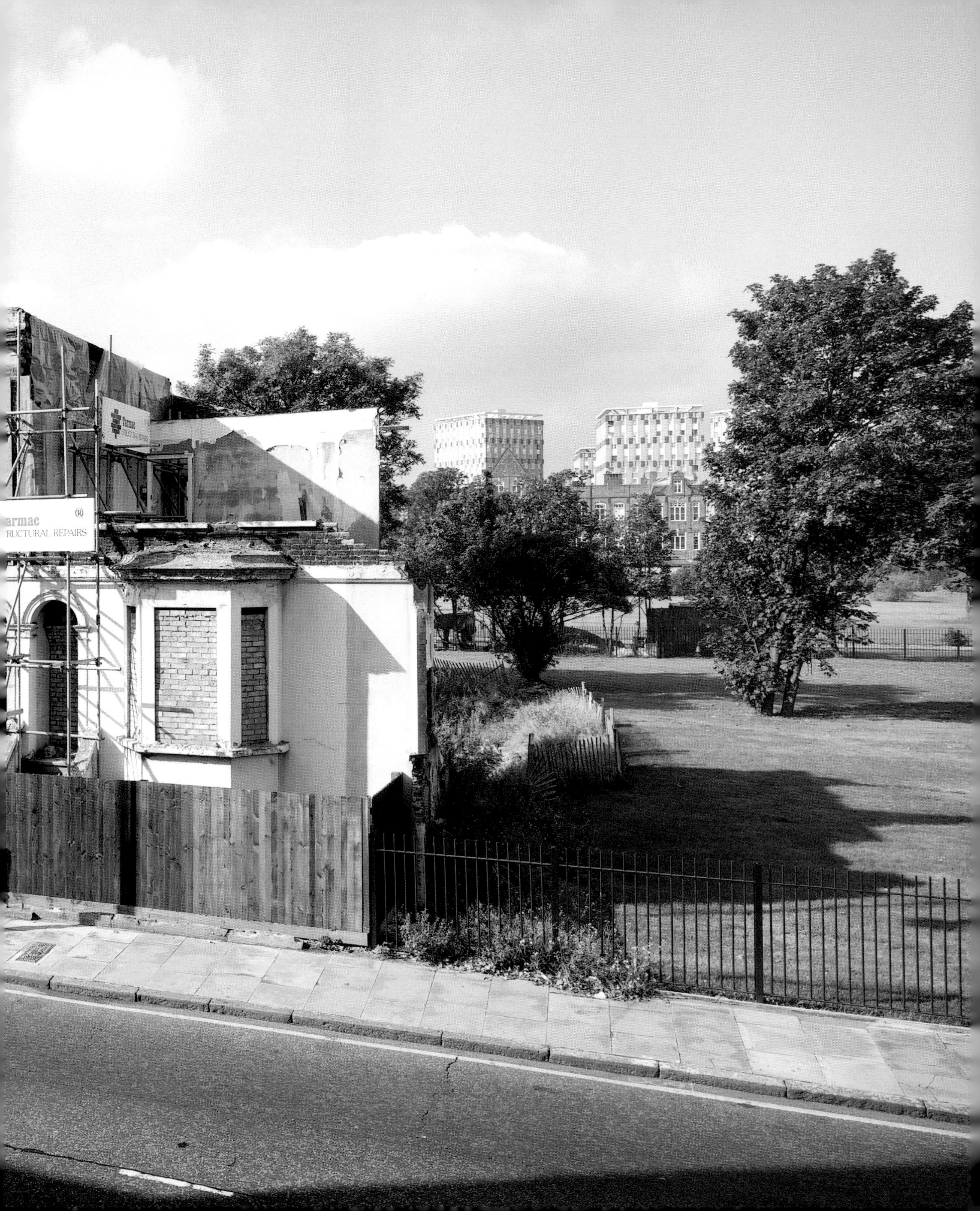
Tarmac
STRUCTURAL REPAIRS
armac
RUCTURAL REPAIRS

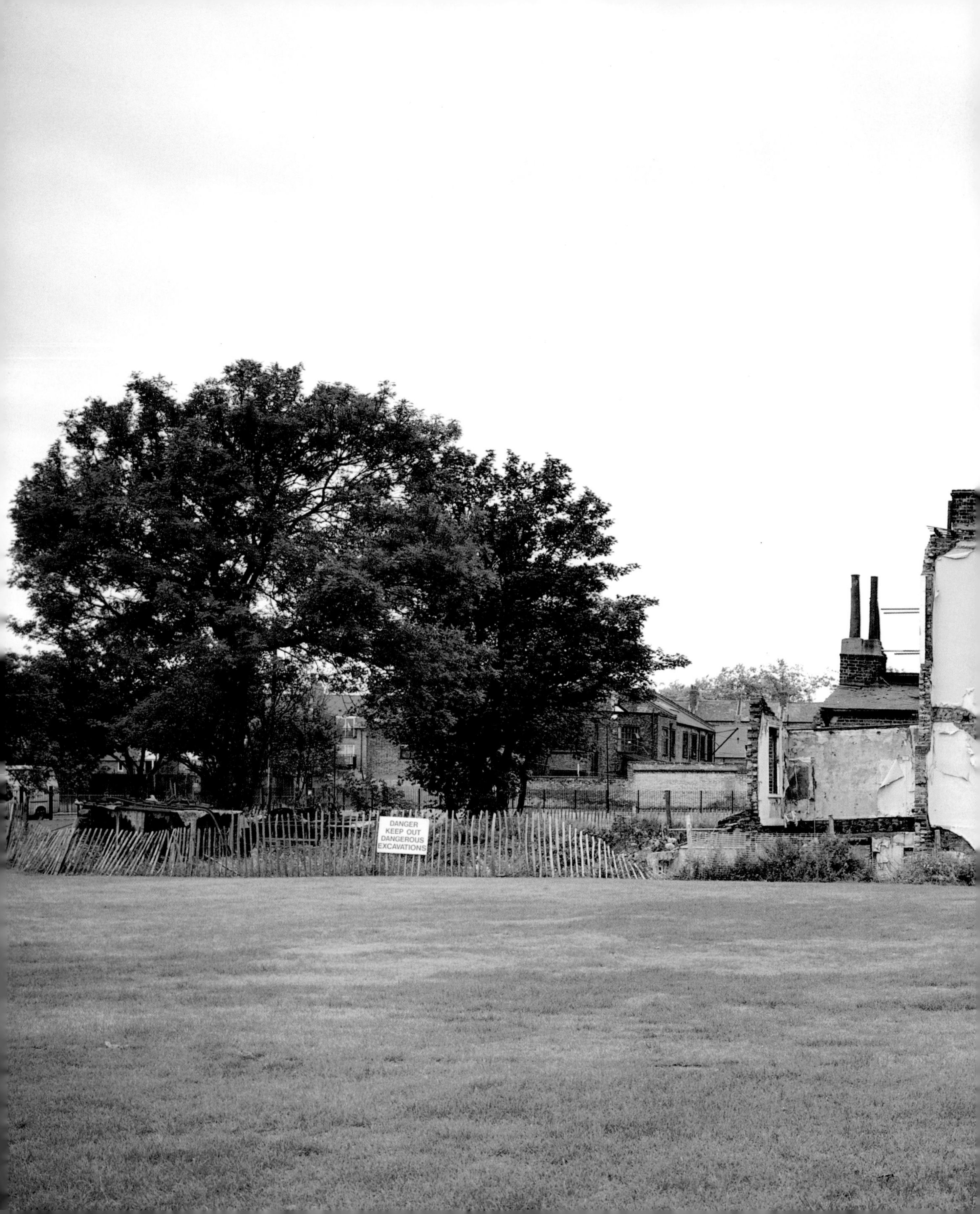
DANGER
KEEP OUT
DANGEROUS
EXCAVATIONS

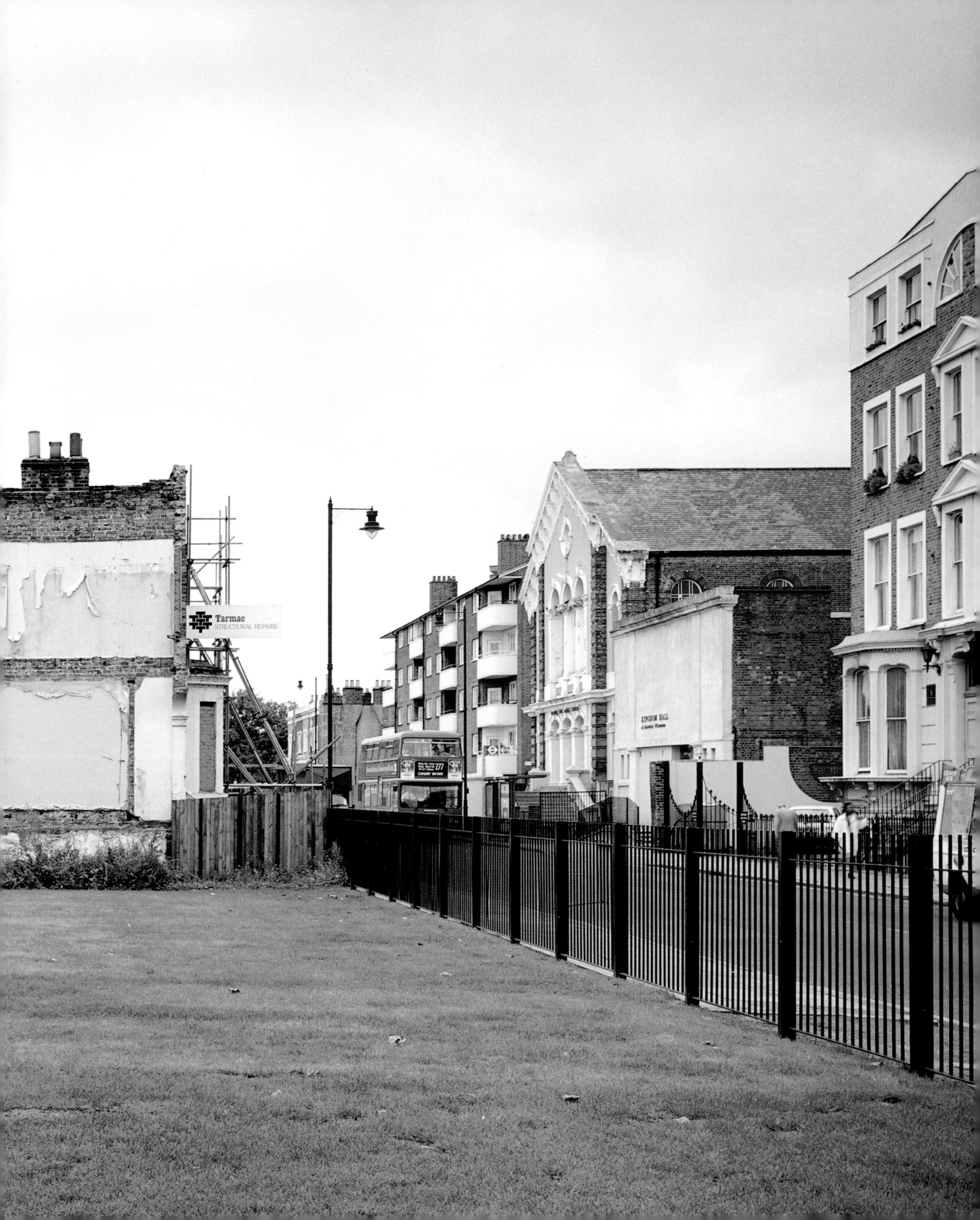
Tarmac
STRUCTURAL REPAIRS
KINGDOM HALL
277
CANARY WHARF

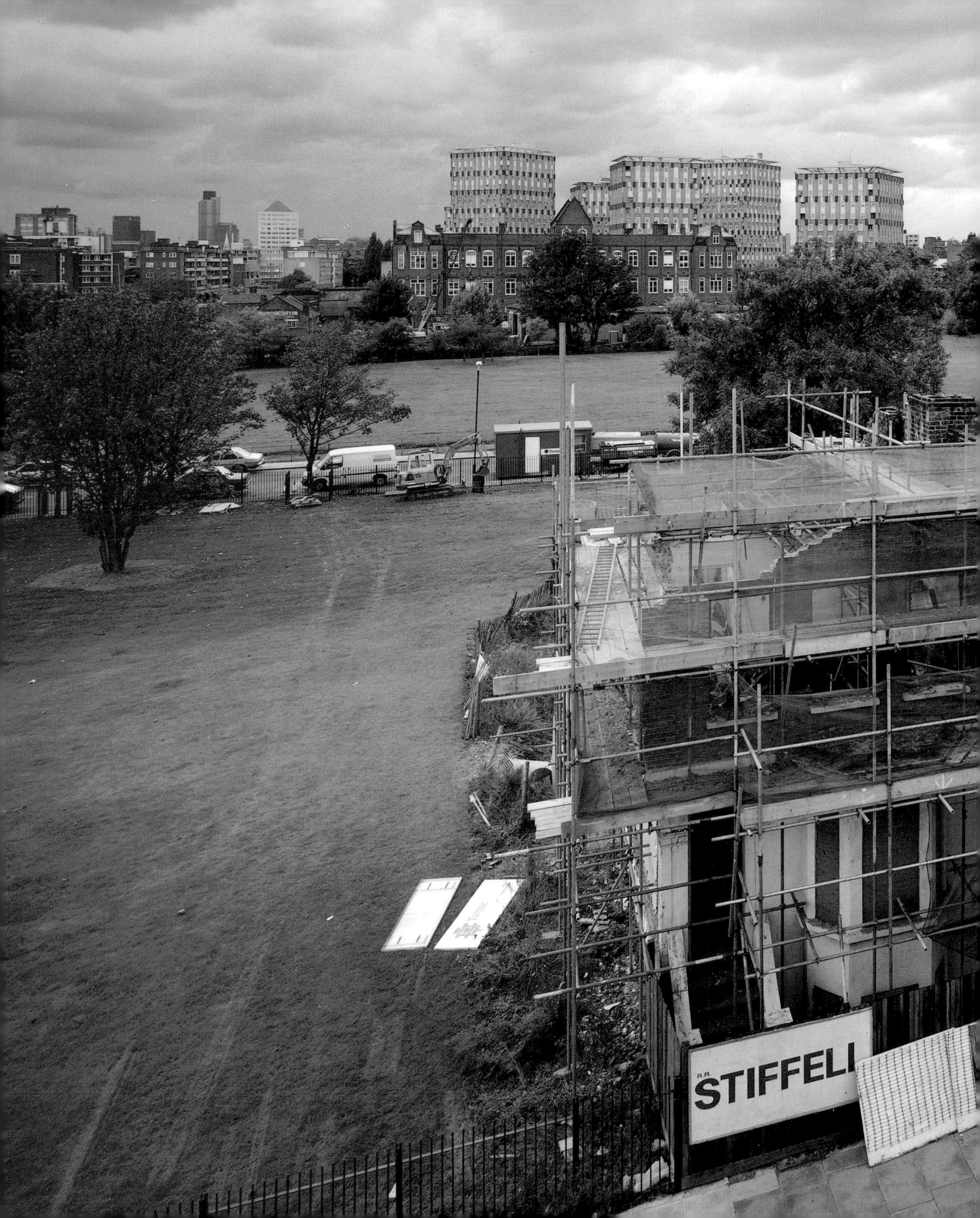
R.R.
STIFFELL

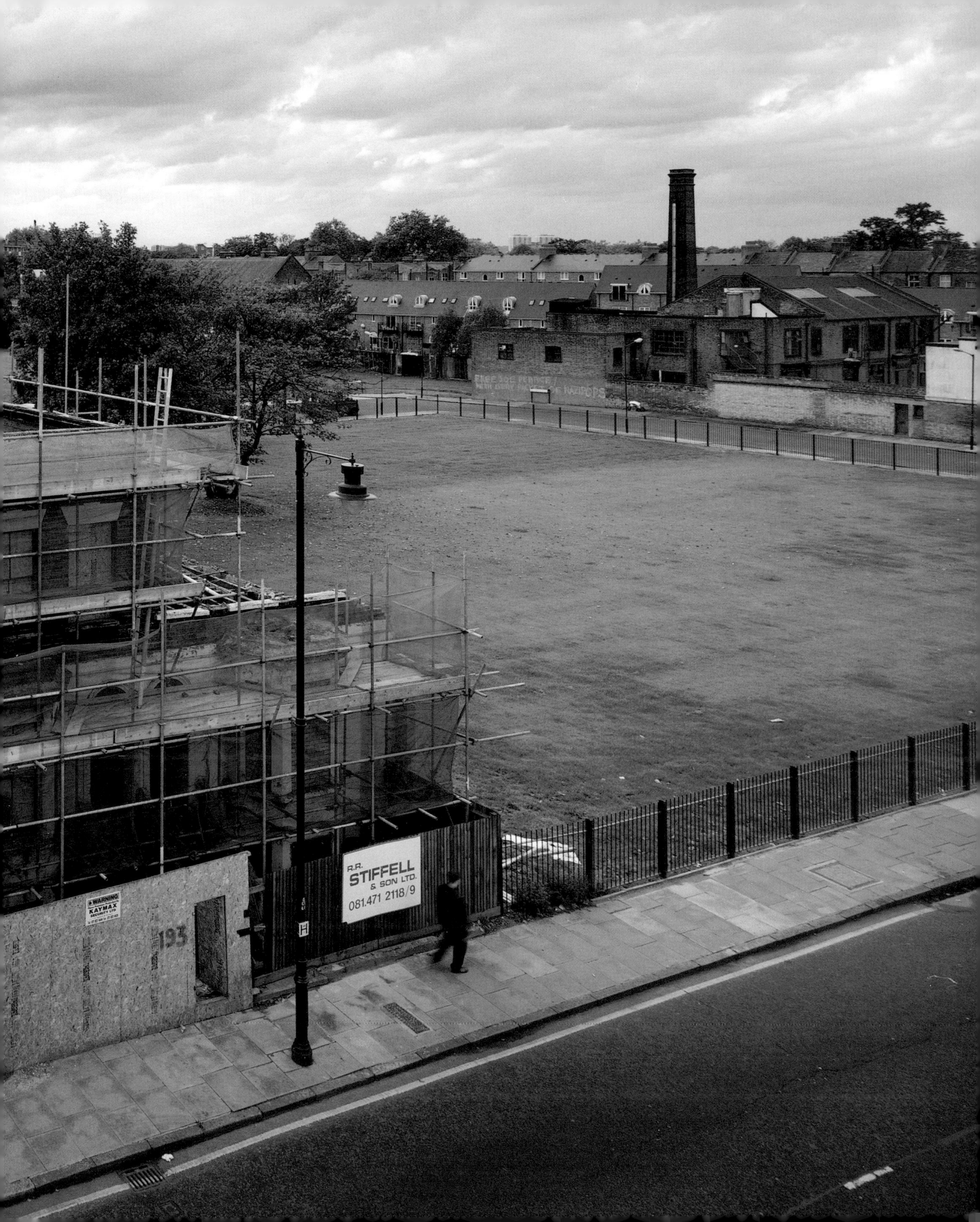
R.R.
STIFFELL
& SON LTD.
081.471 2118/9
WARNING
KAYMAX
SECURITY LTD
193

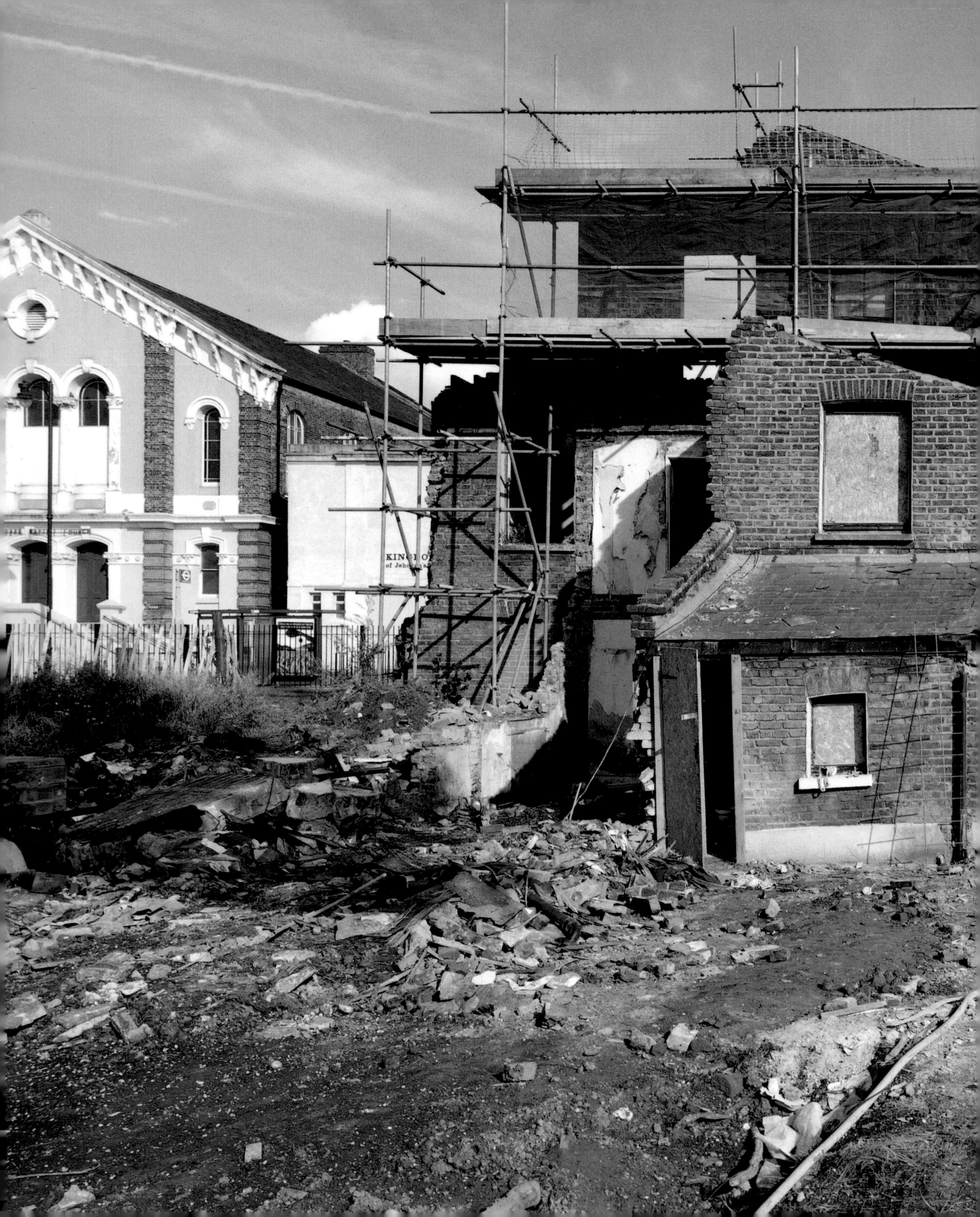

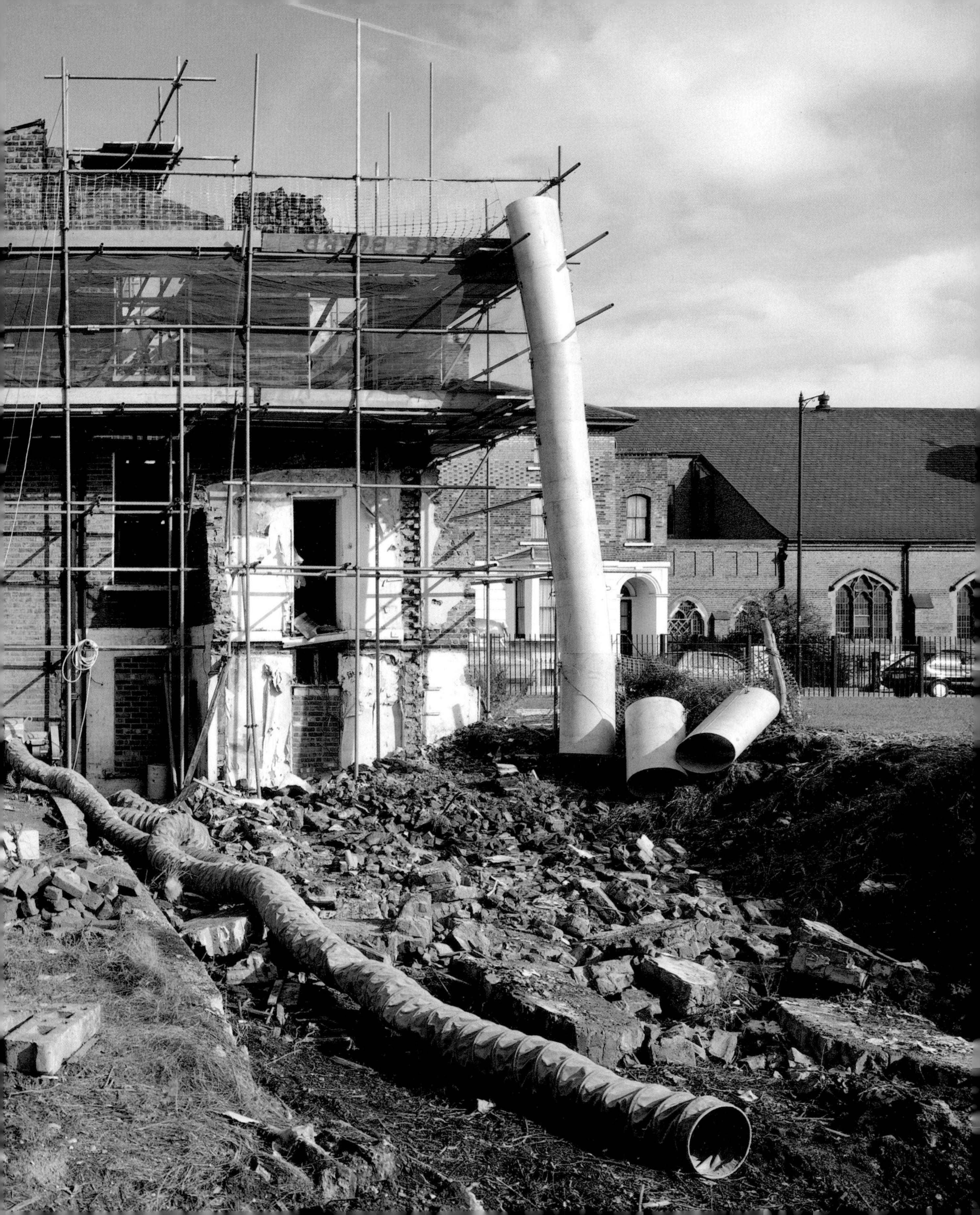

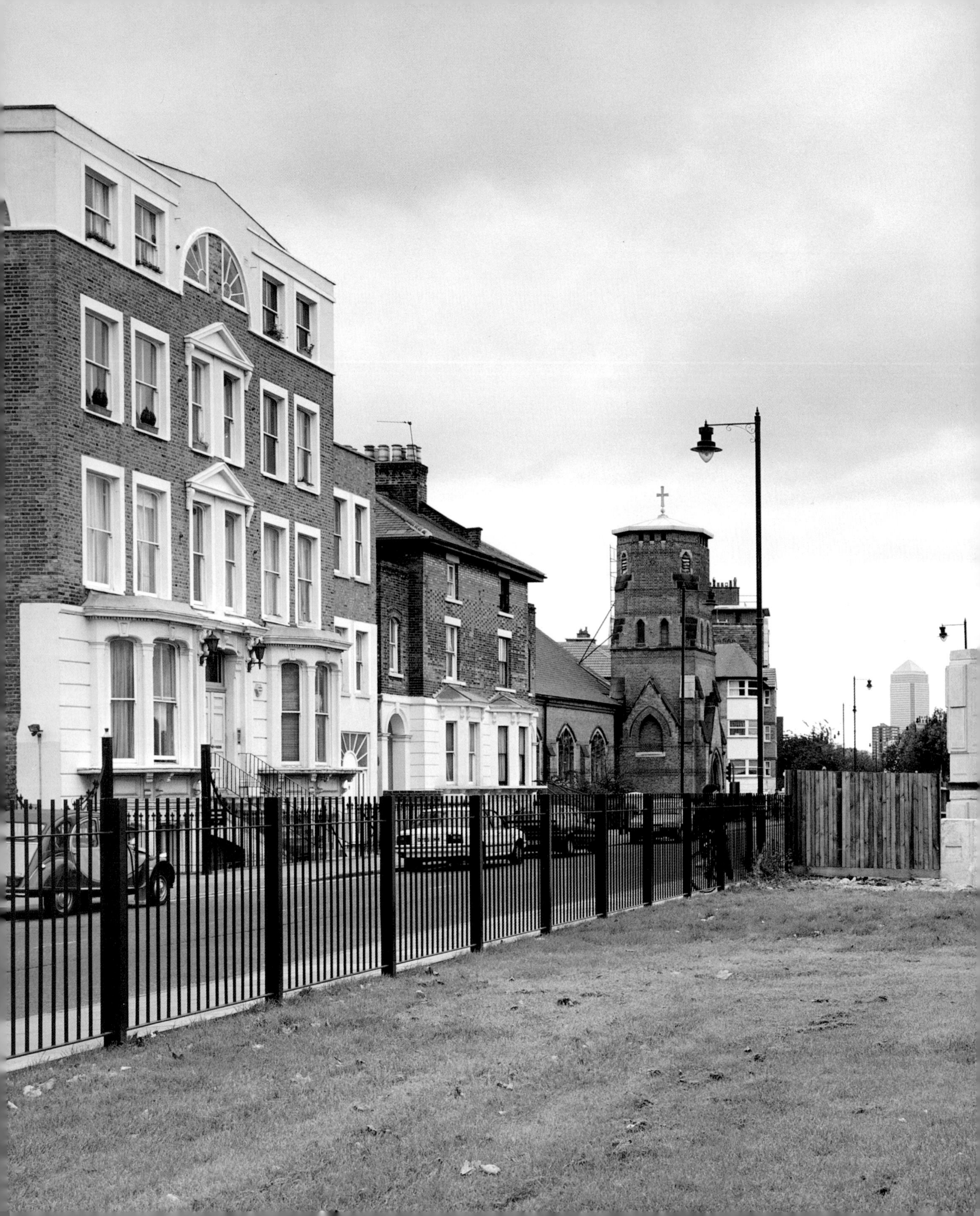

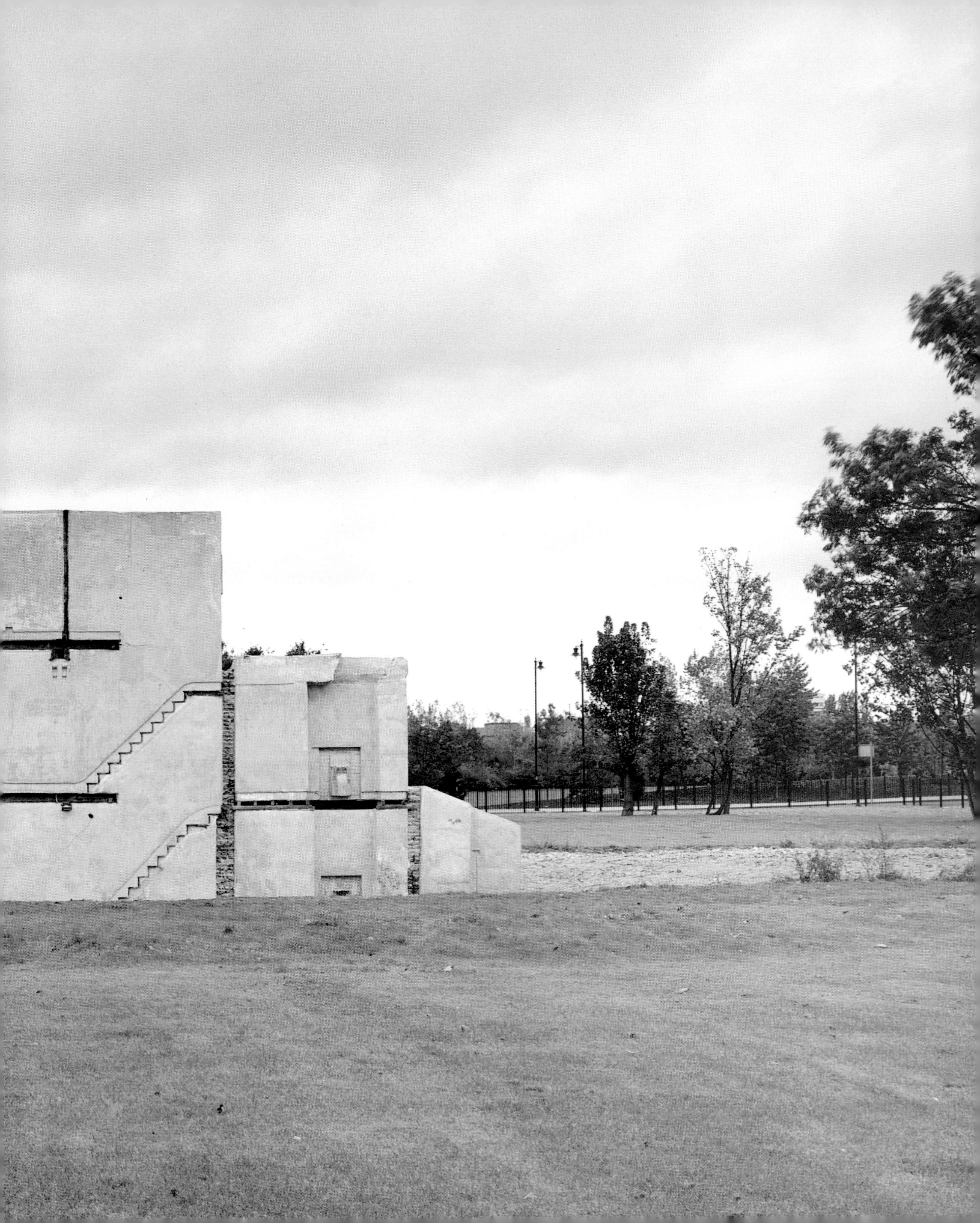

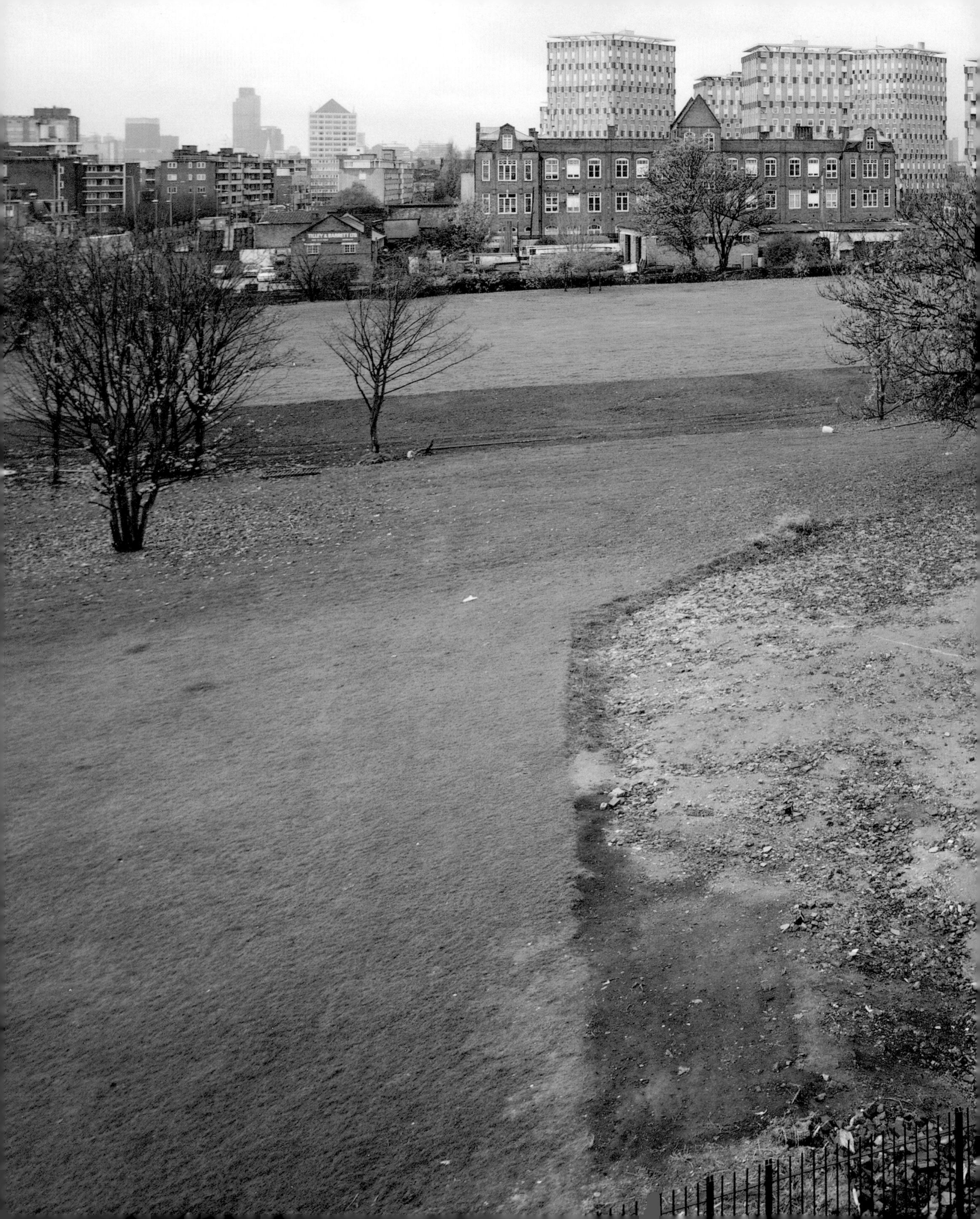
TILLEY & BARRETT LTD

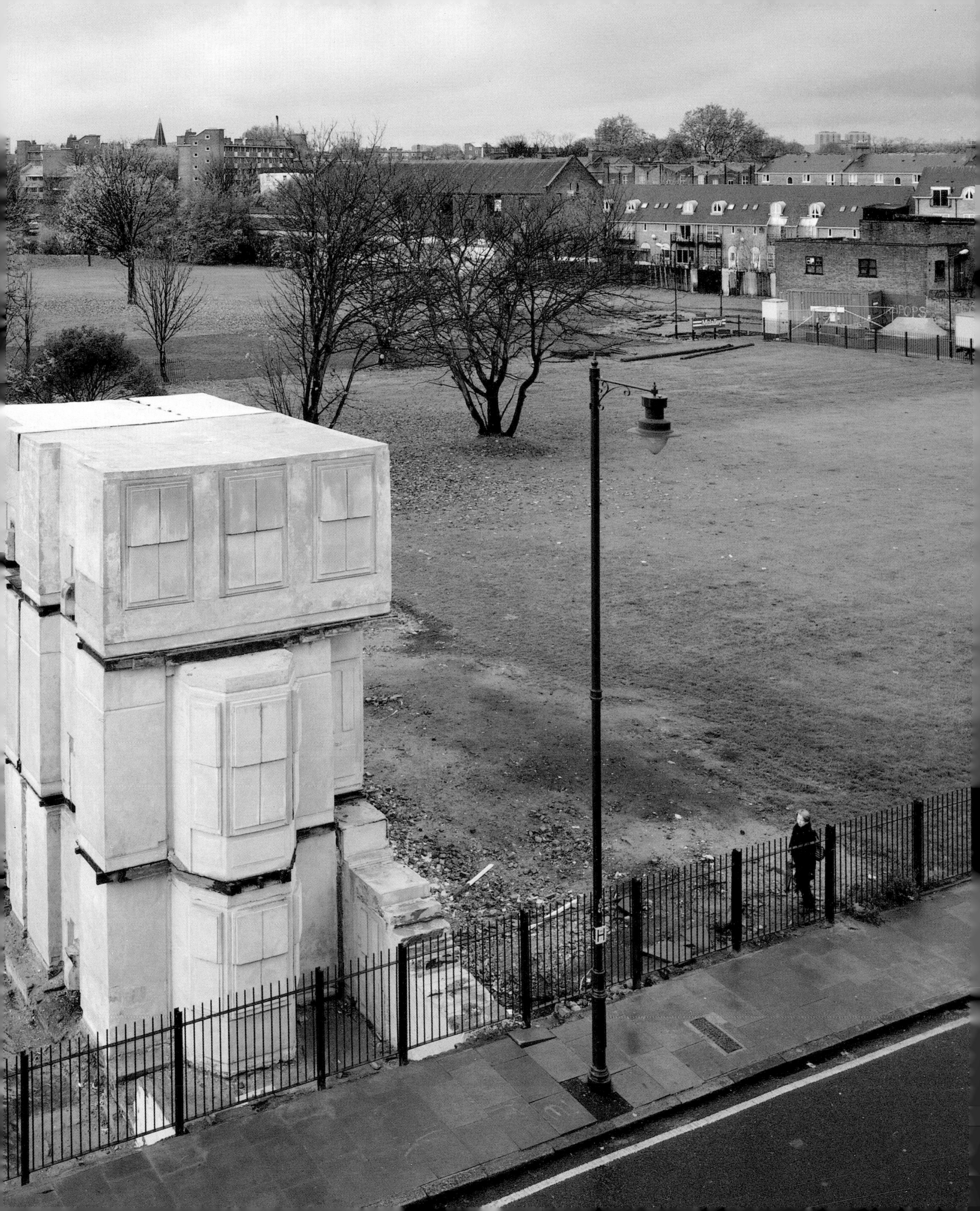

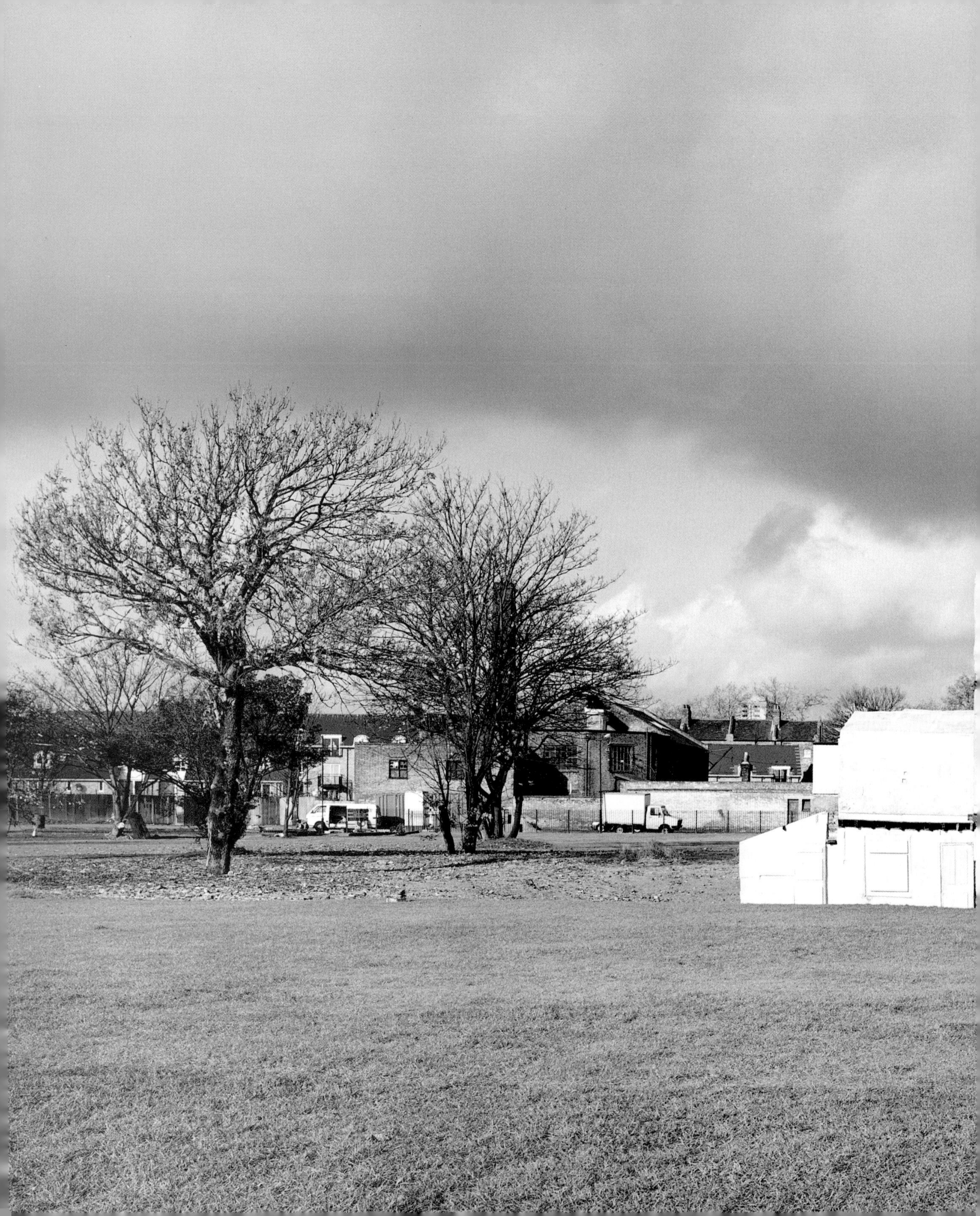

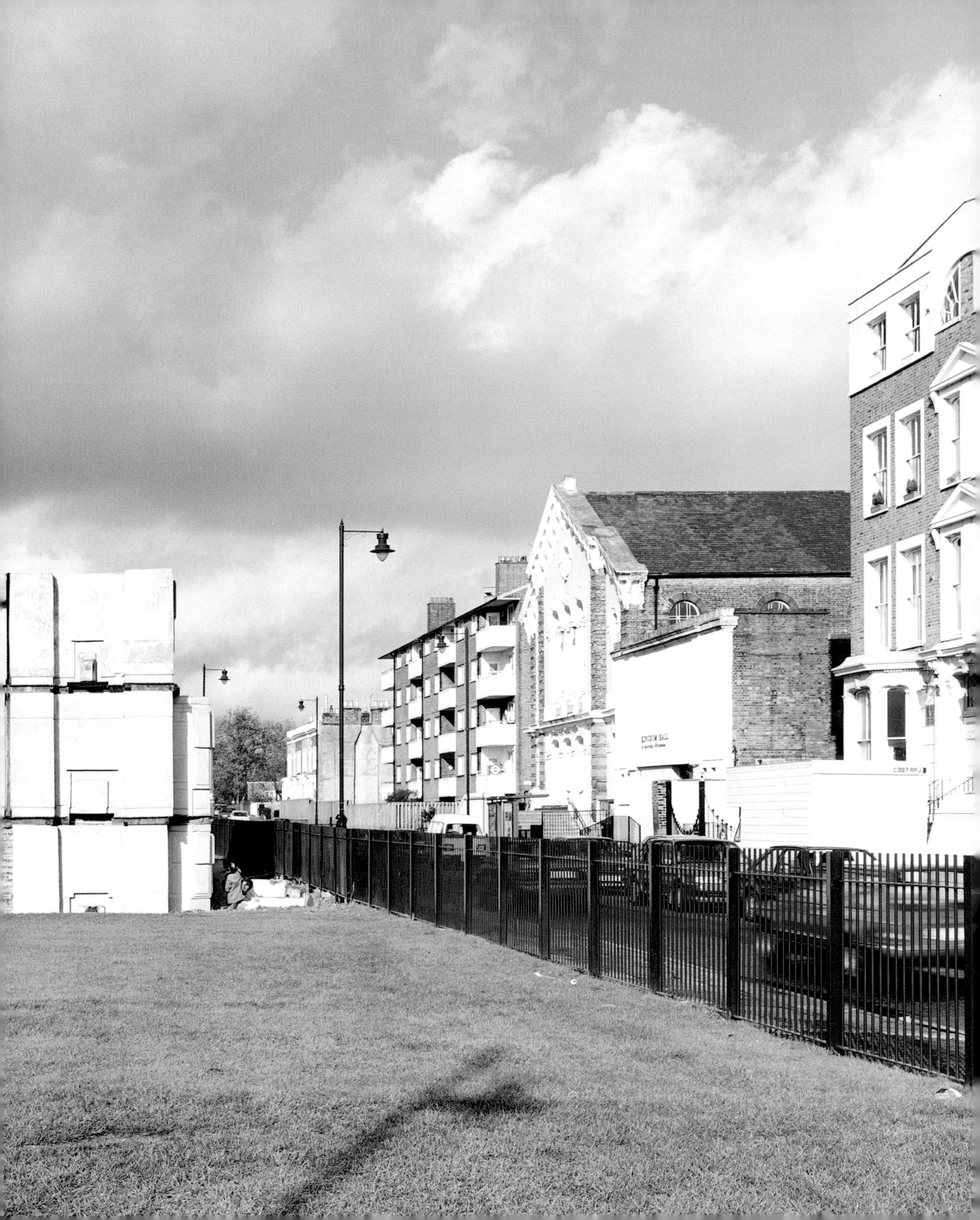
C387 RPJ

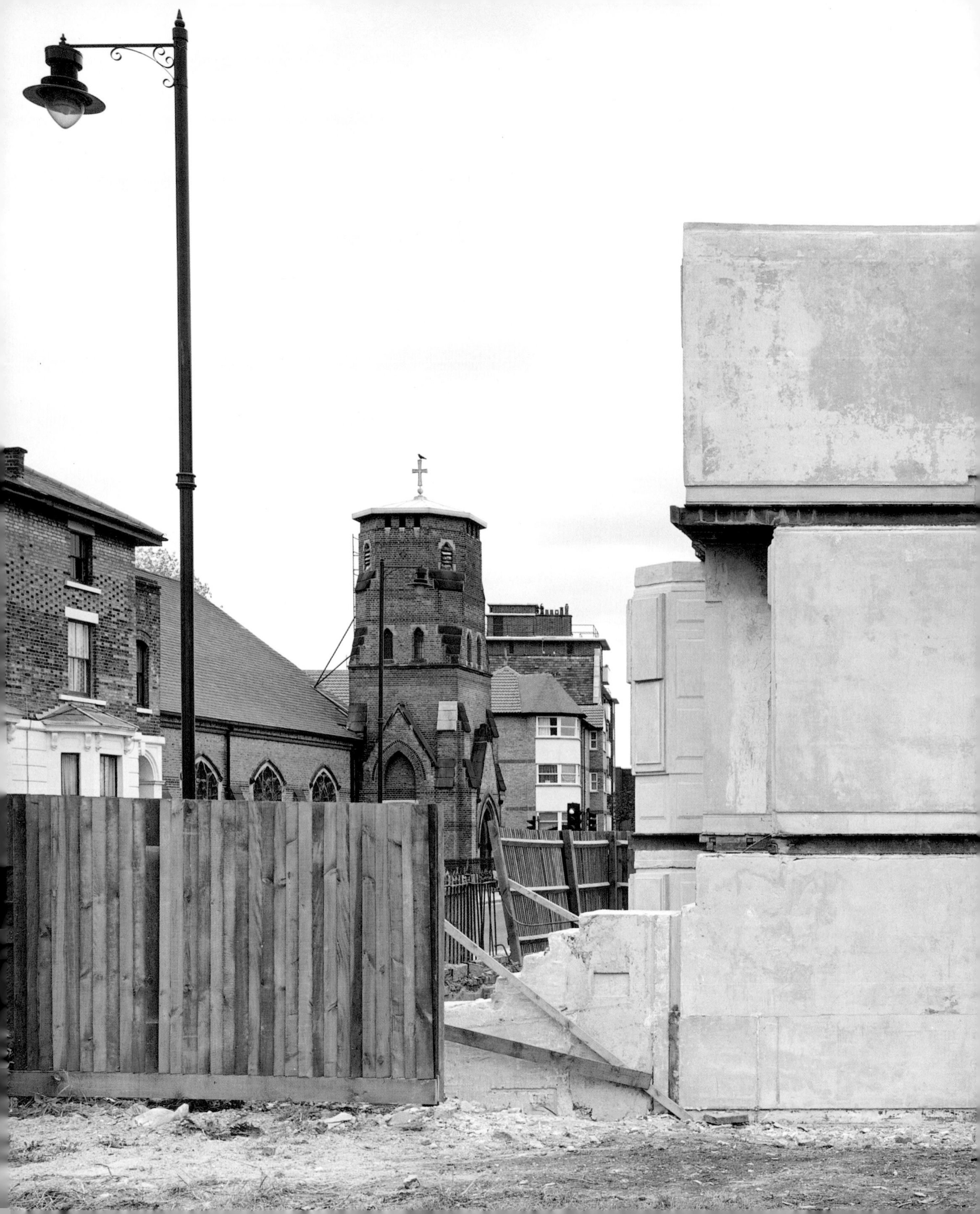

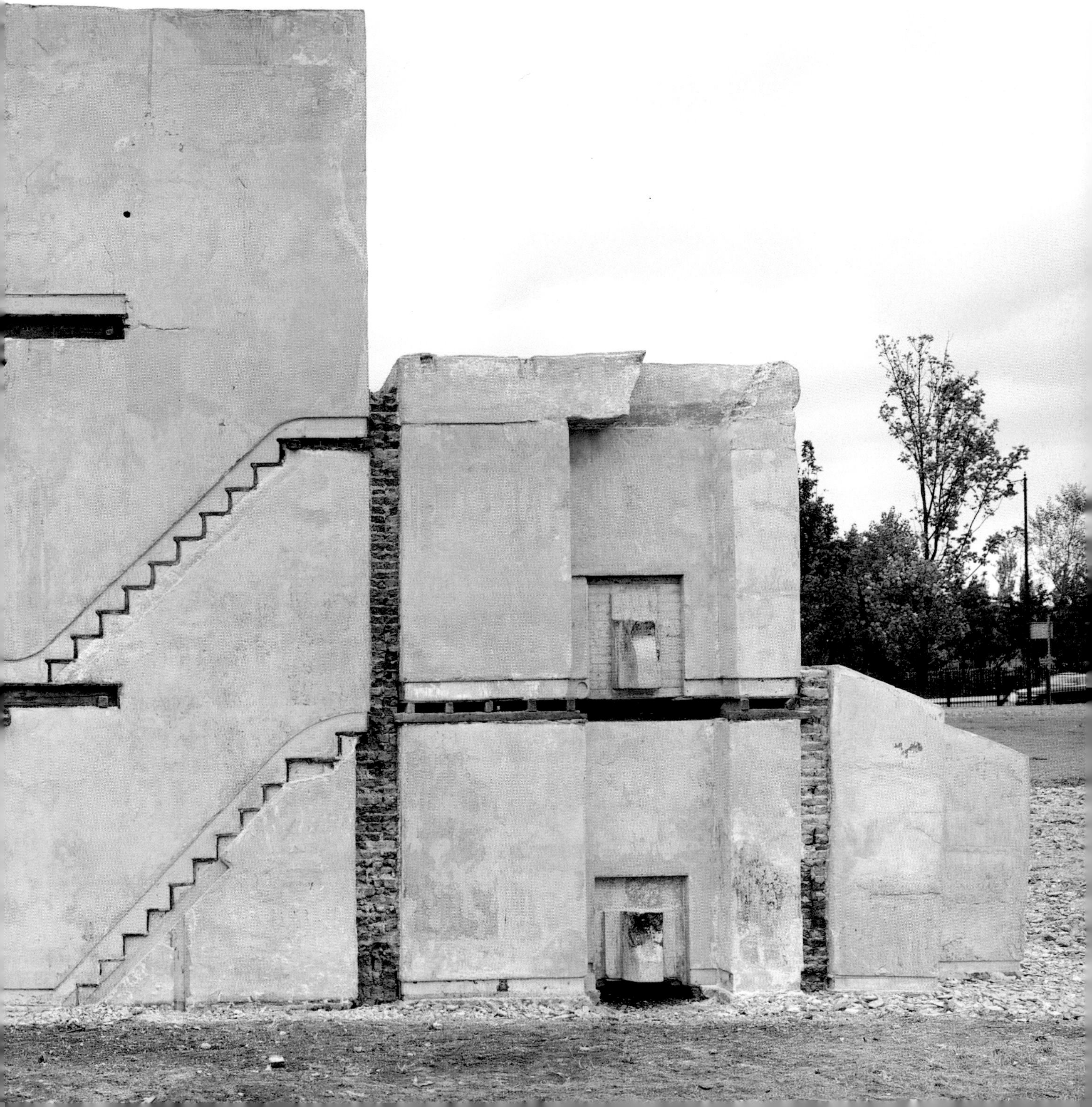

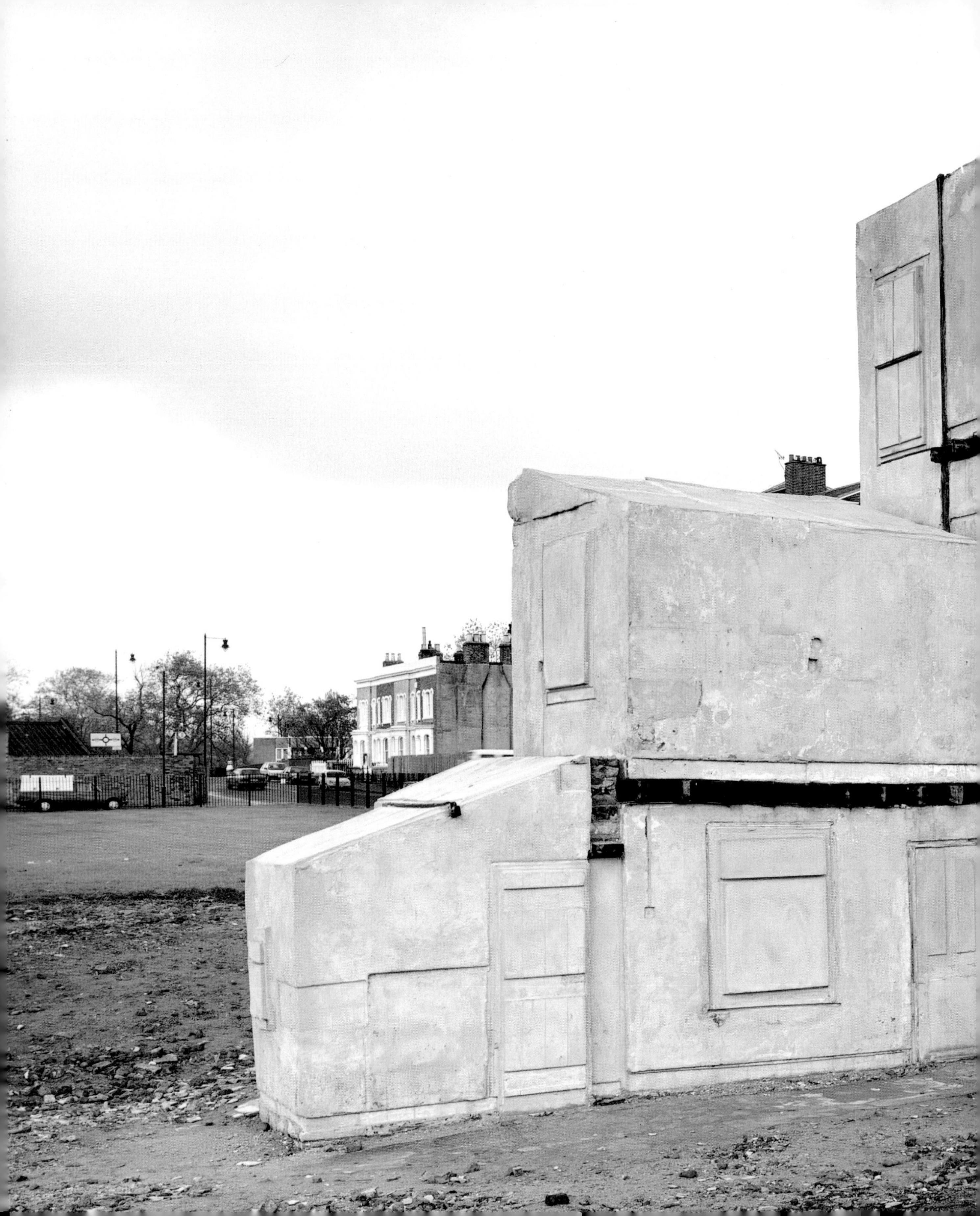

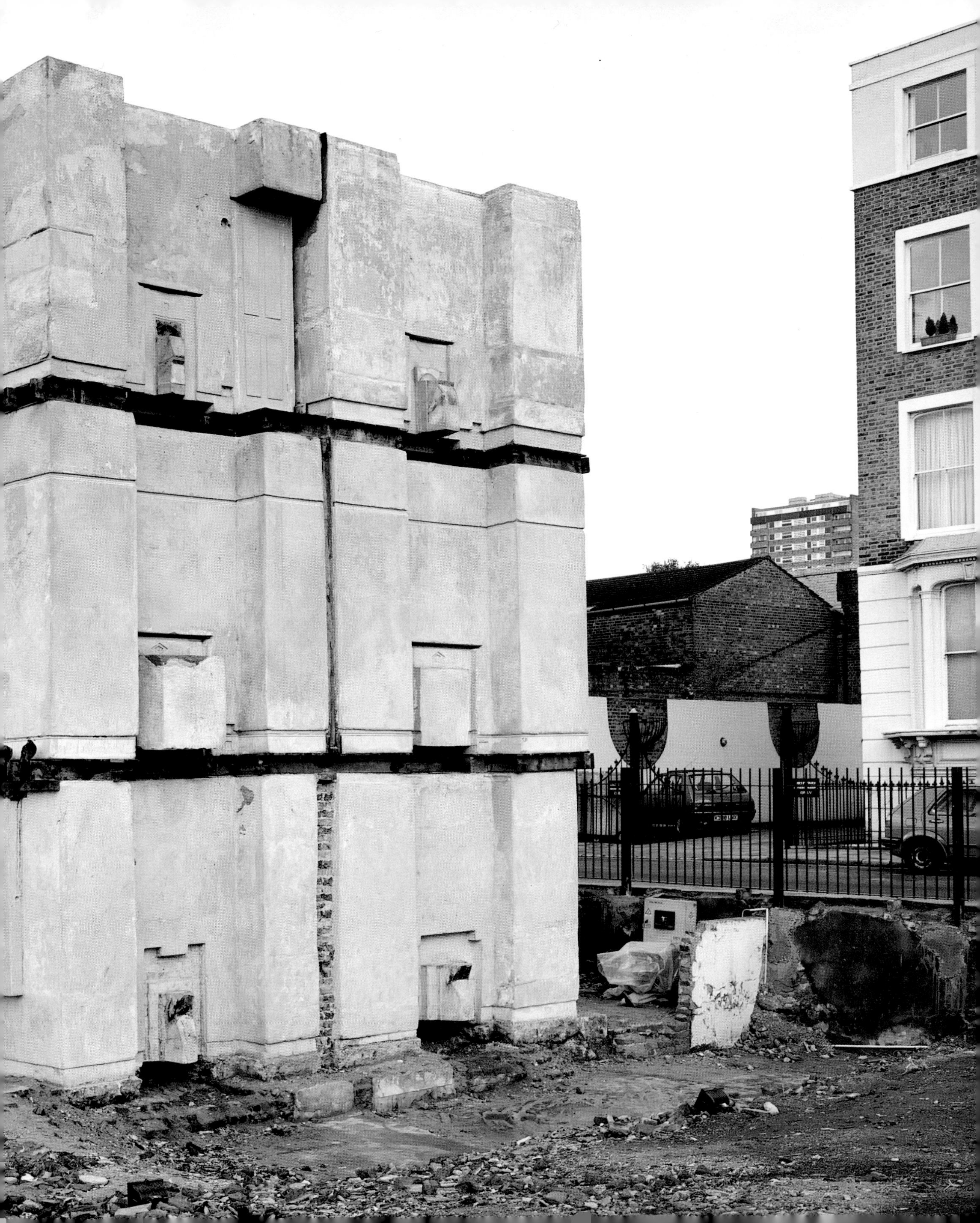

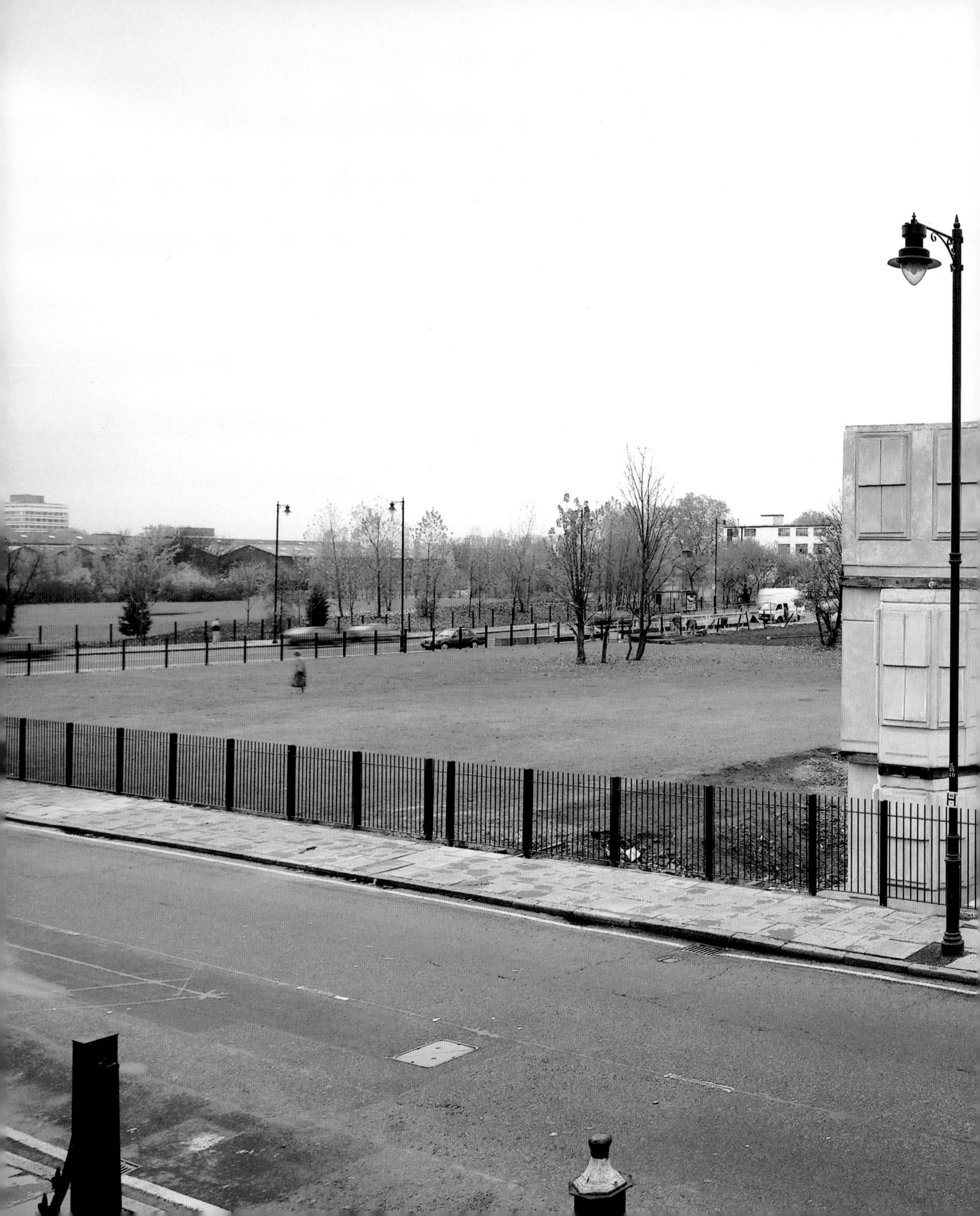

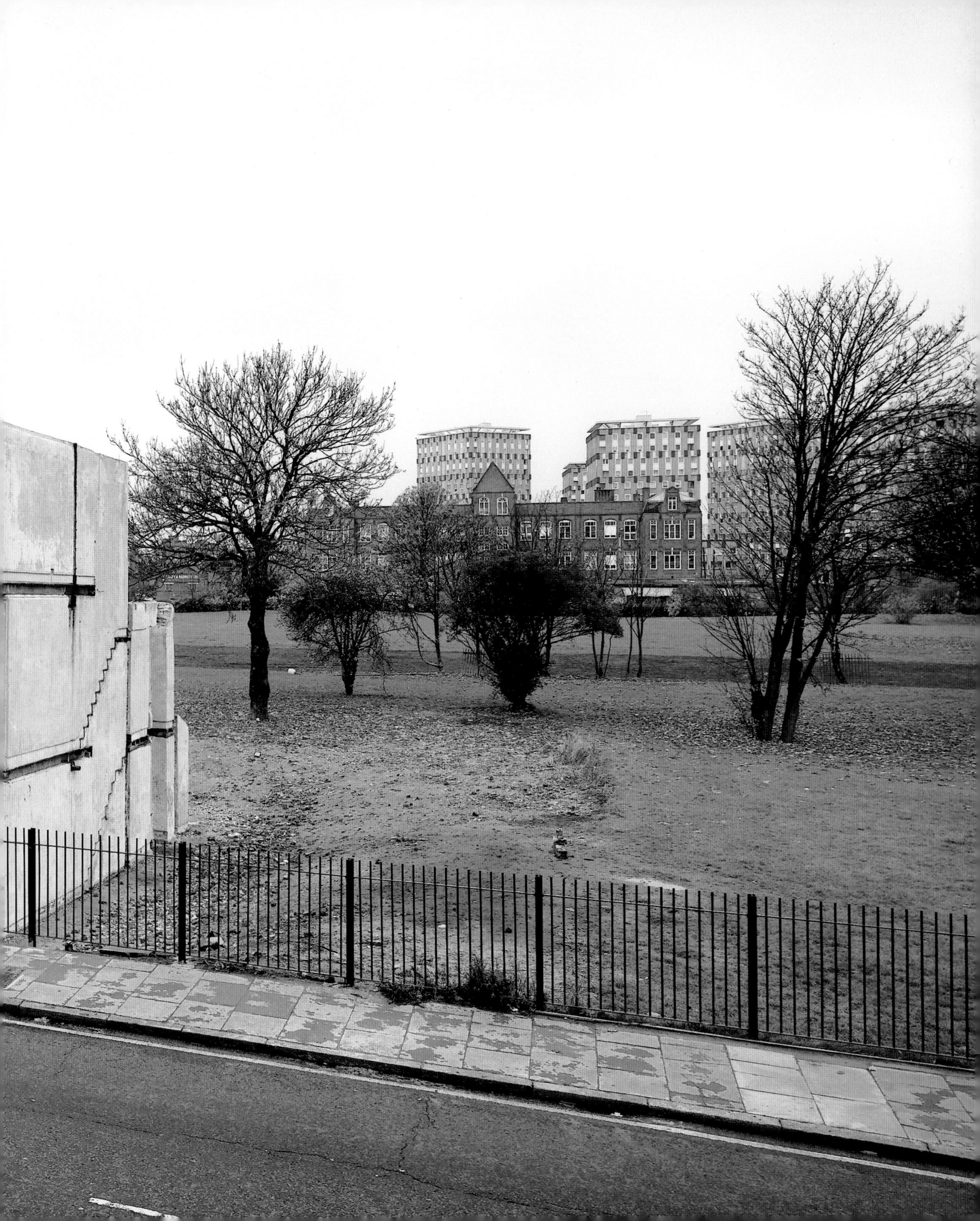

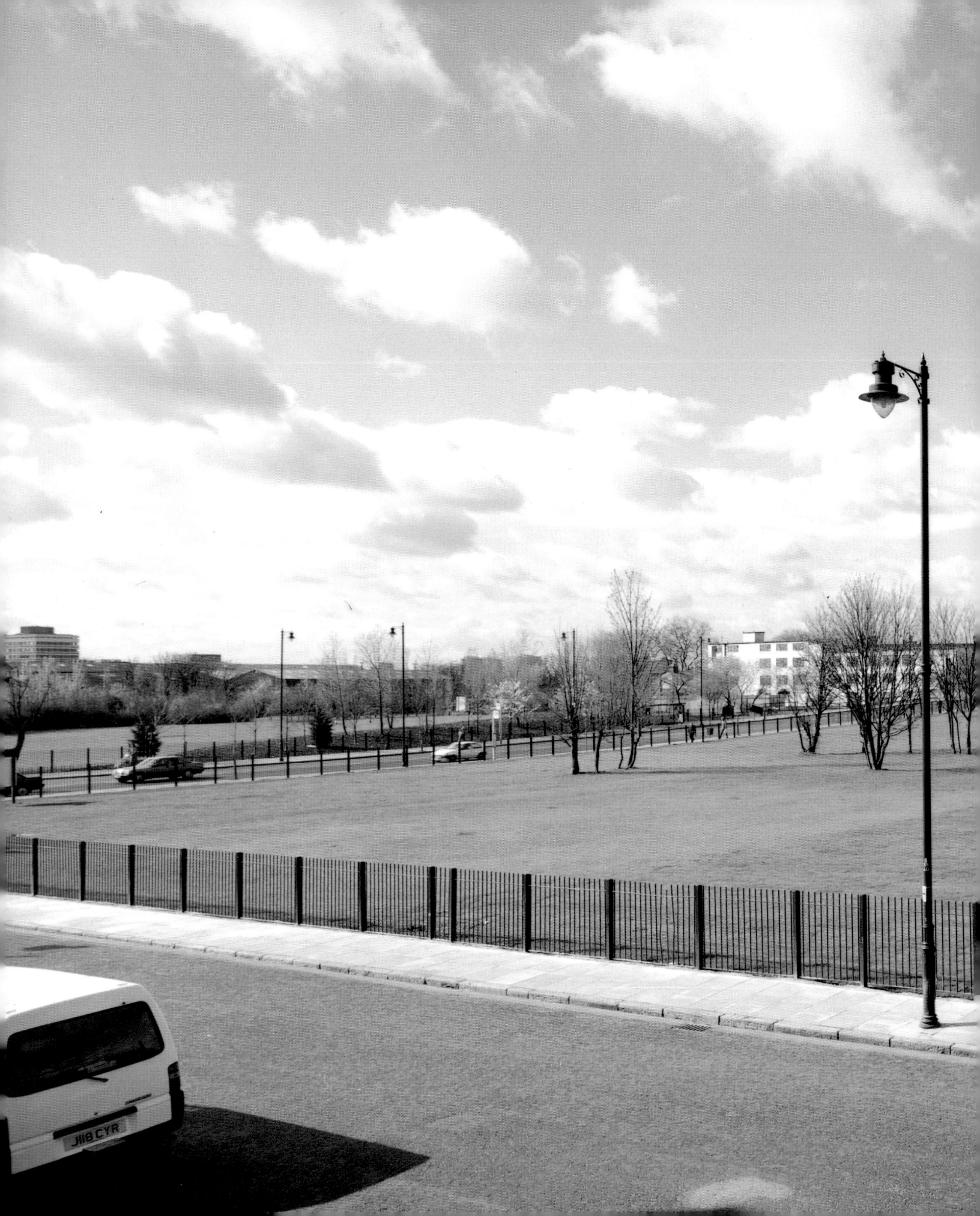
J118 CYR

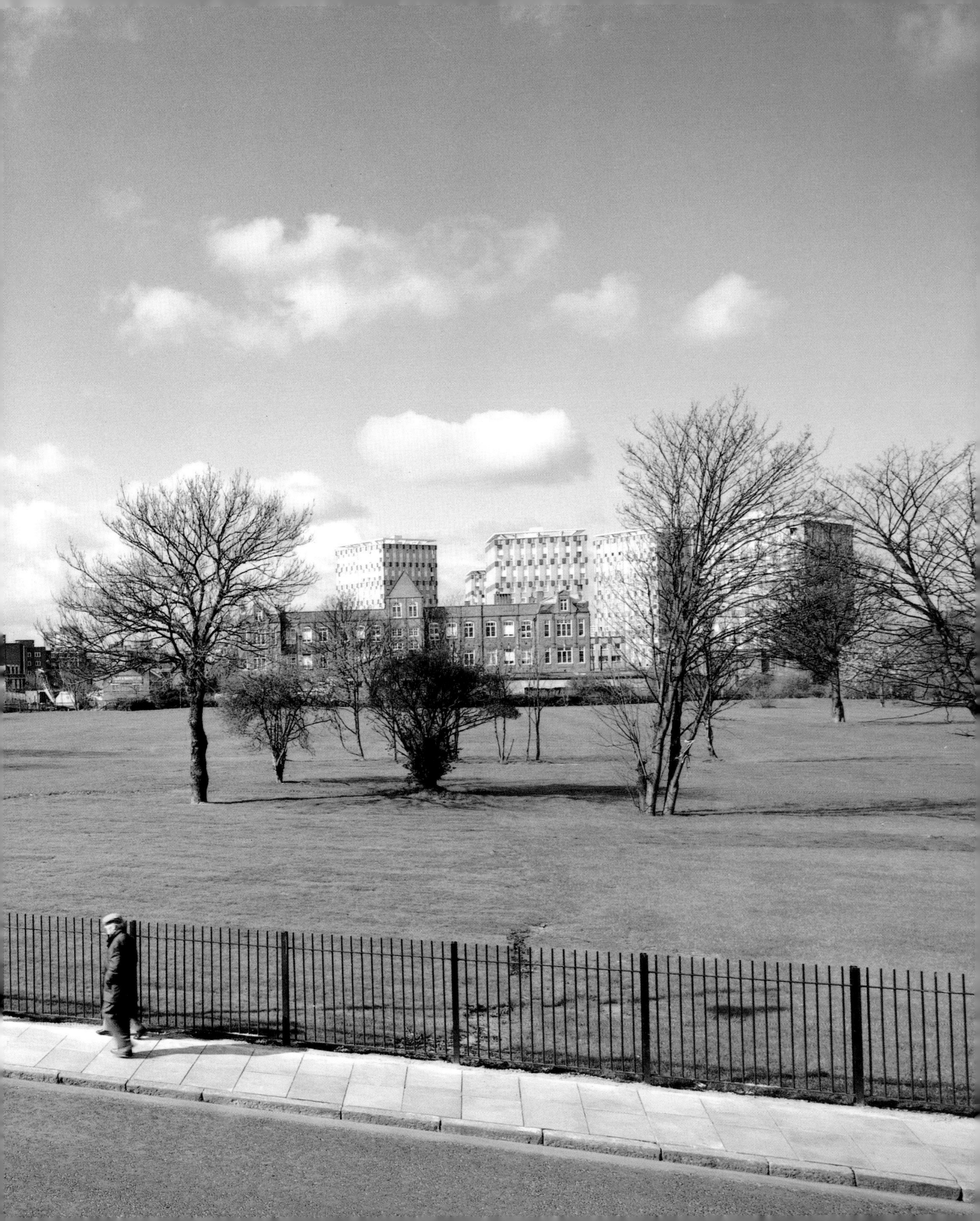

Simon Watney

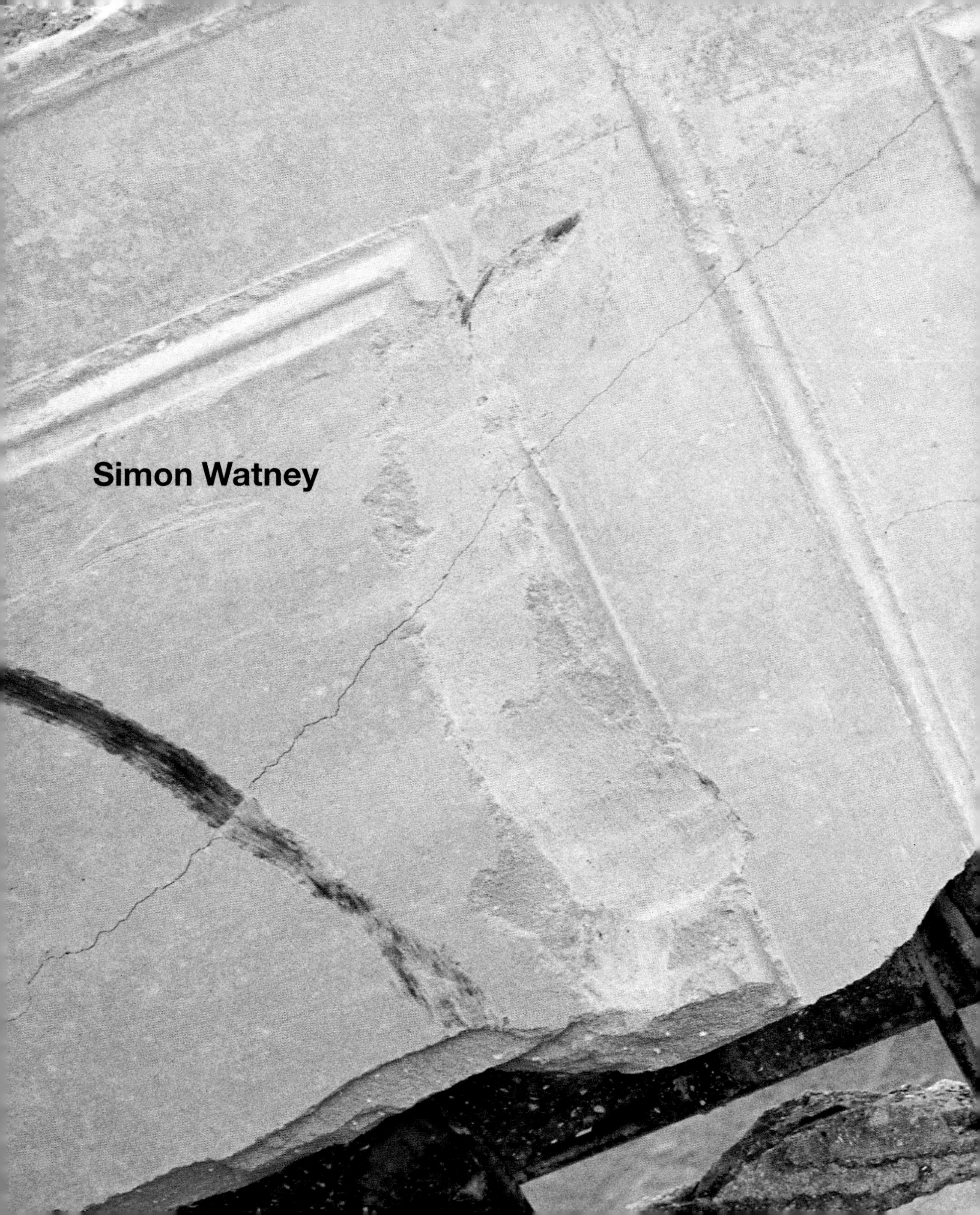

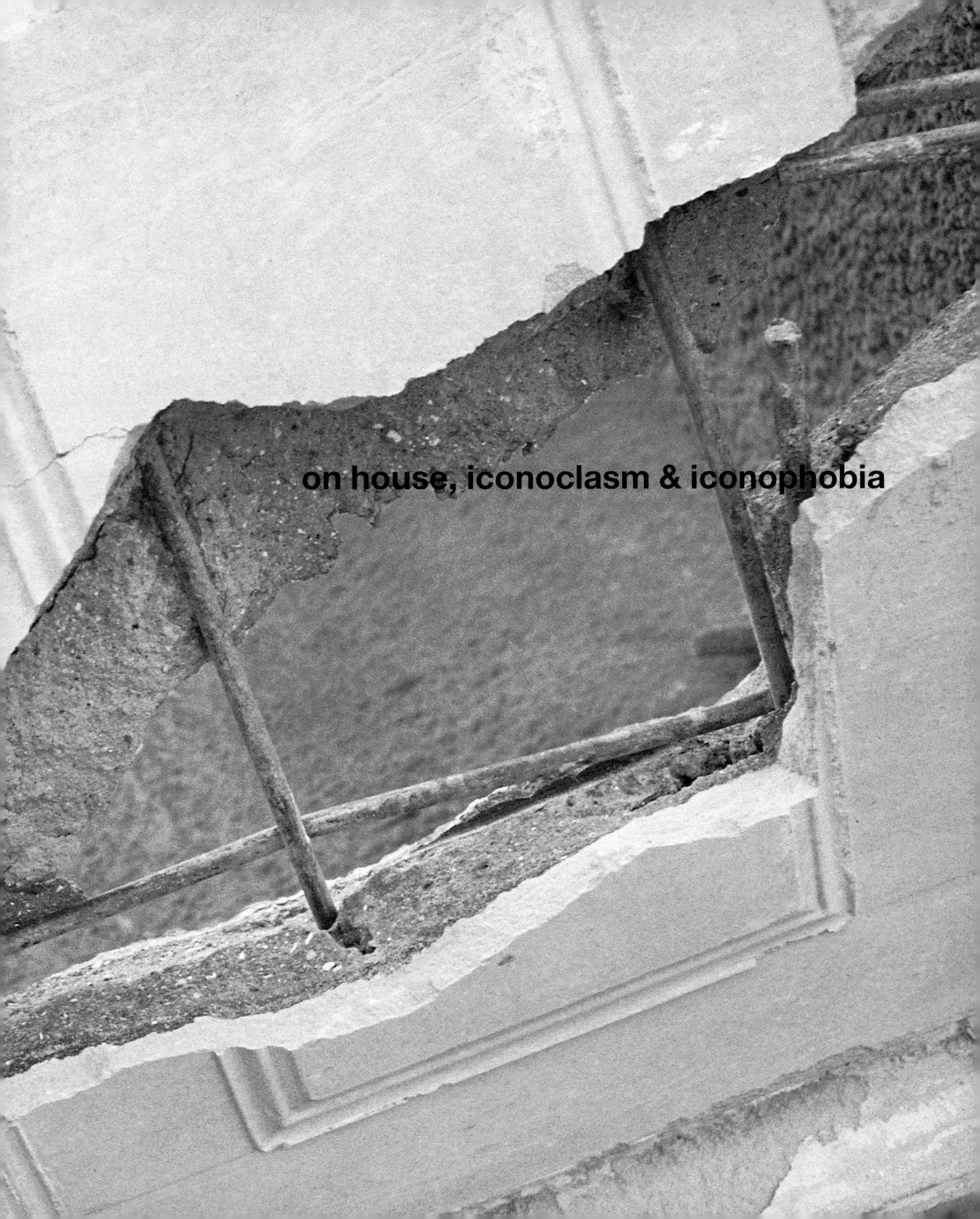
on house, iconoclasm & iconophobia

Introduction: Monuments & Monumentality

Rachel Whiteread's *House* stands within an uninterrupted tradition of public monumental sculpture which is itself inseparable from parallel and closely contingent traditions of vandalism. In his account of the classical monument in European sculpture, Philipp Fehl points out with admirable clarity that:

'Monuments are made for a variety of purposes, not all equally impressive; they may be tombs; marks of honour, affection, triumph or hatred; signs of a covenant; demonstrations of authority or of the possession of property. All, however, have this in common: they are intended to last in time and to signify the importance of whatever memory they wish to pass on to the future (...) The different means of representation which combine to address us from a monument may be equal to that monument's immediate purpose, they may fall short of it, or they may surpass it. Seen at a time removed from the sympathies and disaffections which ruled when it was erected, a monument will, at best, be judged in accordance with the sense of greatness its art is capable of inspiring. I say "at best" because the language it speaks may not be understood. During the Middle Ages, for example, Greek and Roman statues were destroyed because (among other reasons) they were mistaken for idols'.[1]

Evoking and invoking public meanings, monumental sculpture is amongst the most intrinsically vulnerable of the Fine Arts. As Fehl again observes, the monument's capacity to convey meaning '...is not only a source of power; it may also be their undoing, provoking their destruction by the enemies of whatever they stand for. If not actually destroyed, they may be "purified" and dedicated to a new cause; sometimes a simple change of name suffices to re-animate them and give them new dignity'.[2]

'Mors etiam saxis nominibusque venit' (Death comes even to stones and names).[3] In this general context, which informs the entire tradition of monumental sculpture, Fehl concludes that there are only two alternative options, either:

'to do the best one can in an impossible situation and defiantly erect colossal piles against the action of time (the superstitious will, in addition, have recourse to magical practices); or in some manner to make the recognition of the ultimate futility of the monumental effort an element in its subject matter'.[4]

Throughout the history of the *House* project, there was always a certain amount of confusion concerning its actual physical durability, not least in relation to its principle medium, sprayed concrete. Thus the powerful, open-ended ambivalence of *House*'s engagement with issues of housing, domesticity and the relations between 'public' and 'private' were embedded into the piece's very material fabric. Its vulnerable appearance itself signified something basic about the fields of popular memory with which it engaged, and engages still in different ways – now itself in the register of conflicting memories and forgettings. Furthermore, Whiteread's chosen materials inevitably invoke connotations of vulnerability and loss, whether by association with the didactic purpose of making casts of fragile, original sculptural monuments or with the making of death masks. Moreover, the very whiteness of *House* also aligned it poignantly to the major *political* debate in recent years in the East End of London, which has concerned questions of housing and race, as political parties have scrambled to pander to the wishes of those who would regard London as a city of white people, threatened by non-white immigrants. Thus,

House quite evidently became an emblem of sorts, and was taken by its opponents as itself a species of unwanted, illegal immigrant. Thus the supposed 'victory' of *House*'s demolition may be read as a displaced 'victory' for a certain narrow vision of what may appropriately signify 'London-ness' and, by extension, Englishness. In other words, it was inevitable from the start that *House* would mobilize powerful opposition from various predictable sources, especially those troubled by a work of art which so forcefully invites us to meditate on such a potent site of social and psychic conflict as the supposedly inviolate privacy of 'the home'.

The act of casting the last surviving house of a typical terraced row had the effect of contrasting, in situ, the values we habitually attach to the concept of 'home' with the actual emptiness and blankness of much domestic life, remembered or forgotten. Homes conjure up powerful emotions. In the East End of London, these will include folk-memories of earlier 'immigrations' to urban employment, memories of the Second World War and the Blitz, as well as the various municipal housing and rehousing schemes that have proliferated since the 1920s. Families, like whole population groups, tend to move around over time in all cities. I am hardly unusual as a suburban Londoner in so far as the nursing home in which I was born, and the first schools I attended, and several of the houses and flats in which I grew up as a post-war child, no longer exist, save in memory. *House* is a monument which draws attention to such memories, and the complex cultural myths surrounding 'childhood', 'family values', the relations between men and women and adults and children, and so on. It is also fundamentally caught up with questions of

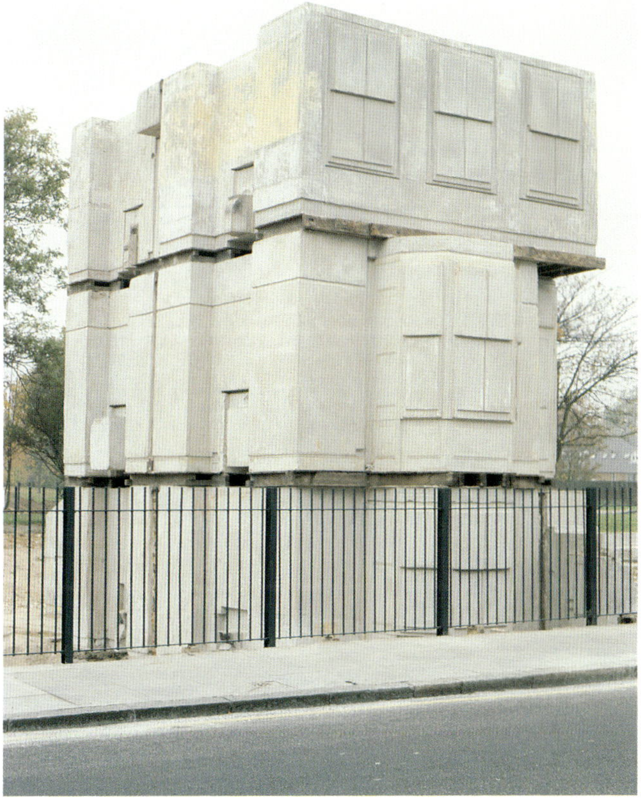

1. Philipp Fehl, *The Classical Monument: Reflections on the Connection between Morality and Art in Greek and Roman Sculpture*, New York University Press, New York, 1972, p.2
2. ibid., pp 3-5
3. Ausonius, *Epitaphs*, 32 1,10
4. op.cit. (1) p.6

class and home ownership in modern Britain, and attendant myths (and realities) of neighbourhood. Alone, *House* has no neighbours. It is the last survivor, but of what? The question of what *House* reminded people of is inseparable from our understanding of those who successfully and vigorously sought its destruction. As novelist Christopher Coe has written:

'There will always be one final everything – the last work, of course, the last breath; there will be one last cheque you write, one last artichoke (...) It doesn't matter how many coins you throw in the fountain. You will make one last photograph, and be photographed one final time by somebody else (...) There will be one final time you will see or will be seen by the woman you have loved, or the people you have known, unless, of course, you outlive them all, which is not likely'.[5]

House condenses such personal feelings about transience with an implicit awareness of the role that institutions such as local government and political parties play in the conservation (or destruction) of those places we remember (or forget) as having been 'home'. *House* evidently offended particular individuals in particular ways. It attracted an especially venomous iconoclastic instinct, an instinct which could not bare to be reminded of the vulnerability and isolation experienced inside many homes, even and especially when they are themselves in close physical proximity to one another. If *House* was, and is, in some important sense 'about' the conflict between simultaneous feelings of both belonging and of exclusion, it could not but have been subject to controversy. If, furthermore, it was also 'about' these issues as they were lived in Britain in the 1990s, its destruction must in turn be regarded as a powerful, if ironic and not directly intended part of its future significance.[6] It is not a monument to a supposedly 'lost' or 'threatened' way of life. Rather, the painfully conflicting realities of working-class domestic life in twentieth-century Britain, as well as the potent myths that surround the entire subject of terraced housing in British popular culture and popular memory, from Coronation Street to Jack the Ripper, to take just two examples. *House* thus also memorializes the unbridgeable gulf between how we lived, and how we live today. It has no inscription. It reaches no conclusions. In these respects it was perhaps most threatening to those who require the consolation of a certain fantasy of family and neighbourhood, and who are prepared to defend such fantasies at almost any cost. As a public monument, it spoke too much for some of its own times, with too much formal eloquence.

Iconoclasm & Iconophobia

Describing the demolition of *House* by a Fiat-Hitachi earthmover as demanded by Bow Neighbourhood Council, art critic Andrew Graham-Dixon drew attention to:

'a venerable history of this sort of thing in England, an old tradition of iconoclasm that stretches back to the days of the Reformation, when religious zealots (...) systematically destroyed the sculpture and painting of the English Middle Ages'.

He concluded that perhaps the ruined site:

'itself amounts to a monument of a peculiarly English kind: a monument to an abiding and virtually fanatical distrust of visual art within the British psyche'.[7]

There is a risk of positing the existence of an immutable,

national psychic mechanism, uniquely hostile to the visual arts. Yet comparisons between sixteenth-century and late twentieth-century England are indeed tempting; not least because there has been no larger transfer of property and other forms of capital since the Dissolution of the Monasteries ordered by Henry VIII in 1536 than took place under the auspices of Thatcherism, involving the wholesale sell-off of almost all our most basic national utilities, from gas and telephone services, to the railways and health care provision.

In his succinct and convincing account of the cultural impact of the English Reformations of the sixteenth century, Professor Patrick Collinson invokes a helpful, clear distinction between Iconoclasm and Iconophobia, understanding the former to imply

'a spirited attack, verbally violent or actually violent, but not the total repudiation of all images, which on my terms is iconophobia. Indeed, iconoclasm in this sense may imply the substitution of other, acceptable images, or the refashioning of some images for an altered purpose. It is hostile to false art but not anti-art, since its hostility implies a true and acceptable art, applied to a laudable purpose'.[8]

There are certainly fascinating parallels between the intensity and the objects of cultural debate in mid-to-late sixteenth century Britain, and in late twentieth-century Britain. For example, Collinson lists some of the many justifications Elizabethan Protestant iconoclasts gave for attacking the theatre. These included objections to drama as:

'pagan or even "devilish" in origin, Sabbatarianism, concern for public health and order, dread of prodigality and idleness, an ever-increasing sensitivity to anything "filthy", that is, suggesting and inciting sexual licence, the rejection of dramatic fictions, as (in effect) lies, with a particular objection to the transvestite life; and, most significantly for a discussion of incipient iconophobia, resistance to the theatrical appeal to what has been called "the idolatrous eye" ... Anthony Munday concurred: "there commeth much evill in the eares, but more at the eyes".'[9]

Thus we may fairly detect a cluster of concerns which goaded sixteenth-century Protestant iconoclasts – anxieties that evil influences could come into the body through the eyes, and corrupt the viewer. Offending materials were those with attention to sex and sensuality, which were responded to with excessive appeals to purity and cleanliness, the ancestors of our modern cultural regimes of domestic hygiene. And not far behind the fanatical hostility to certain types of imagery, including paintings of the Madonna and Child, lay a deeper anxiety about the religious acceptability of representations as such. Indeed, it seems that paintings and works of art were comparatively rare in late Elizabethan English houses. Thus was the Puritan polemic against popery and superstition translated from the destruction of monastic culture in its entirety, to the field of popular culture. Art must improve and give example. It may reflect Creation, but not distract from the Creator. In one broad current of English Theology, aesthetic pleasure was closely bound up with appetites associated with sensuality, and thence with corruption. By contrast, art which satisfies base appetites such as vanity and magic must be destroyed, or else subjected to a programme of correction.

At the same time we have to recognize that such attitudes, and the types of legislation it enacted, coincided with the greatest

5. Christopher Coe, *Such Times*, Hamish Hamilton, London, 1993, p. 73. I would like to thank Edward King for drawing this passage to my attention.
6. See Adrian Searle, "Rachel doesn't live here any more", *frieze*, London, Issue 14, January-February 1994, pp. 26-30.
7. Andrew Graham-Dixon, 'Artless earthmover finally brings "House" down', *The Independent*, London, 12 January, 1994, n.p.
8. Patrick Collinson, *From Iconoclasm to Iconophobia: the Cultural Impact of the Second English Reformation*, University of Reading, 1985, p.8
9. ibid., pp. 11-12

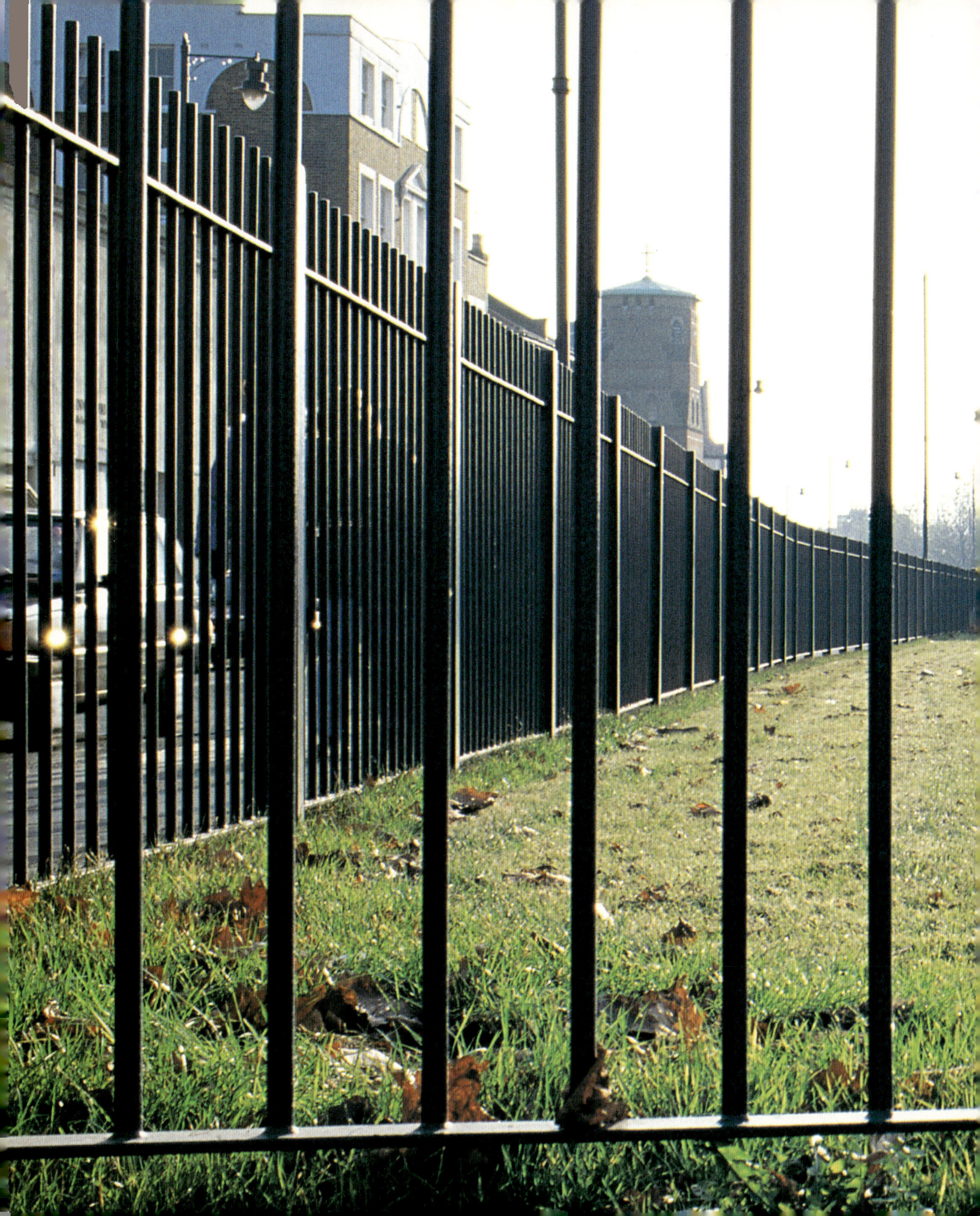

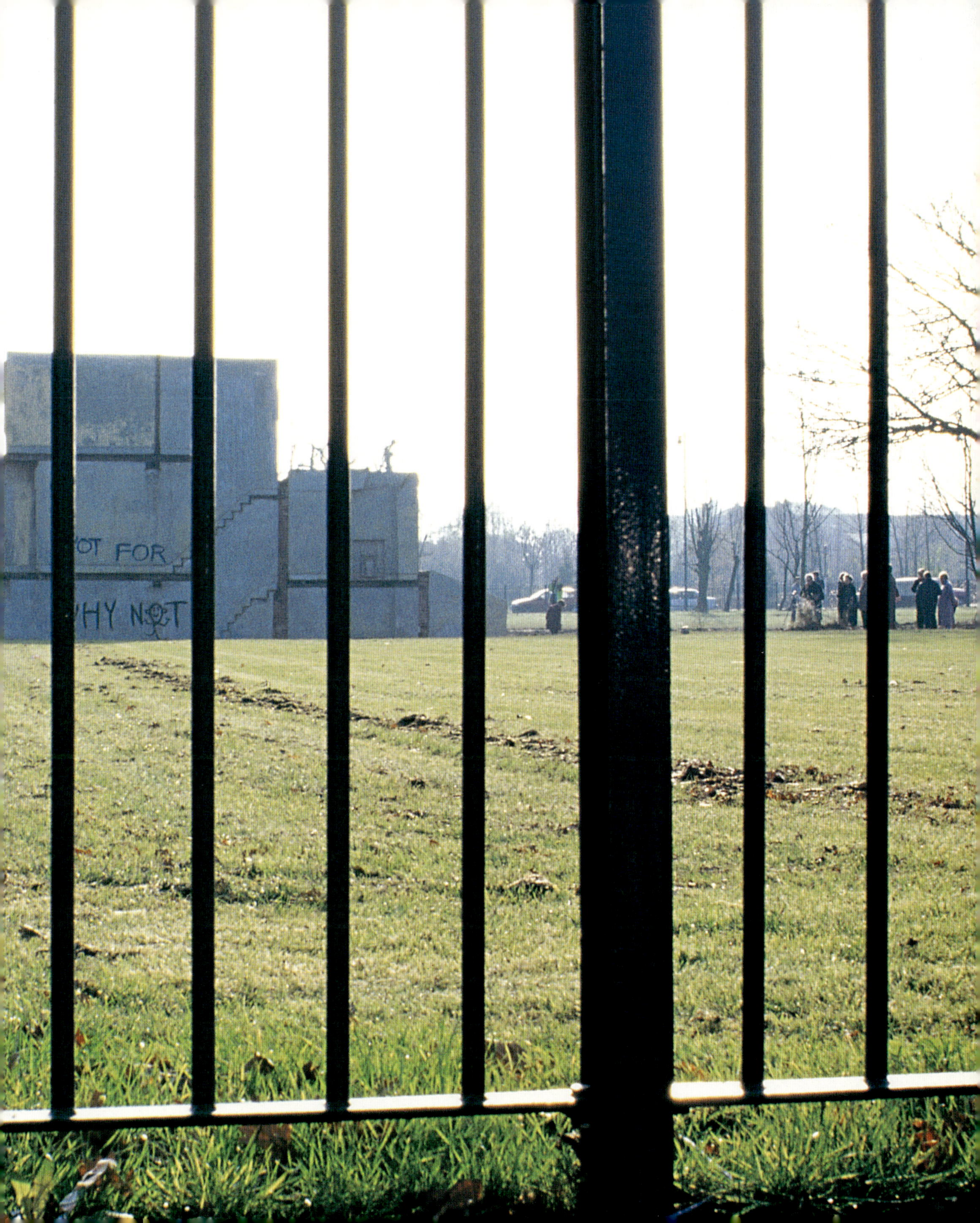
OT FOR
HY NOT

flowering of English Renaissance literature in the theatre of Marlowe, Shakespeare and the playwrights of early Jacobean theatre in London and at Court. For an unrelenting theological, political and cultural war against Roman Catholicism did not mean that nobody went to the theatre. Then, as now, there were powerful moral and political disputes taking place both within and between classes concerning disputed standards of public 'decency', often focused on the domain of visual representations, rather than in relation to actual social relations. Certainly it would appear that we can, as it were, recognize certain continuities of human nature – the enthusiasm with which some will embrace systems of belief that can rationalize fear of and hostility to *all* images of human sensual pleasure. At the same time it is not entirely fanciful to trace an institutional and intellectual line of descent from the original Reformers, to the puritans of the seventeenth century, gradually secularized into philanthropic agencies and ultimately into political parties and social movements, including large sections of the contemporary English Left and the Women's Movement. Indeed, with few exceptions, the aristocracy of English Left and feminist culture responded with significant timidity to the destruction of *House*. For if American historian George L. Mosse is correct, the culture of the modern English labour movement is largely constituted within notions of *respectability* that *House* could only serve to trouble. 'Respectability' involves rigid divisions of gender, and of age, and frequently of race and sexuality. The 'respectable' household is always clean. It is thus also always sterile. It cannot acknowledge affection, or displays of sensuality. Yet it is not embarrassed to be seen reading *The Sun* or the *Daily Mail*, though *The Daily Telegraph* is best. Doubtless the housewives of Grove Road, like my grandmother's family in nearby Commercial Road, kept their front doorsteps bright red with fanatical zeal because this was the only way they could demonstrate their social superiority over those in neighbouring streets where dirty door-steps spelled out unemployment and descent into depravity. And somehow the scrubbing, the tut-tutting at Page Three girls, the obsessions with the imagined evils of extreme pornography, the deep hatred and fear of the body and its pleasures, are not unconnected. And all this is 'acceptable', and 'normal' and 'English', according to the respectable – a constituency which has little respect for the boundaries of race or class or gender. For 'the respectable' read 'the Saved'.

We are witnessing what amounts to a new era of English puritanism, in which the ever-censorious forces of anti-sensualist iconoclasm are met only by a Leftist-Feminist intelligentsia which is itself almost equally distrustful of monuments and which tends to dismiss them as if they were intrinsically 'nationalistic', and probably guilty of many other 'isms' as well. When the legal concept of 'Listed Buildings' was defined in the Town and Country Planning Acts of 1944 and 1947, this was regarded at the time as a direct result of awareness raised by recent wartime threats. It is frequently pointed out with some pride that England has far more listed buildings than other comparable countries. But might this not be because England also has fewer ordinary cultural protections than other countries, and a far less developed sense of the worth and value of its own national cultural achievements?[10] We are endlessly exhorted to rally to the protection of Venice, whilst more or less ignoring the virtual pillage since World War Two of cities including Gloucester, Newcastle-upon-Tyne,

10. See Martin Robertson et al. 'Listed Buildings: The National Resurvey of England', *Transactions of the Ancient Monuments Society*, Volume 37, 1993, London, pp. 21–95. I would like to thank Mandy Merck for drawing this article to my attention.
11. Eric Flounders, 'Letter', *The Independent*, London, Wednesday 17 November, 1993.
12. Nigel Glendinning et al. 'Letter', *The Independent*, London, 20 November 1993.

Brighton, Exeter and so on. In such circumstances it was unlikely that *House* would attract much support, and this too seemed to inform its sad, defenceless form.

Representation & Representativeness

House's most implacable adversary was Councillor Eric Flounders, proudly self-proclaiming Chair of the Bow Parks Board and the Standing Neighbourhood Committee. For Cllr. Flounders, *House* was beyond question a 'monstrosity', and unwelcome in Bow.[11] He also described it as an 'excrescence', frequently claiming to speak 'on behalf' of local opinion. It is, however, doubtful how far an elected local Councillor who chairs both a Parks Committee and a local Standing Neighbourhood Committee may actually be understood to 'represent' his or her constituents in matters of public taste. Throughout the newspaper coverage of the *House* affair, some journalists would go out looking for outraged local opinion, whilst others, more sympathetic to *House*, could write up approving local sentiments. As one large group of Bow residents explained in a letter to *The Independent* in November 1993:

'Councillor Flounders has every right to express his personal dislike for Rachel Whiteread's *House* in your columns, but it seems an abuse of his local authority office for him to imply (...) that he speaks for the Bow committees he chairs in this matter, and that he represents the views of the electors he is meant to serve (...) Nobody knows exactly what the balance of local feeling is towards *House* at this juncture. Opinion is divided in Bow as it is nationally. But the response to the work's challenging presence is strong, and its power and validity are hotly debated'.[12]

In a previously unpublished response from Cllr. Flounders to

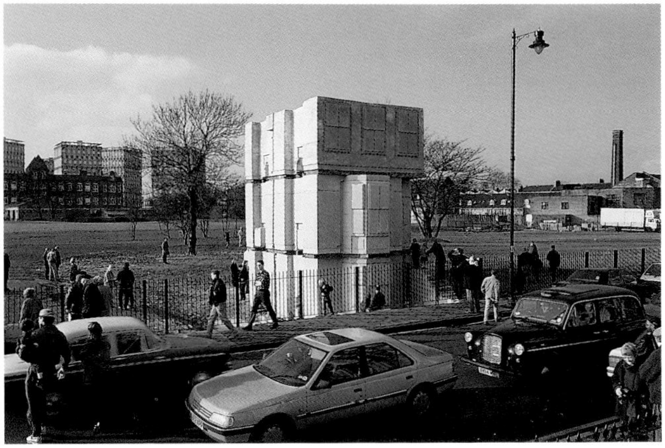

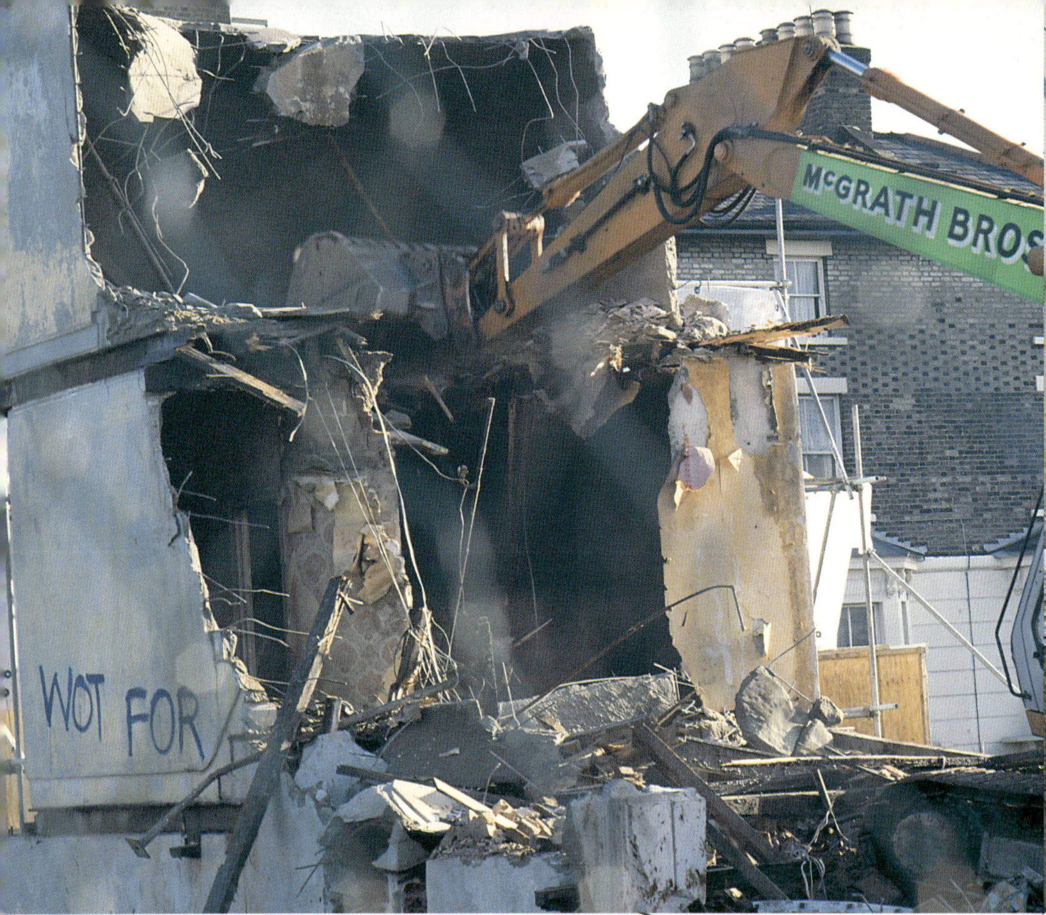
McGRATH BROS
WOT FOR

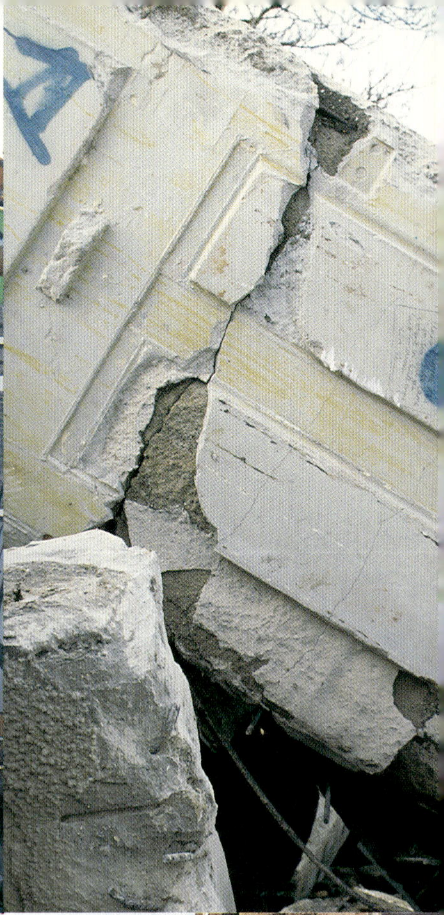

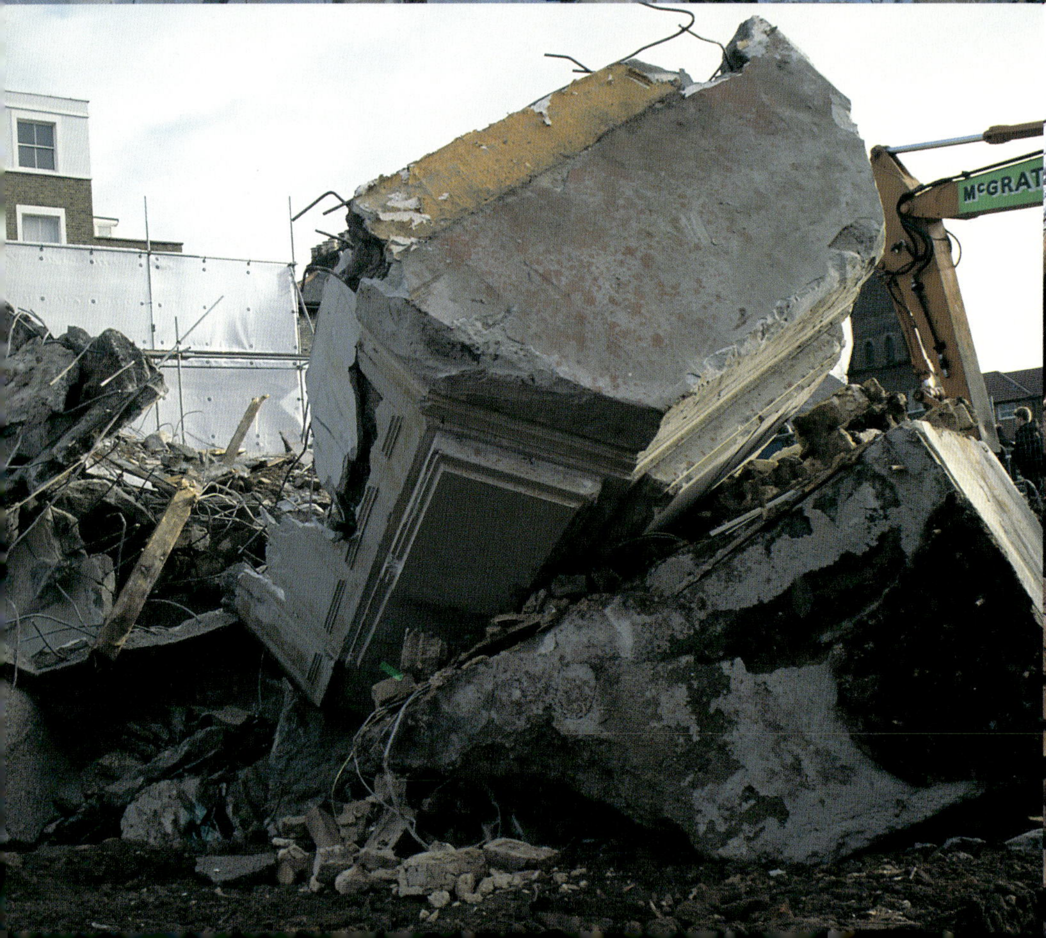
McGRATH

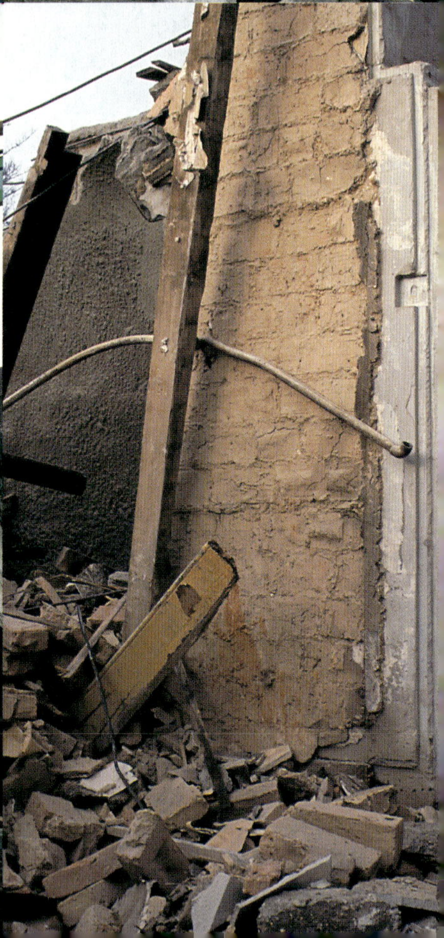

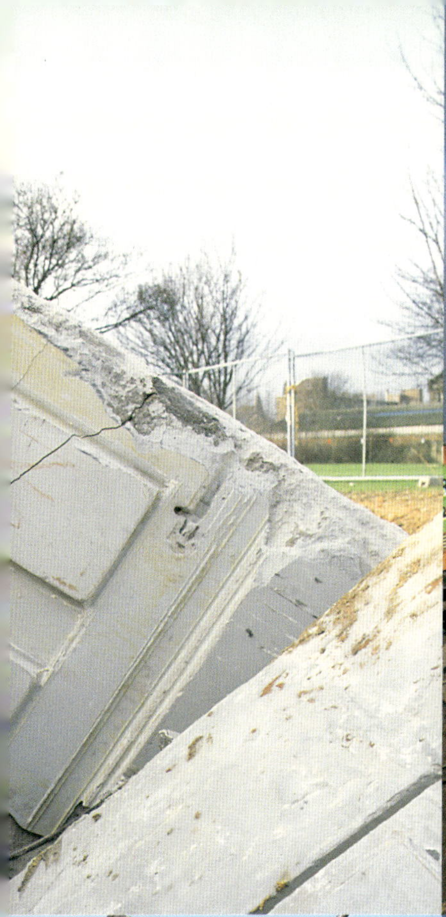

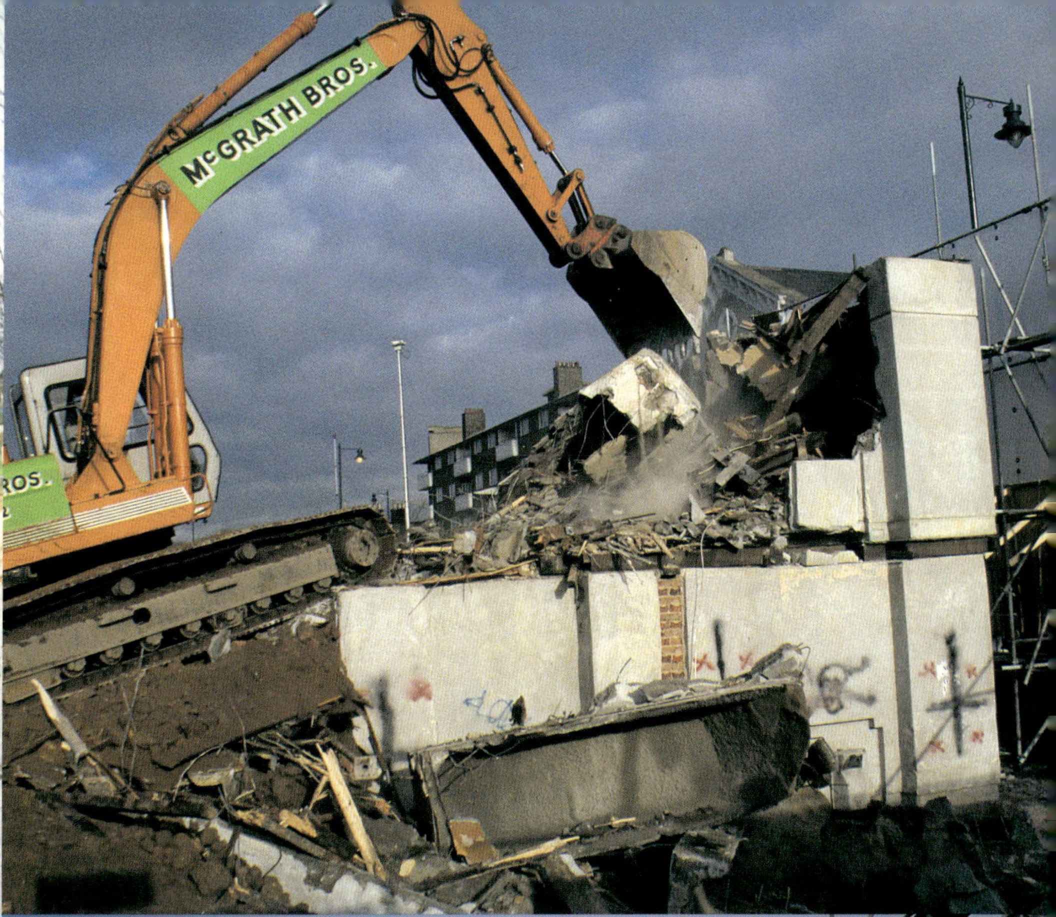
McGRATH BROS.
ROS.

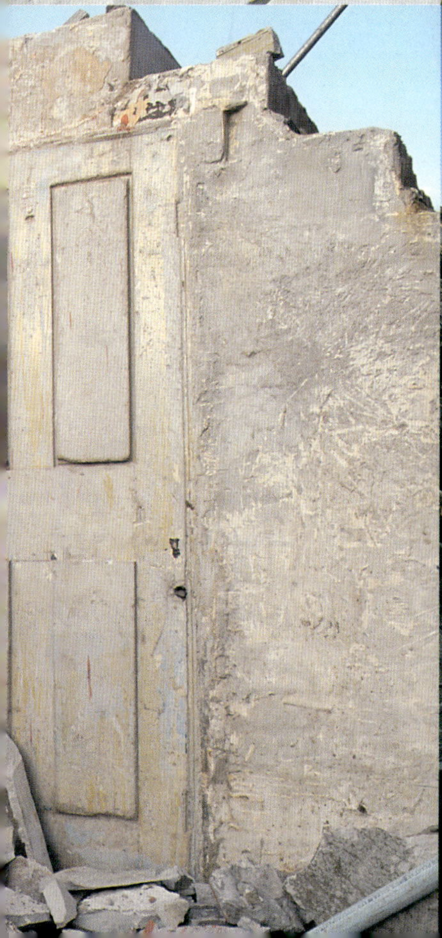

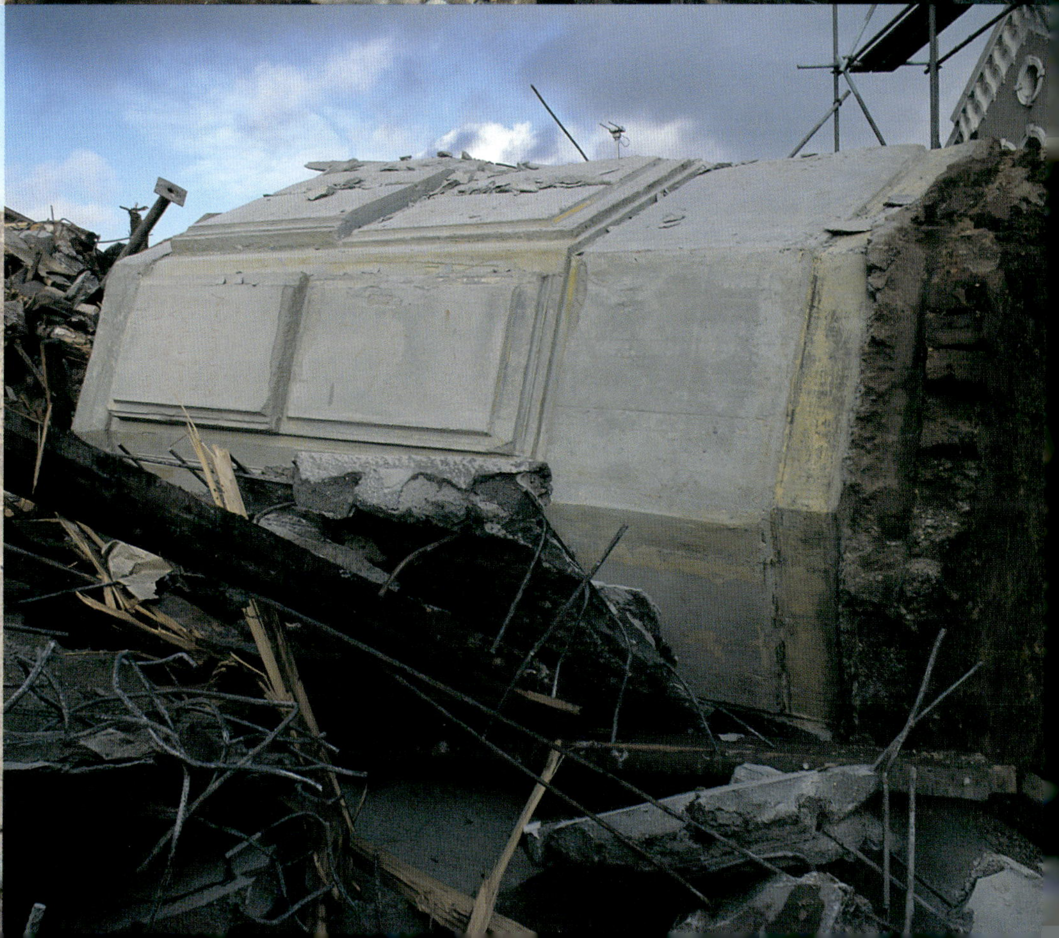

one of the hundreds of letters asking for a stay of execution on *House*, he described how he could not imagine why someone '... from the leafy elegance of South Edwardes Square, where a lump of concrete of this type would never be tolerated, feels able to inflict this monstrosity on a local community which has clearly said it does not want it. Public sculpture is answerable to those whose environment it inhabits, and on that basis *House* has no place in Bow. Nor, for that matter, do the disruptive crowds who come to see it. The argument that it "makes people talk" is equally absurd. A 10-foot pink plastic penis in the middle of South Edwardes Square would make people talk, but I doubt if you'd favour it'.[13]

One cannot but note the contradictory claim of representativenesss in the face of large crowds of people who had evidently gone to see *House*. For Cllr. Flounders such people are necessarily dismissed as 'disruptive' visitors, outsiders with funny, alien ways ... Furthermore, the slippage from the actual Cistercian austerity of *House* to the fantasy-image of a 10-foot tall pink plastic penis is also highly revealing. *House* is deemed obscene because it exposes an interior, because it shows us something we are not supposed to see, because it fails to operate as proper, decent, 'public sculpture', in the interests of the moral and political claims of an administrative system which imagines its constituency in the homogeneous likeness of 'the public' whose uniform views and opinions must at all costs be expressed in 'public' art in 'public' places. The only problem in all of this is that 'the public' *only exists* as a discursive device. There is no more uniform 'family life' or 'general public' in Bow than anywhere else, save in the delusions of party politicians, and others who wish to mobilize the chimera of 'public opinion' as the legitimizing externalized form of their own volatile prejudices and phobias.

1 Previous pages: Demolition of *House*, January, 1994 **2** Engraving of the demolition of Reculver church in 1809 **3** Shrine of St. Wite, Whitchurch Canonicorum, Dorset, 13th century

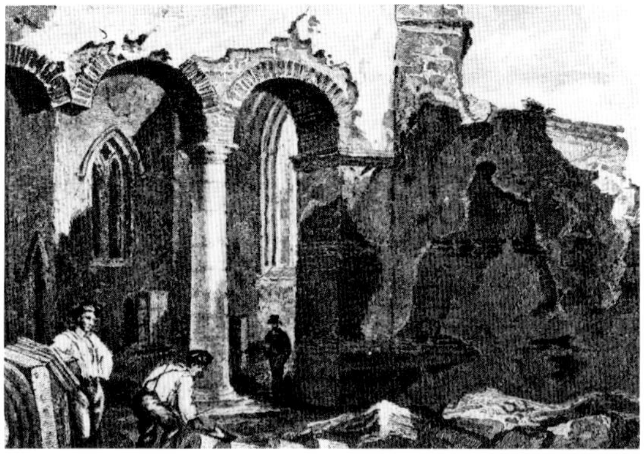

2

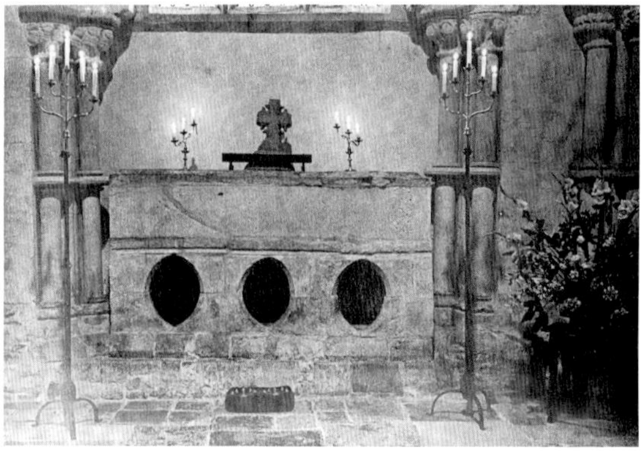

3

None of this is exactly new. For example, until 1809 a seventh century Saxon church founded by St. Augustine and his converts stood near the Kentish cliffs at Reculver, until most scandalously, in the words of the appalled parish clerk:

'Mr C.C. Nailor be'en vicar of the parish, his mother fancied the church was kept for a poppet show, and she persuaded her son to take it down'.[14]

A print exists, illustrating the vandalizing and demolition of the building. Only a few architectural fragments survive in the crypt of Canterbury Cathedral, including six pieces of what was once a unique sculpted cross of a quality unknown in Europe since the fifth century, save in the remote outposts of Northumbria and its sphere of influence. In other words, in the early nineteenth century, people came to see St. Augustine's surviving church, and this was enough to seal its fate in the eyes of someone for whom such interest was evidence of idolatry, a 'poppet show'. Popery and superstition.

One strongly suspects that Mrs Nailor and Cllr. Flounders would have got on famously together, for what they both actually objected to was the very idea that people might travel to look at works of art, or that such 'attendance', as it were, is any kind of valid evidence of value. On the contrary, it was precisely as monuments in the mainstream of the European classical tradition of monumental sculpture that the sculpture at Reculver, and later the church itself, and more recently *House*, were vandalized by the projective consequences of an iconophobia passing itself off as mere iconoclasm.

It is however, of some importance that we do not impute such cultural continuities simply to the workings of some innate national psychological mechanism, operating uniformly over the course of the centuries in the English. Rather, we need to be more searching in our analysis of the ways in which currents of anti-sensualism may be articulated in relation to particular cultural forms, and of the ways in which cultural beliefs (including magical beliefs) are transmitted over time through different institutional discourses and other practices. The complex relations between our national Protestant history as a nation, and later Social Purity and Reform movements, and attitudes towards art and representation in general remain almost entirely uncharted.

Rachel Whiteread's art is intrinsically melancholic. By its very nature it preserves and holds out the image of the lost object, in simulacrum. It cannot let go, or forget. Perpetually it draws us back to what has been lost, in all its uniqueness, and all its typicality. If our *House* has been turned inside out, how can we ever go 'home'? If the last time we saw single houses standing where once there were rows was in childhood, after the war, what might *House* mean? Or if our parents had been forcibly resettled to Dagenham in the 1960s, or scooped up into tower blocks in the 1970s? There is no single answer to such questions. What matters is that such questions may still be raised with such deceptively reticent precision by sculptural means.

In Whitchurch Canonicorum in Dorset, there is an extreme rarity, a surviving complete medieval stone shrine, containing the remains of the church's founder and patron, St. Candida, better known as St. Wite. She came from the north of France, and one day simply strolled across the waves to the rolling hills of the west Dorset coastline. No passports, or immigration controls. One rather fears that if the anti-European zealotry of much contemporary British populist politics, feeding a powerful motive of anti-sensualism, were still targeting churches, the beautiful plain shrine of St. Candida would not survive much longer than *House*.

13. Eric Flounders, letter to Richard Salmon, December 1993
14. John Newman, North East and East Kent, *The Buildings of England*, Penguin Books, London, 1983, p. 430

Jon Bird

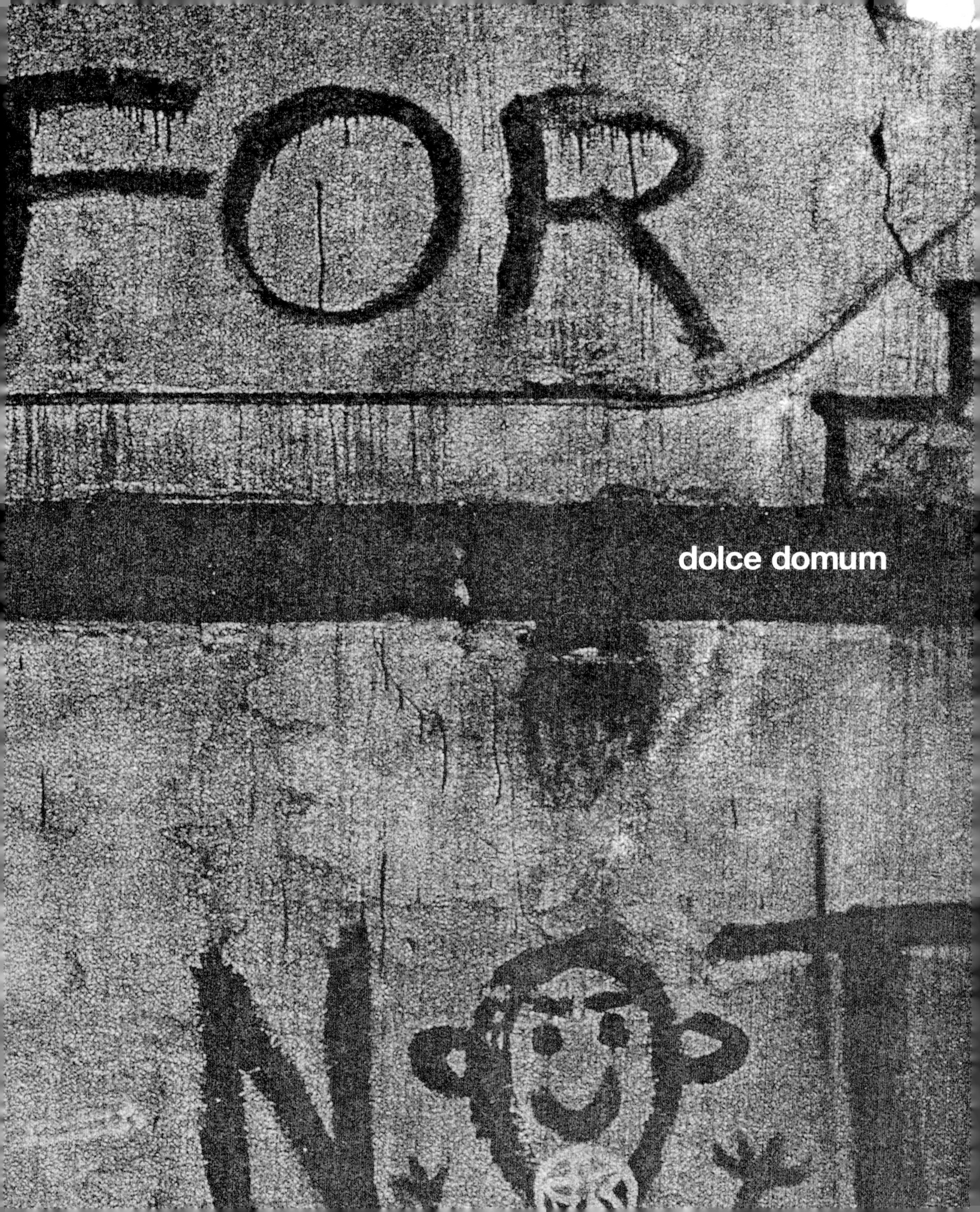

dolce domum

Introduction

> 'All great simple images reveal a psychic state. The house, even more than the landscape, is a 'psychic state', and even when reproduced as it appears from the outside, it bespeaks intimacy'.[1]

> '... the uncanny is that class of the frightening which leads back to what is known of old and long familiar ...'[2]

Many people tell *House* stories.These range from testimonies of participation – the day of the petition, the letter to the newspaper, opening night, demolition day, of witness as the foundation of oral history – to additions to the mythology: estate agents, advertisements, empty milk bottles outside the front door, the threat of squatters, or the general 'commonsense' that framed the cultural history of *House*, from the philistinism and bureaucracy of local councils to the role of art and artists at the end of the twentieth century. *House* lives on as a focus for story-telling, linking fact and fiction, personal experience with media coverage, an imaginative interweaving of reason and fantasy that replaces the material object with its narrativization in critical discourse and collective memory. It has become a work that marks a moment – creates a space – beyond the confines of the art world, spilling over into the general culture to become an icon of popular reference and symbolic meaning.

There are no souvenirs of *House*, at least not in the form of 'relics', other than our individual and collective memories of the event. Susan Stewart argues that our desire for the souvenir arises from the unrepeatability of an event, of a longing for a vanished original, a nostalgic denial of loss which refers back to the original lost object, the mother.[3] Souvenirs are traces of events, locations, experiences, objects which replace authenticity with narrative, a narrative which commences with the personal pronoun and statement of witness – 'I was here'. As I'm writing this I have on my desk my own reminders of *House* – a photographic archive composed of official documentation and personal photographs taken at various moments throughout the three-month period of its existence. By far the most evocative are a group that I took on a dreary afternoon in mid-December. The wet road, the spongy suction of the grass underfoot, a few curious onlookers, the damp cold numbing fingers as I fiddled with the camera trying to keep water off the lens, the gradual fading of *House* into the grey East London sky.

The Uncanny

Memory, childhood experiences, staging the scenes of origins and endings, these are fundamental themes that run through Whiteread's work: spaces of concealment (she recalls an early memory of hiding in a cupboard), of sexuality and death – mattresses, baths, mortuary slabs, the home as the site of memory and our formative experiences. Simple objects reveal ambiguities that shift their identity and introduce an element of uncertainty. Invested with shared meanings – the functions of the body, familial experience, the patterns of everyday life – they are sufficiently strange to evade the closure that accompanies classification, like a memory trace that hovers at the edge of recall, or the moment of waking when a dream image slips out of consciousness to leave a residue of uneasiness and intrigue.

The implied referent for Whiteread's sculptures became explicit in *House* as the

1. Gaston Bachelard, *The Poetics of Space*, trans. Maria Jolass, Beacon Press, Boston 1969, p.70
2. Sigmund Freud, 'The Uncanny', *Standard Edition*, vol.XVII. All references to Freud are from *The Standard Edition of the Complete Psychological Works*, trans. James Strachey, et al. The Hogarth Press and The Institute of Psycho-Analysis, 1953
3. Susan Stewart, *On Longing: Narratives of the Miniature, the Gigantic, the Souvenir, the Collection*, Johns Hopkins, Baltimore, 1984

cultural space of the home, an identifiable place and place of identity. The home represents a key component in the constitution of identity, a point of reference amongst the shifting patterns of our social and cultural formation, a focus for desires and longings, a point of origin and return, the universal experience of acquiring a place in the world. The home is the context for initiating social relations, a microcosm of all possible worlds and the space in which we make our first differentiation between interiority and exteriority and learn to distinguish between safety and danger, pleasure and pain, desire and gratification. Many children's tales traverse the realms of violence and joy, interchanging the animal and the human, upturning conventions of the material and emotional world, putting words to nightmares and powerfully invoking the transitional rites of early life. Throughout the classic story, *The Wind in the Willows*, the space of the home differentiates between the known and familiar and the loss of security and innocence:

> 'But ere he closed his eyes he let them wander round his old room, mellow in the glow of the firelight that played or rested on familiar and friendly things which had long been unconsciously a part of him.'[4]

The disturbing effects of repetition and the strangeness of certain everyday occurrences are the subject of Freud's famous essay on 'The Uncanny'. Tracing the word's complex etymology, Freud reveals a process of transposition of the familiar into its opposite. The lengthy entry in Sanders German Dictionary that provides the starting point for his investigation offers a definition of *heimlich* as 'belonging to the house... familiar... friendly...' then, in the process of elaboration, turns into something 'concealed... kept from sight', finally becoming the negative compound *unheimlich*: 'gruesome fear... ghostly'. An 'unheimlich home', literally an 'unhomely home', is translated as a 'haunted house'. Freud concludes, 'thus *heimlich* is a word the meaning of which develops in the direction of ambivalence, until it finally coincides with its opposite, *unheimlich*'.[5]

Freud starts this paper by relating his enquiry to the subject of aesthetics as the theory of the qualities of 'feeling', the

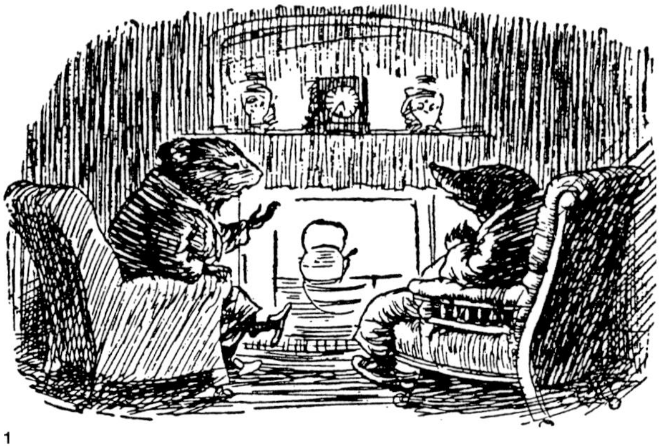

1

1 Arthur Rackham, illustration from *The Wind in the Willows*, 1939

'uncanny' being a special case of emotional response to an object or event within the general field of the aesthetic. Proposing two lines of investigation – the genealogy of the term, or a consideration of all the examples to which the term might apply to establish common characteristics – he suggests that either approach will lead to the same conclusion that 'the uncanny is that class of the frightening which leads back to what is known of old and long familiar'.[6] Two stories from Hoffmann, 'The Sand-Man' and 'The Devil's Elixir', provide examples of the uncanny and lead Freud along the associational chain of object and effect. 'The Sand-Man' is the tale of an automaton, the doll Olympia, which acts as a disturbing love-object for the student Nathaniel. Immediately, doubts about the possibility of inanimate objects coming alive provide a common instance of the uncanny, but Freud argues that there is a more fundamental fear underlying the narrative which revolves around the recurrent and threatening presence of the Sand-Man. This is both a fantasy figure conjured up by Nathaniel's nurse, throwing sand in children's eyes so they pop out and become food for his own offspring, and a mysterious visitor to Nathaniel's father, the repulsive lawyer Coppelius. At a later stage in the narrative, the lawyer becomes identified with the optician, Coppola, who provides the eyes for Olympia. After many twists and turns the story ends with Nathaniel's madness and suicide. Freud argues that it is the fear of losing our sight, a childhood fear which reaches into adulthood, that is the uncanny in the narrative, and that this fear 'is often enough a substitute for the dread of being castrated'.[7]

In 'The Devil's Elixir' it is the phenomenon of the 'double' that confirms the hypothesis of the uncanny as the return of 'what is known of old and long familiar'. The effect of doubling comes from assuming likeness from resemblance, the loss of self from an over-identification with another or from the repetition of features, character traits, names, etc. For Freud, doubling and repetition are guarantees against extinction, an insurance against the destruction of the ego which he relates to primary narcissism. Although repetition does not immediately connote the uncanny, we are invited to consider the feelings of unease we experience when everyday occurrences become repetitive.

Two final examples of the uncanny conclude Freud's essay and they are of great significance. Paradigms of the culture's neurosis as a whole, not just at the moment when Freud was writing in the immediate aftermath of The Great War but for us as we stagger towards the millennium's end, the uncanny is most generally and most intensely experienced in relation to death, the body and the fears and fantasies of a return to life; spirits, ghosts and monsters, the realm of the abject. The other example is from psychoanalytic experience – the male fear of the mother's body, her genitals: the *unheimlich* is what was once *heimlich*, the prefix is the sign of repression.

Memory

> 'There is no imagination that is not, overtly or secretly, melancholy…'
> (Julia Kristeva)[8]

House was a lost object. Freud's writing is saturated with mourning and loss, with the life-death dualism of pleasure and pain, sexuality and destruction. 'The Uncanny' ends on a sombre note that could almost

4. Kenneth Grahame, *The Wind in the Willows*, Methuen, 76th edition, 1944, p.124
5. Freud, 'The Uncanny', S.E. Vol XVII
6. Freud, op. cit.
7. Freud, op. cit.
8. Julia Kristeva, *Black Sun: Depression and Melancholia*, Columbia University, New York, 1989, p.6

act as a summary for the findings of psychoanalysis: 'Concerning the factors of silence, solitude and darkness, we can only say that they are actually elements in the production of the infantile anxiety from which the majority of human beings have never become quite free'.[9] In the process of mourning we experience an ambivalence towards the lost object, sometimes turning the loss inwards as a violence against the self, which in its extreme manifestation can lead to annihilation; or we may project onto the world all the varieties of our destructive intent. Why did it become so necessary for *House* to be destroyed? There was something excessive in the Council's determination to ensure that this took place, a desire which was matched by the intensity and extent of the campaign to preserve it beyond the agreed date for demolition.

House appeared to function as the metonymic link between both the particular and the shared experience of the realities of city life at the end of the twentieth century, and the remembrance of other patterns of neighbourhood and community; an expression of longing for the lost spaces of childhood and the rhythms of street life that characterized a certain image of London's East End. Of course this can easily slide into nostalgia, a profoundly ideological form of narrative that strips historical experience of its specificity and idealizes lived experience. But there was nothing nostalgically idealized in *House*, its very mundaneness attested to the material structure of social reality: this home, these dimensions, this location; this is how it was.

House eloquently memorialized the presence of the past in the present, but also marked the loss of a past, the passing of a 'habitus' that had come to represent a pattern of metropolitan working-class culture. It is through the institutional forms of memory that we collectively re-encounter the past in the course of its articulation. Memorials stage the past, objectifying individual and collective experience within the flux of the historical process. Public monuments tend to speak the voice of authority, they are a representation of power in symbolic form, documents of a culture's historical experience. They provide instruction into the official narratives of

2 Cenotaph, Whitehall **3** 'Tommy' at Home in German Dug-outs, First World War postcard **4** Canary Wharf and terraced housing

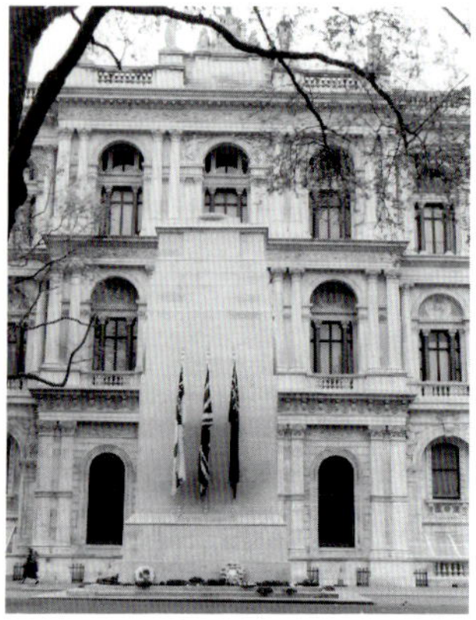

2

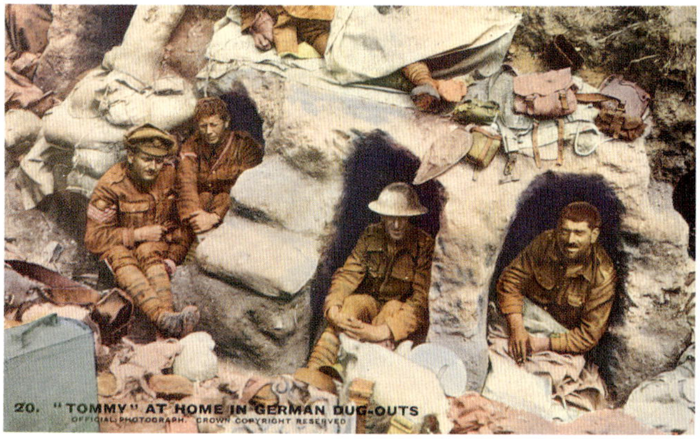

3

the past. Memorials freeze-frame historical narrative, cutting through the web of events to single out a moment (an incident, an individual) which then becomes the personification of memory itself. Consequently, artworks placed in the public domain have constantly to negotiate with the discourses of official culture (which, in this period of global capital and the severe restriction or loss of a public sphere, means the dominance of corporate culture), and the possibility of initiating or correlating with alternative or critical discourse. However, the other side of the memorial as a rendering of collective memory is the tendency to forget and the symptoms of denial. Revolutionary and reactionary crises are often marked by the destruction of the sign of the threatening other, or the denial of history. The postmodern critique of legitimacy and certainty suggests that the only viable forms of public memory are those that embody paradox and the ephemeral. *House* provided a poignant reminder that the material values of permanence and stability were little defence against the power of ideology.

The City

'Architecture positions its ensembles – houses, towns or cities, monuments or factories – to function like faces in the landscapes they transform'. (Deleuze and Guattari)[10]

Space has a history. Henri Lefebvre has observed that the town or city only becomes a subject, a unity of the public and the private, in Europe in the sixteenth century, a model of social and topographical relations that persisted up until the early twentieth century.[11] The First World War marked the cataclysmic loss of what Lefebvre terms the 'commonsense of space'; the battlefields of the Western Front shattered the experience of place and identity as relatively fixed and hierarchically ordered, most poignantly expressed in the designation of areas as 'no-mans land'. The landscapes of Ypres, the Somme, Paschendale, etc., were the spaces of death. The depth of our attachment to home as a source of identity is illustrated by the imposition of a domestic topography onto the alien environment of the trenches, street names and places creating a dreadful pastiche of neighbourhood and community. This was a part of the history of *House*. From such Edwardian terraces an endless procession of men and boys responded to the call for Kitchener's Army, then later fought in the campaigns of the Second World War. Decimated by machine guns and mustard gas, blitzed and bombed, such streets became the standard iconography of resistance and resilience. (An aerial photograph from the 1950s used in the publicity material for *House* shows the terrace of Grove Road backing onto a sprawl of pre-fabs, the urban index of intense bombardment.) London's East End also carries the imprint of other battles – the suffrage movement and the dockers disputes of the 1920s, the opposition to Mosely's fascists in the 1930s and their echoes in the racism that has disfigured the area intermittently in the post-war period, and now another kind of war signified by the looming presence of the tower of Canary Wharf and a mutation in our subjective sense of space.

If space has a history, it also has a politics: 'We must be insistently aware of how space can be made to hide consequences from us; how relations of power and discipline are inscribed into the apparently innocent

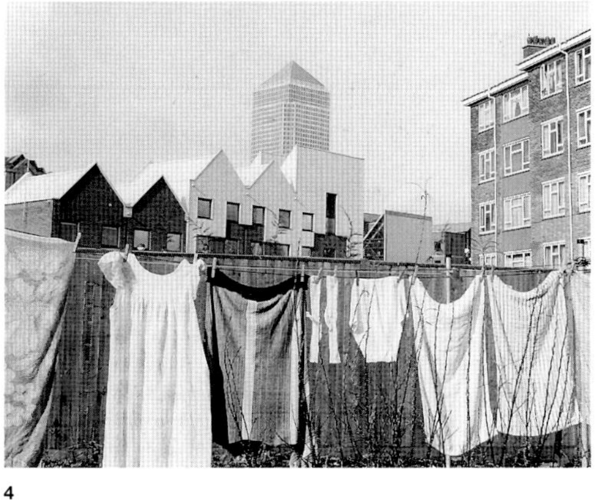

4

9. Freud, op. cit.
10. Gilles Deleuze and Felix Guattari, *A Thousand Plateaus: Capitalism and Schizophrenia*, trans. Brian Massumi, Athlone Press, London, 1988. p.172
11. Henri Lefebvre, *The Production of Space*, Basil Blackwell, Oxford, 1991

spatiality of everyday life, how human geographies become filled with politics and ideology'.[12] Increasingly the conflicts and tensions of Postmodernity produce empty or 'waste' spaces at an equal or excessive rate to planned or speculative urban development, indeed the one is too often the outcome of the other. The economic viability of an area has generally been the dominant factor in determining patterns of decline and the politically expedient strategy of 'regeneration', with housing as the battleground caught between the ideologies of fiscal policy, electorial profiling and social need.[13]

In the speculative land developments that characterized the 1980s, London's East End, particularly the Docklands, became a war zone as embattled councils and resident associations vainly attempted to oppose or restrict the activities of the development corporations who were massively supported by Government grants and generous tax incentives. As apartment and office blocks started to dominate the riverside and panoramas of a 'twenty-first century waterside city' which enticed the financial and investment community out of the city, down-river to the Isle of Dogs, what was mourned was the loss of the street as a site for the life of local communities and the social interaction that transforms an area into a neighbourhood.

The sense of place that defined the history of these localities, a history which included waves of migration and defensive strategies against ethnic, class and economic exploitation has, over the last two decades, surrendered to market forces. Transformed into landscapes made in the image of global capital, much of this area became, in the 1980s, the largest building site in Europe, a chaotic vision of the city as a disembowelled body, a memorial to the fantasies and desires of the corporate will. *House* was on a sight-line to Canary Wharf with its silver-topped tower and elegant profile a dramatic contrast to the surrounding depressed inner-city boroughs. Here the local is locked into the global, with homelessness as the social corollary to privatization. As Canary Wharf added floor to floor to become, briefly, the tallest office building in Europe, so street after street of local housing was abandoned or levelled as local authorities were starved of the funds necessary for the realization of adequate housing policies. What had been *heimlich* became *unheimlich* as derelict areas marked the ghostly presence of the lives and social relations that define a sense of place. *House* articulated this geo-politics of origin and identity, inscribing historical memory on the cast surfaces of 193 Grove Road which, besides the imprint of doors, windows and rooms, carried the faint traces and remnants of the domestic lives of former inhabitants. These ephemeral indices of family life were charged with meaning, hieroglyphic clues to a half-remembered, half-forgotten past.

Another telling juxtaposition occurred during the brief period of the existence of *House* as a media event as its image appeared on the TV screen following footage of the war in Bosnia. As the broadcast media emptied evidence of the world's broken cities into our private spaces, the fragility of homes and homeland was painfully evident in the images of wholly or partly destroyed buildings, villages, towns and cities; of once solid structures perforated and penetrated by shell and bullet, of homes with their eyes put out and their mouths agape, and the endless columns of refugees – the homeless of the world.

House/Body

Lying at the edge of the Dockland's redevelopment area, these spaces – the fall-out from capitalism's uneven development – were divested of their false utopianism and reappropriated in the symbolic vocabulary of *House*. Viewed frontally, isolated and set against the sparse linearity of the surrounding park, it dominated the viewer's field of vision, asserting a kind of monumentality, the steps leading to the blank front door suggesting the visual rhetoric of memorials and civic buildings, a vernacular classicism that effected the transition from the public space of the street to the private space of the home. Side-on, the squat geometry of *House*, with its vertical and horizontal divisions and interior details, offered a reassuring familiarity – we know this vocabulary and can imaginatively recreate the routines of daily life. But there was a difference. This might be registered as a disturbance located between perception and cognition; as the uncanniness of the object invaded the symbolic field leaving the viewer estranged from everyday normality – the everyday itself becomes strange. Uncannily familiar, *House* signified the shadow of history and the pathos of memory.

The house is the primary unit of measurement and point of reference for a spatial politics, a human scale which determines the nature of our relationship to the immediate environment and beyond that to the culture as a whole. 'Where do you live?' figures amongst the key questions which momentarily arrest the narratives of identity, how we answer determining our place within a grid of co-ordinates which plot social subjectivity. Homelessness begs the issue of where home might actually be. The common experience of the homeless and the migrant is to be made to feel out of place. Home not only becomes the mythical point of origin (the fundamental question every child asks the parent – 'Where did I come from?') but also a utopian projection, a homeland. Home is a fiction, a concept we carry around with us, our narrative of identity and (be)longing: 'For our house is our corner of the world... it is our first universe, a real cosmos in every sense of the word'.[14]

Bachelard's poetic constructs the home as a metaphor for the creative imagination – 'the house allows one to dream in peace'

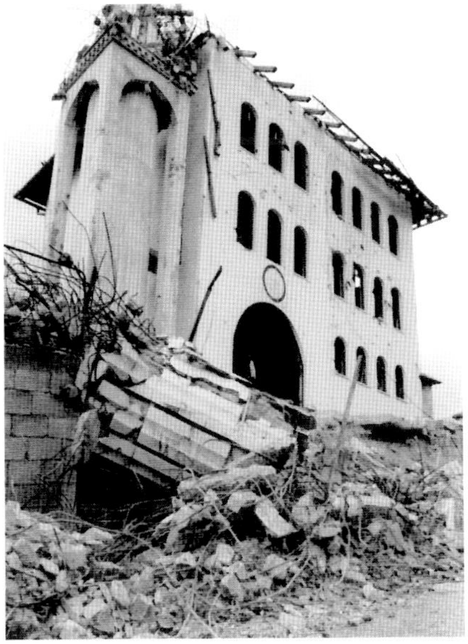
5

5 Bosnia, February 1995

12. Edward Soja, *Postmodern Geographies*, Verso, London 1989, p. 6

13. The politics of space is most blatantly evident in the 'homes for votes' policy operated by, in particular, Westminster Council, and the related practice of 'gerrymandering', (adjusting electoral boundaries to the advantage of the governing party). Throughout the 1980s, Westminster Council attempted to create owner–occupiers by selling off council houses and moving council tenants out of the borough into leased accommodation in East London.

14. Bachelard, op. cit. p. 4

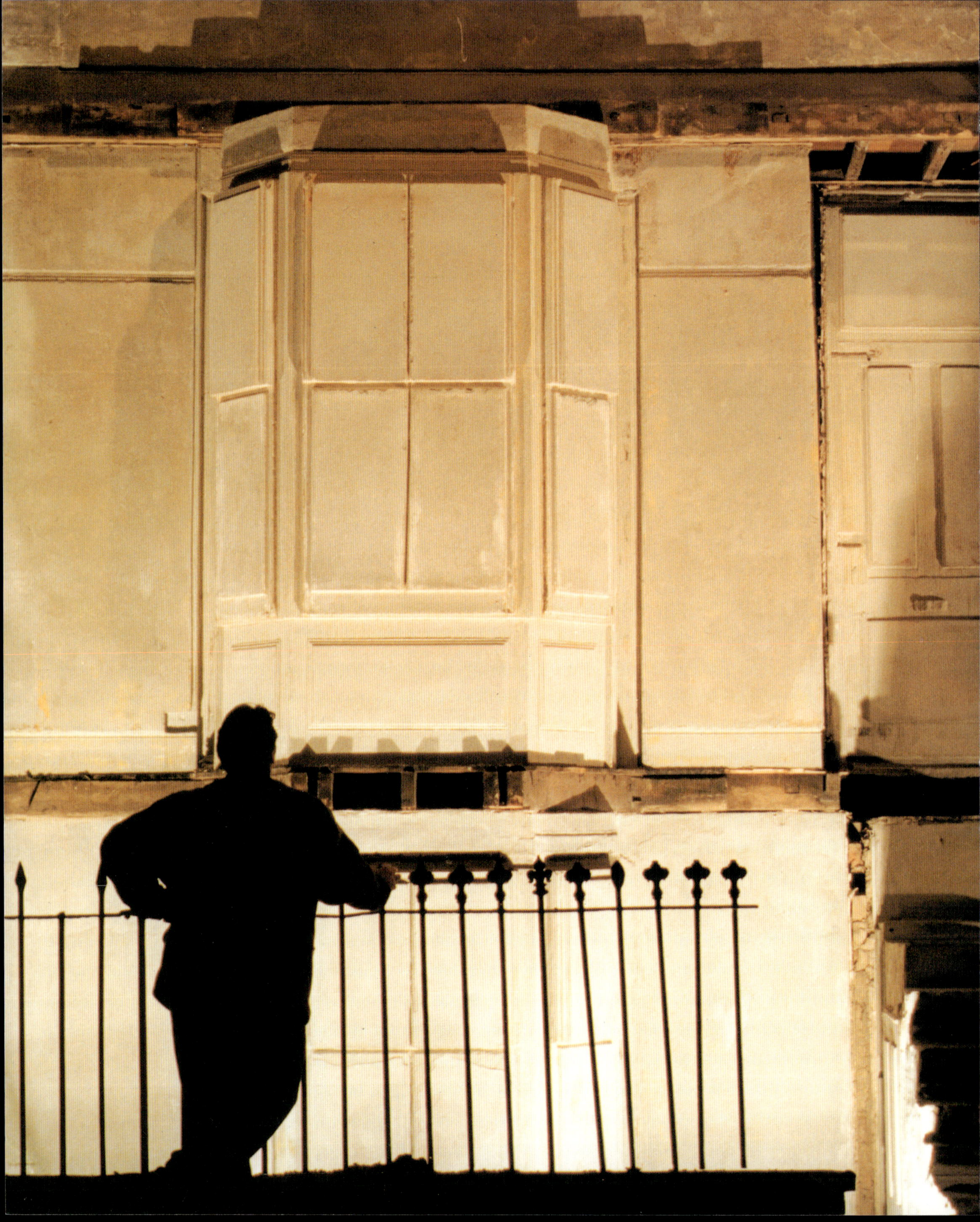

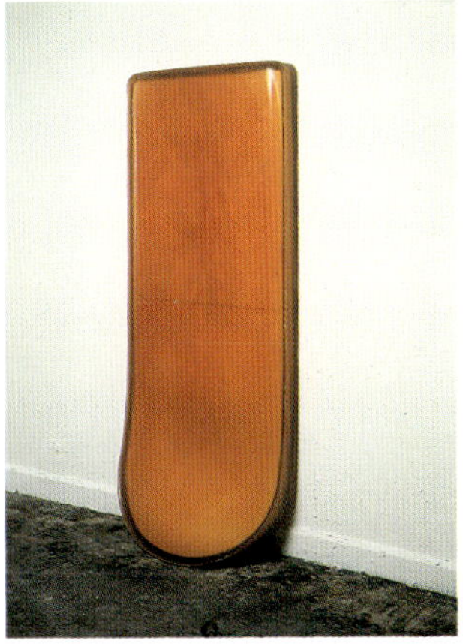

6

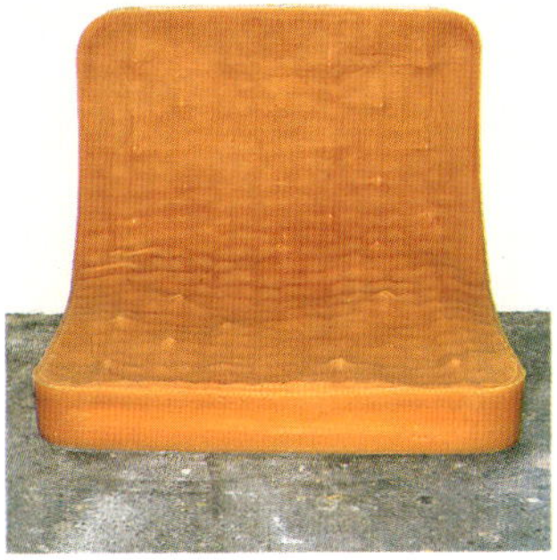

7

Rachel Whiteread **6** Untitled (Amber Slab), 1991, rubber and high density foam, 194.4 x 74.4 x 10.8 cm **7** Untitled (Amber Double Bed), 1991, rubber and high-density foam, 112.8 x 129.6 x 98.4 cm

– a fantasy of childhood, replete and secure, a boundary against the loss of innocence amongst the urban spaces of social reality. Early infancy is the period when the boundaries are in the process of formation, when interior and exterior coalesce in the 'imaginary', a convergence of the infant with the maternal presence prior to the processes of separation that mark the entry into the symbolic. The ghost of this connectedness will haunt us forever, occasionally materializing in a momentary perception that has the psychic force of a memory trace in the unconscious. These memories can be stimulated by any of the senses. Embedded within the substance of material culture, social memories can be as easily awakened by a taste, touch, sound or smell as by an image.

Childhood is the period when the boundaries between self and other, body and space, inside and outside, are in the process of formation. Children constantly make places (dens or tents) or discover places within the home for solitude or escape – from parental authority, sibling rivalry, unwanted friends – utilizing cupboards, wardrobes, beds; the marginal spaces underneath, between, inside the object world. The representation in dreams of a desire for invisibility (hiding or being unfindable) is seen by Freud as an intimation of mortality – 'another unmistakable symbol of death'.[15] These discoveries – of edges, borders, boundaries inside and outside, visibility and invisibility – are all recurrent activities that possess particular significance (symbolic meanings) during childhood, providing the template for experiences in adult life. If the first lost object is the mother, then the first lost space is the maternal space. An early and formative work by Whiteread was the cast of the interior of a wardrobe (*Closet*, 1988), and the precedent for *House* was the cast of an entire room of a derelict house in north London (*Ghost*, 1990) The casting process itself repeats the play of presence and absence. Traditionally the mould is discarded and the cast is left as the 'supplement' to the original. Whiteread utilizes this familiar technique but introduces an alarming twist, for what is the cast supplementary to: the original is a space, a nothingness or void.[16] Her working methods start with viscous material which is transformed into either

15. Freud, 'The Three Caskets', S.E. Vol. XII
16. After Derrida – in any set of binary oppositions it is the second term that comes as a 'supplement' to the first, the first is privileged. Derrida argues, however, that there are no unsupplemented terms, that there is always within a text a supplement that works to contaminate any claim to a fundamental truth based an an essential identity, or the purity of a concept; neither presence nor absence, the supplement is the play of difference. See Jacques Derrida, *Of Grammatology*, trans. Gayatri Chakravorty Spivak, Johns Hopkins, Baltimore, 1976

the silky hardness of plaster or the springy resistance of rubber, metaphors of flesh and bone. What is striking about Whiteread's casts is the constant reminder of interiority, absence is made presence as solidified space inviting the spectator constantly to decipher the relationship of sign to referent, to try and make sense out of ambiguity and contradiction. *House* was profoundly contradictory, offering a *gestalt* of wholeness and coherence followed by the negation of that apparent accessibility: doors that didn't open, reversed fireplaces and doorknobs, blank windows, unoccupiable rooms, perception was constantly frustrated as *House* slipped categories and subverted meanings, a hybrid object whose temporary status provided an unsettling closure to its perceived permanence and material presence. Houses and bodies are porous entities traversed by the currents and flows of other histories and memories. The walls and surfaces of the house conceal a secret – an umbilical network of pipes, cables, electronic signals and power lines which connect with the local and the global environment. Like the orifices and passages of the body that connect us to the material and social world, the house is a corporeal structure linked to a grid of energy and communications, its life-support system. Whiteread's *House*, however, severed these patterns of exchange, shifting the associations from the libidinous body to the political body: a body differentiated from other bodies and the object world. Although not actually a solid form (the casting material was aproximately 10" thick), *House* suggested a mass that resisted rather than accommodated its surroundings, a muteness that testified to levels of shared experience beyond the realities of everyday life. *House* signified a metaphorical inversion of the body, a reversal of interiority and exteriority, structure and void, that rendered the private public and made the public a site for democratic exchange.[17]

Whiteread's works persistently refigure the dialectic of inside/outside in terms of a mundane object world defamiliarized through a casting process that redirects our gaze to that which was an absence, a void, the uncanny spaces beneath the surface of everyday life. These objects carry the marks of history written on the social body,

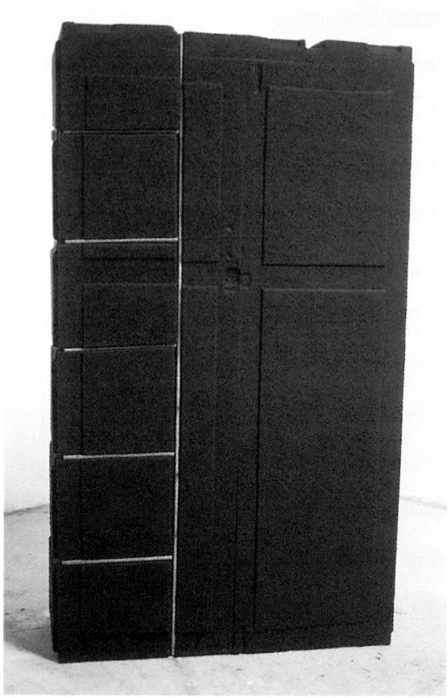

8

8 Rachel Whiteread, Closet, 1988, wood, felt and plaster, 151.2 x 113.4 x 50.4 cm

17. Jurgen Habermas has argued for the importance of the 'public sphere' as a space for discursive interaction between all members of the society, for open and critical exchange free from the state and market relations. Despite the idealised and universalizing implications of this concept, the debate over public space as essential for a participatory democracy connects many of the urgent issues relating to identity politics today. One argument for the role of public art is the contribution works can make to the formation of a public sphere with real emancipatory potential. See Jurgen Habermas, *The Structural Transformation of the Public Sphere: An Inquiry into a Category of Bourgeois Society*, trans. Thomas Berger, Cambridge, Mass. 1989

at times infused with a melancholic presence, at others connoting a darker intuition of the macabre. What at first appears an abstract notation upon a surface becomes, on closer inspection, a clue to the social. For example, at one stage Whiteread made three casts of mortuary slabs, simple uniform blocks that formally referenced Minimalist sculpture of the 1960s. But whereas the Minimalist surface tended to signify the precision of machine production, these surfaces carried the indexical signs of the knife and surgical instruments that carved the body on the slab.

Cuts, cracks, incisions, apertures, slits, gaps, fissures, these are the 'erotogenic' zones of the body, liminal orifices where the exchange between inside and outside takes place. All of Whiteread's sculptures carry such traces – the 'supplement' which can unravel the threads of meaning and create the tension of an ambivalence as the object oscillates between abstraction and figuration, seeing and knowing. The properties of scale, weight, mass, volume, texture and surface are the semiotic imprint of the body's pleasure and mortality: the memories of place, the fundamental and repetitive experiences of childhood, the intimations of death within the rituals of our daily habits and routines, the sites where matter is subjected to signification.

The processes of socialization from infancy proceed partly through a continuous projection of the body onto the external world, we thus read the body's image mediated through the culture. Bachelard's psychology of the house relies upon two principal connecting themes – 'verticality' and 'centrality' – and a dynamic tension between extremities: 'the polarity of cellar and attic'. In this schema the roof is the signifier of rationality, 'up near the roof all our thoughts are clear', the cellar the irrational – 'the dark entity of the house'. These oppositions also traverse popular culture. In many horror movies the cellar is the place of the abject, the attic often the scene of a discovery or revelation resulting in the recovery of a lost memory from the contents of cases, trunks or albums of old photographs. *House*, however, did not have a roof. The levelling off of the building above the first floor was the single significant structural alteration. Originally the roof formed a 'V', the converse of the line of roofs running the length of the terrace, and Whiteread decided at an early stage to dispense with a form that would have carried unwanted connotations – to crowns, castellations, spires, etc. Architecturally this decision annexed *House* to the codes of the Modern Movement, the right angle functioning as an expression of rationalist ideology emphasizing gravitational weight and the ground plane. Combined with the building material (mesh reinforced concrete under fine white locrete), *House* was the negative imprint of a small turn-of-the-century dwelling, but also suggested a functionalist iconography through oblique references to bunkers (the armoured body) and prisons (the incarcerated body).

As a sculptural and conceptual work, *House* referenced some of the concerns of Minimalism. The apparent solidity and sense of wholeness, the emphasis upon material presence and repetition of unit structures echoed the language of the Minimalist works of the 1960s with their constant play between perception and cognition that defined the object/viewer relation. Bob Morris's 'Notes on Sculpture' defined the quality of 'wholeness' as the strong *gestalt* produced by simple polyhedral forms: 'In the simpler regular polyhedrons such as cubes and pyramids one need not move around the object for the sense of the whole, the gestalt, to occur. One sees and immediately 'believes' that the pattern within one's own mind corresponds to the existential fact of the object'.[18] Morris argued for a detached opticality free from the determinations of the body and history. Subsequent accounts of Minimalism have contextualized the gaze and situated the body of the viewing subject centre-stage, a critical reading of the triangular relationship between work, viewer and location that defines site-specificity as conjunctural. It is this re-reading that connects with *House*. Whereas the typical Minimalist object rejects associational meaning for the immediate apprehension of totality, *House* skewed these codes, demanding from the viewer an imaginative projection within the body of the work in order to comprehend the connotational references of the external surface. The overall structure marked a tension between 'objecthood' and the sum of its parts: as the viewing field altered, so the meanings shifted between relations of form and a recognition of the trace of human presence – registered as a discharge on the material fabric itself. One way of describing this is to suggest that *House* required both the 'gaze' and the 'glance': the detached contemplation of the object by a knowing subject constantly disturbed by the fleeting and flickering glance of desire and the body.[19]

Whiteread's works are very much about surface and the significance of the detail. Their three-dimensional facticity does not primarily function as spatial division but reinforces surface: a surface for inscription. Despite Minimalist allusions her works do not emphasize an 'objecthood' that implicates the viewer's bodily presence but, rather, the absent body. The spectral presence of the body haunts the work as surface details offer enigmatic clues to the repetitive and mundane acts of everyday life.[20] What disturbs meaning in Whiteread's work, and was the case with *House* in particular, is the psychopathology that lies beneath the everyday; the repressed fears, desires, prohibitions and transgressions that lurk within social routines as the uncanny stalks the familiar, and the inanimate threatens to come alive.

On reflection it seems appropriate that *House* only remained for its intended three month period, that it really is a 'lost object', a memory that touched lives and experiences across many publics and constituencies. Endings are always hard – we resist all finality, retreating into metaphor or denial in the recognition of an impossible relation. But the work of mourning and remembering can only come from the acceptance of loss, that there is within the social a fundamental instability that, through the practices of culture, can have an emancipatory effect. And, occasionally, the semiotic and symbolic richness and diversity of a work of art can testify to an affective reality, to be both of and for its historical moment and speak to the strangeness of everyday life.

18. Robert Morris, 'Notes on Sculpture' in *Uber Kunst: Artists Writings on the Changed Notion of Art After 1965*, ed. Gerd de Vries, DuMont International, Germany, 1974, p196
19. For definitions of the 'gaze' and the 'glance' see Norman Bryson, *Vision and Painting: The Logic of the Gaze*, Macmillan 1993
20. Perhaps a less obvious but more significant sculptural reference for Whiteread is Eva Hesse who also employed plaster and rubber as materials that flow, emphasizing viscosity and tactility. Other references – formal and conceptual – might include the relation of *Untitled/Floor* (1992) and the *Bed* works (1992) to Carl Andre's *Equivalent VIII* (1966), Martha Rosler's exhibitions on 'The Homeless' in New York (1987–89), Krzysztof Wodiczko's *Vehicle for the Homeless*, Christian Boltanski, and, recently, Antony Gormley's indexical casts of the lost body, *Home of the Heart* (1992–93).

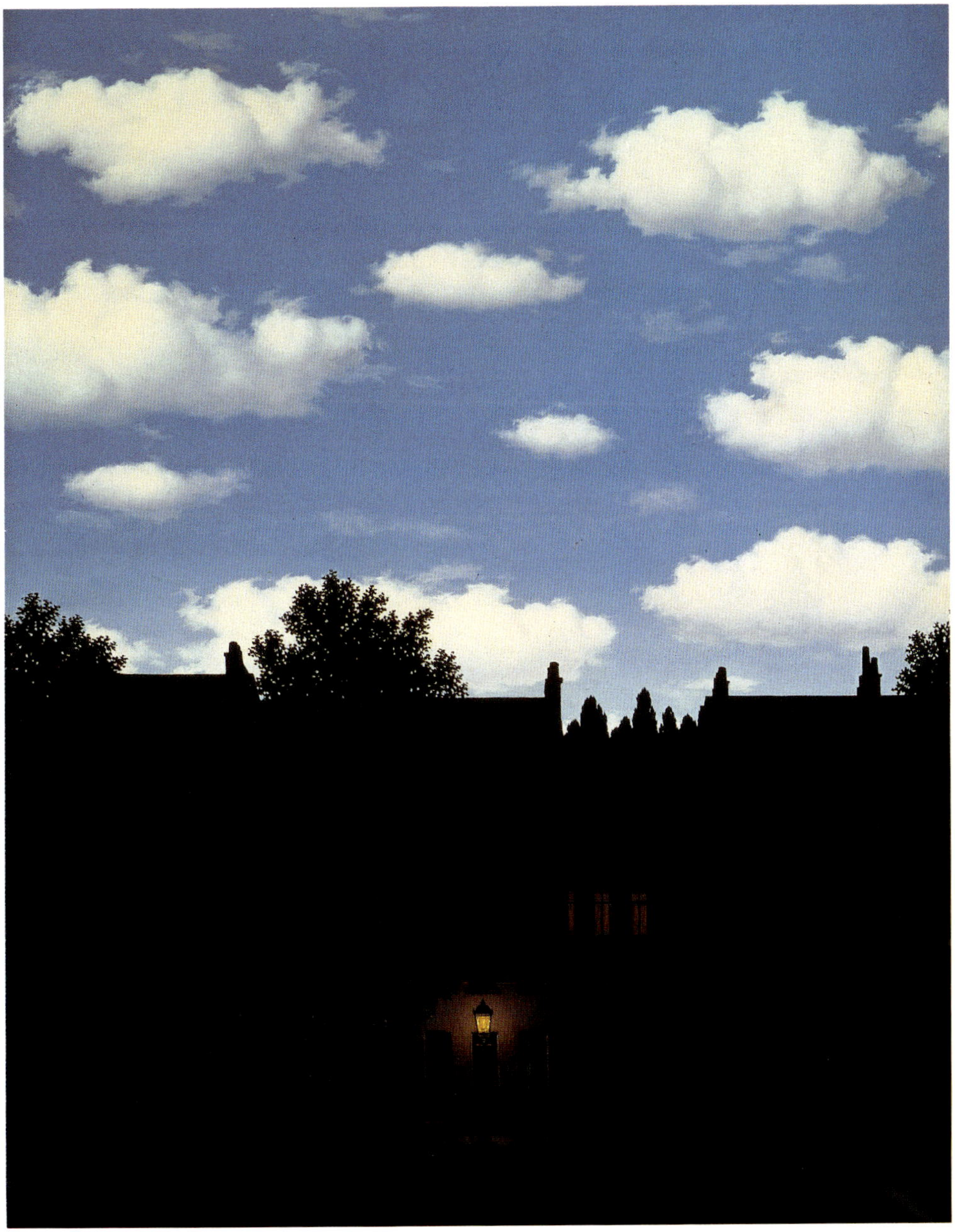

9

9 René Magritte, The Empire of Lights, 1954, oil on canvas, 146 x 114 cm

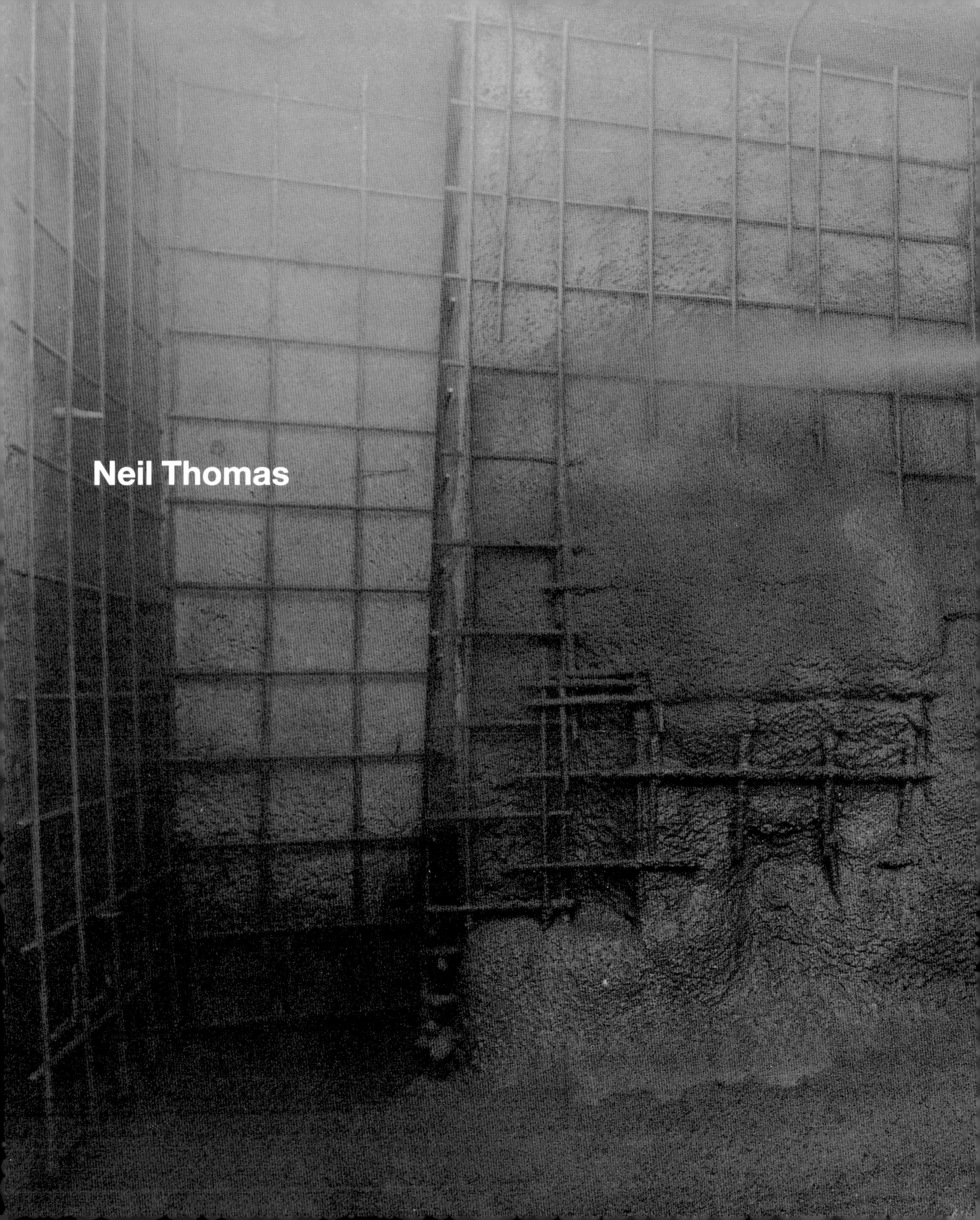

Neil Thomas

the making of house: technical notes

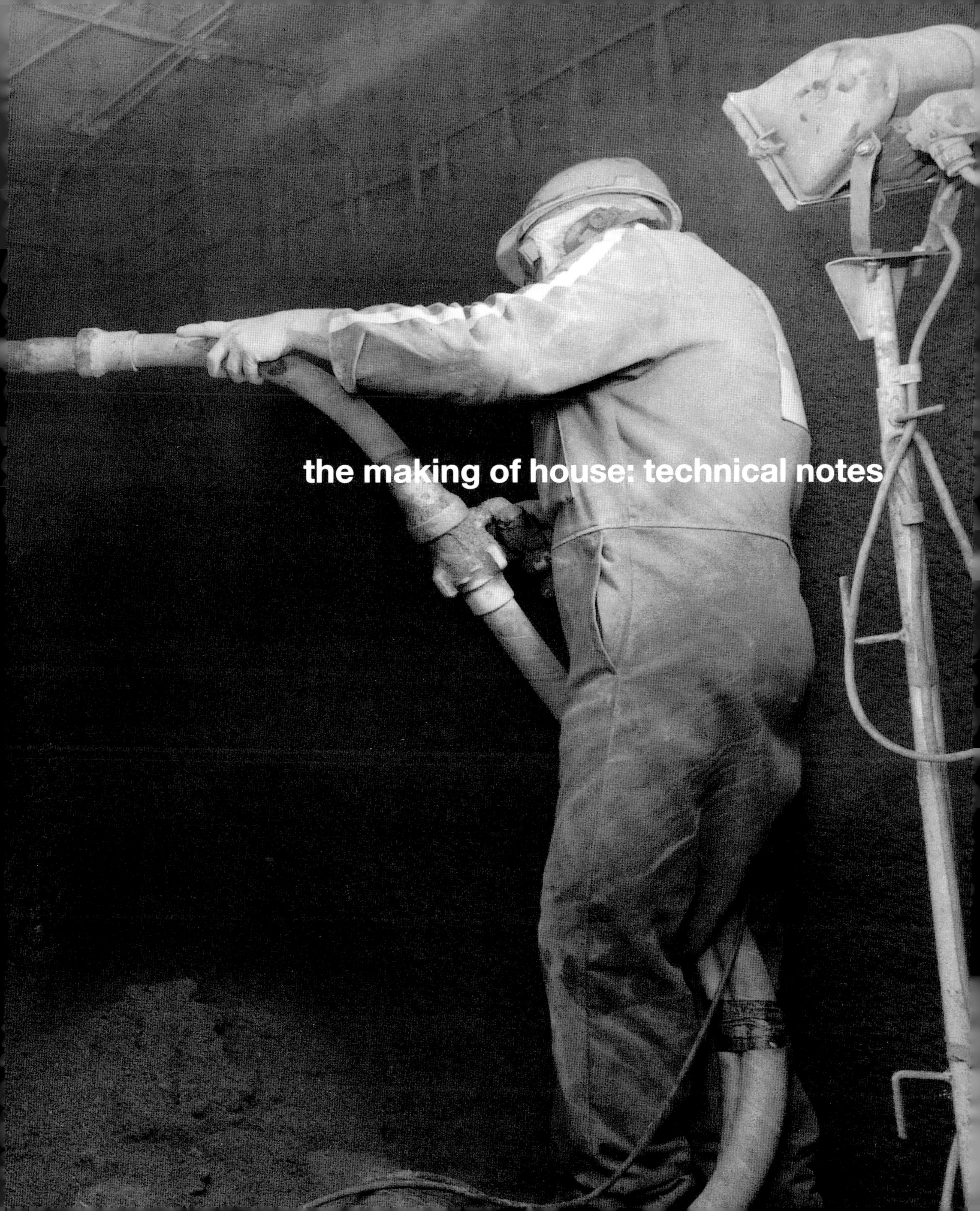

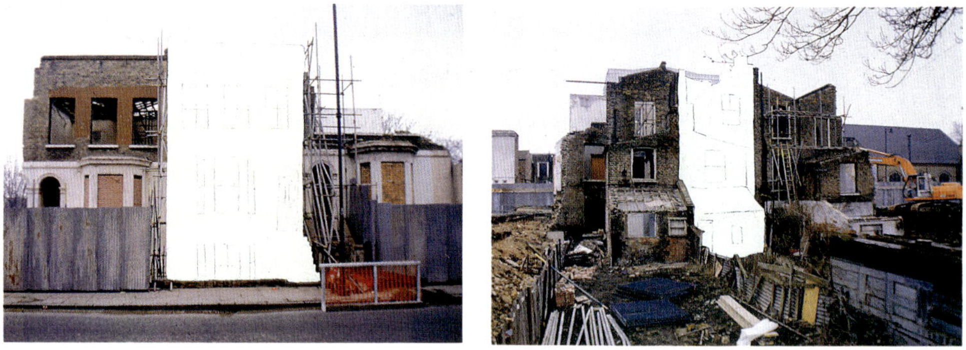

1

1 Rachel Whiteread, sketches for House, 1992-93

Rachel Whiteread and James Lingwood approached Atelier One in 1992, through the recommendation of Will Alsop, then a trustee of Artangel.

Rachel then described the method by which she had created *Ghost*, a sculpture made in 1990, and her proposal to make a cast of an entire terraced house in situ in East London.

Artangel spent more than six months in late 1992 and early 1993 searching for a property suitable for Whiteread's new project. During this period Atelier One worked with Rachel to develop a principle with which the proposal could be successfully realized.

Ghost involved the casting of the negative of a single room. Without the constraints of a traditional building site and without limits on time, the room was cast in plaster as a series of panels in discrete sections which, when placed together, would recreate the negative space. An armature was formed which supported the parts in their original configuration.

Clearly the process of casting individual parts in plaster, allowing a period for curing, and the treatment necessary to fix to a predesigned armature was an extremely lengthy one. Early discussions about realizing *House* included considering the building of an armature within the existing building and casting elements of the skin in a similar way to *Ghost*. However, with *House* the logistics of restructuring by discrete translation of load from one point to another until a total restructuring of the facade was completed would necessitate an extremely sophisticated system, likely to be very expensive and to involve significant amounts of time. The commodity of time was not available in large measure for the new project.

In early discussions about the project of making *House* the idea of a sprayed concrete skin was introduced. The process known as 'gunniting' had been used previously by Atelier One in an application which had immediate associations with the technical ideas involved in *Ghost*.

In order to remove a step in the underside of a concrete ceiling in a building in the Middle East a reinforcing mesh was hung beneath the existing concrete and bonding agents applied to the surface. Concrete was then sprayed under pressure and directed through a nozzle at the surface. The pressure, used along with very precise constituents in the concrete, allows the spray to stick firmly to the bonding agents and remain in place, building a series of layers until the step is reined. Following early curing of the concrete, the surface was smoothed to match the existing adjacent surface and this created a continuous concrete plane. However, this applied layer of concrete has little or no integrity, with the additional concrete layers simply holding themselves to the original structure and therefore basically acting as a ceiling panel.

The concept of concrete shell structures has long been employed throughout the world. One of the greatest exponents, the Spanish-American architect engineer, Felix Candela, has produced shell surfaces as long as 30m from a concrete skin only 10 cm thick.

The integrity of those shells at this size is taken from plastic properties of the concrete with the rigidity provided by reinforcing steel mesh when combined and the concrete hydrated. This alone would not allow the substantial spans shown possible by Candela. These are achieved by combining the material properties with the

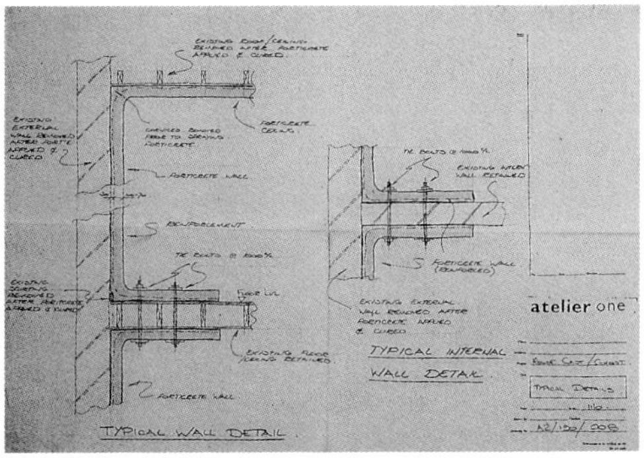

2

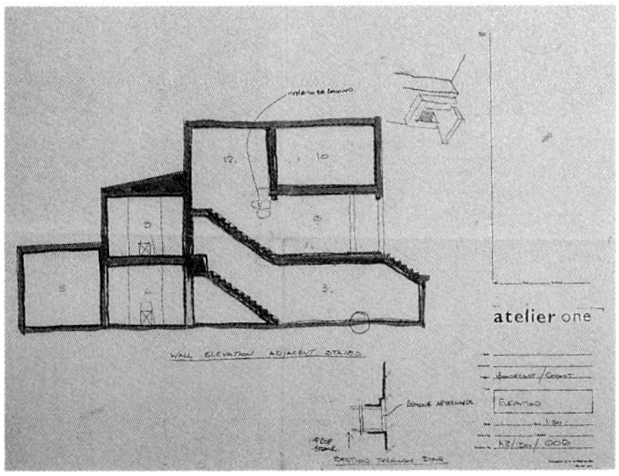

2, 3 Atelier One, computer-generated drawings, 1993

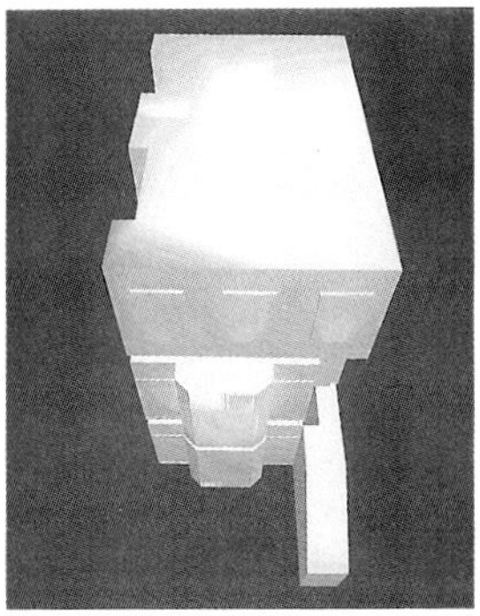

3

geometric form of surfaces. These doubly curved surfaces are capable of spanning such distances with so little material.

A potential solution to the problem of forming *House* emerged through combining the principle of shell structures with the facilitation of spraying the concrete to form the shell. The idea of spraying a concrete shell to the inside of a house is fraught with problems, and the next few weeks were spent addressing these issues.

The detailed proposal was to cast a series of independent concrete boxes which form the negative of each room. Each of these units would have adequate stiffness to stand alone whilst still being capable of transferring the imposed load and their own weight to the ground, and having adequate rigidity to act as a completely stable unit once exposed. Both physical and computer models were then made of the discrete boxes to investigate some of the potential problems with this idea.

When Artangel obtained permission to use 193 Grove Road, it was possible to survey the specific building both dimensionally and materially to ensure the feasibility of this proposal. 193 Grove Road stood between partial elements of the two adjacent terraced houses. The actual integrity of the existing building itself was accepted as adequate. Then careful investigation was made into the conditions of another condemned building to ensure that during the construction of *House*, unforeseen problems would not be encountered.

Although damaged through lack of repair, the primary elements of the building – timber floors and masonry – were sound. Given that the concrete shell sits inside the loadbearing skin of the existing building (and that the existing skin is to be removed) then the dead weight of the wet concrete during construction must be supported by the existing structure. Therefore detailed analysis of the new loads was carried out. Further, a sequence of casting each of the rooms was developed to ensure that the existing structure would not be distressed in any way.

Once the new shell was in place, and the existing building skin removed, the loads from the shell would be eccentric to the original foundations. Investigation into this proved that the existing foundations were inadequate to deal with the new loads and therefore it was necessary to lay a new foundation at the base of the 'boxes' of *House* inside the existing arrangement.

How could the loads from each room be transferred from one floor to the next through the existing floor plates? Would the gunnite achieve the quality of finish necessary for the final representation of *House*? Normally gunnite is designed to attach to existing structures. Would the process work in reverse – sticking to the surface for casting but allowing a delayed debonding when the original building was to be removed?

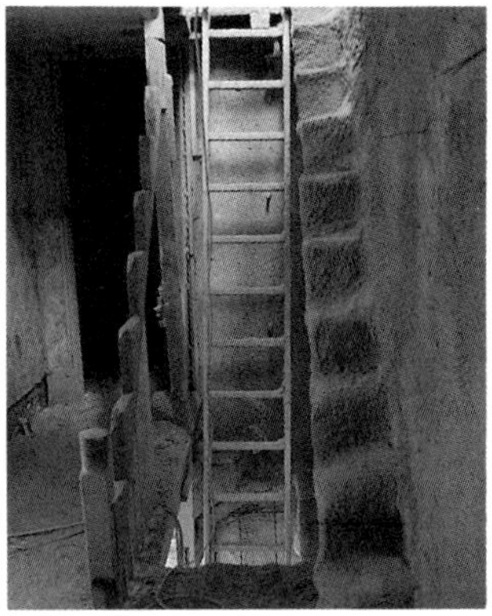

4

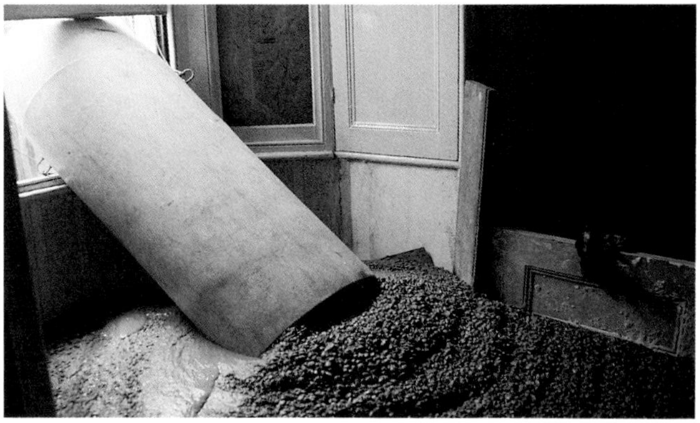

5

4,5 Casting in progress, September, 1993

Work began on site with the clearing of all rooms exposed to the outside surface. The building was prepared very carefully prior to concreting. Each room to be sprayed was stripped of all secondary trappings and cleaned up to provide a smooth finish throughout to which the concrete would be bonded. Windows were filled with plywood to ensure the spraying did not merely blast the glass out through the frame.

All re-entrent corners and recesses were infilled to ensure that when lifted away the external skin would not pull elements of the concrete with it.

The walls were coated in a debonding agent as advised by Tarmac Structural Repairs with several layers being soaked by the existing wall until a thin continuous surface was left over the walls. The concrete could then be applied through the gunnite spraying process.

To avoid the necessity to stiffen the existing floors and to transfer concrete load through the timber, 25mm bolts were drilled through the floor. These carried washer plates and nuts at either end. The ceiling concrete would then be cast around the bolt and the concrete in the floor around the other end. Once the walls were removed the much higher modulus of elasticity (less change in length) would transfer the load from the compressed timber to the steel bolts. These bolts were designed stiff enough to transfer lateral bending between the boxes.

Next a new foundation strip was cast into the ground, adjacent to the existing in the conventional way.

Reinforcing mesh was fixed to the walls where the concrete was to be sprayed. This mesh continued throughout to ensure shell section in each box. As previously explained the bolts provided movement continuity.

During this period of construction the District Surveyor from Tower Hamlets visited the site on numerous occasions with a surprising number of different colleagues. When asked about the reason for such close inspection, they explained that no one could believe the project and wanted to see it with their own eyes.

The concrete was then sprayed onto the mesh in consecutive layers, over several weeks, the sequence being developed to ensure distribution of loading and also access for the operatives. A small opening in the roof was left for the last exit from the fully sprayed interior.

The concrete then cured for the necessary period of 10 days and scaffolding placed around the *House* to allow protected removal of the original building in a way reminiscent of archeology.

The one remaining question concerned the efficacy of the agent to allow initial bonding with a delayed release mechanism. Tarmac Structural Repairs developed with their research facility a bonding agent with a retarder which would delay the action of the release agent until the concrete had gone off.

The delayed release mechanism functioned as planned and the outer walls of the original building were removed room by room with relative ease to reveal an excellent representation of the negative of each room forming *House*.

compendium of press and cartoons

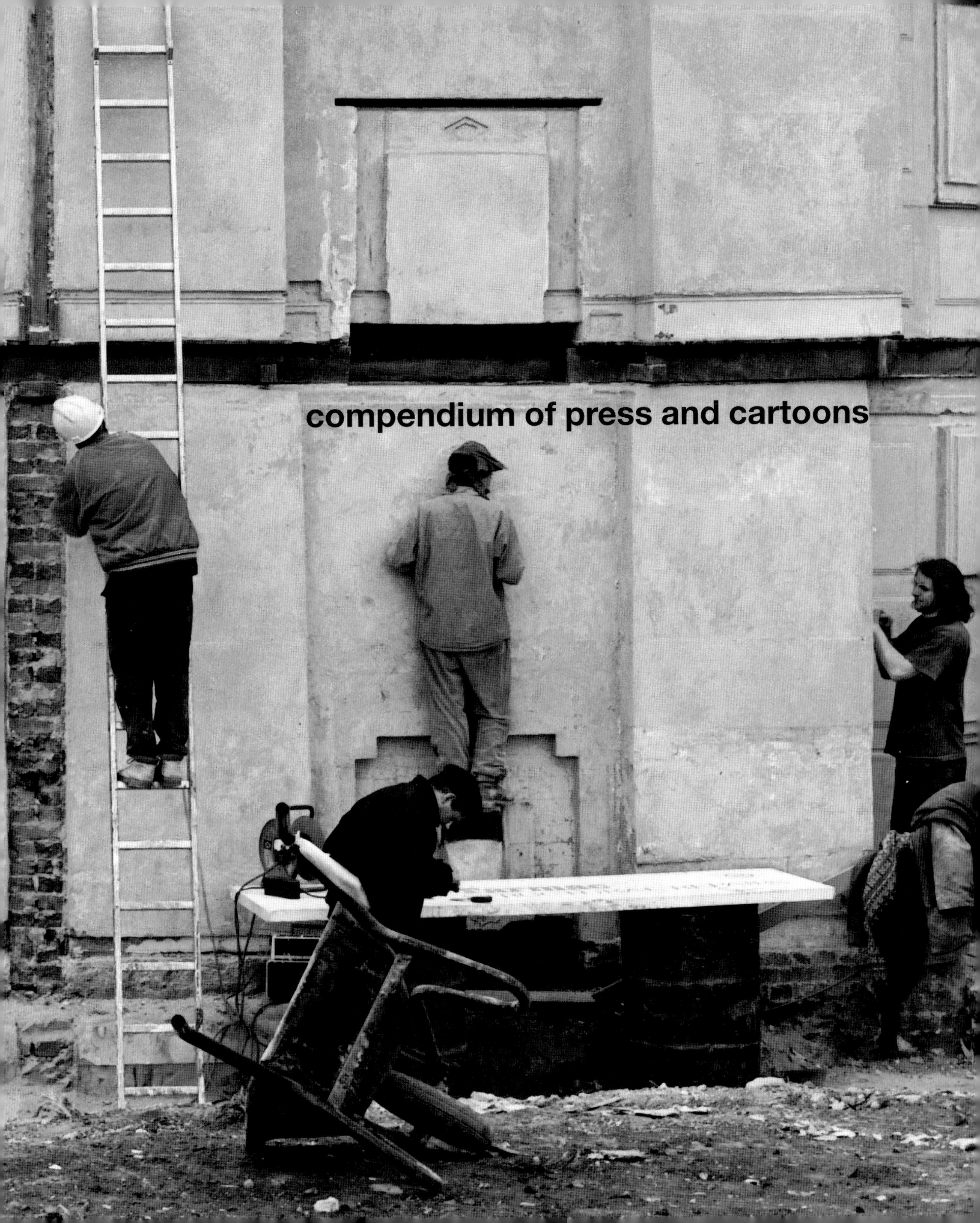

Sunday Telegraph, 24 Oct 93

ARTS

The house that Rachel unbuilt

Rachel Whiteread should win the Turner Prize for her cast of a house, thinks John McEwen

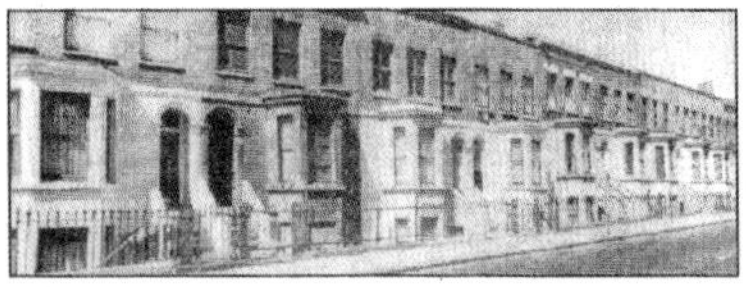

YOU CAN hardly call it a park, just a small, newly turfed, grass space tidily set aside behind incongruously grand railings next to a road junction in the heart of London's East End; and yet six months ago half of it was a pretty Victorian terrace, like thousands of others, with back extensions and garden plots. In September when I visited, only one house remained, an object of blitzed desolation amid the lapping green, the tangled roses disappearing under debris, boardwalks and muck.

To make a cast of this house is the artist Rachel Whiteread's latest and most ambitious project. She had the general idea four years ago, has planned it for two, and since August has been working on site alongside the men, hard hat on head and mobile phone in hand.

Whiteread came to prominence with *Ghost*, a plaster cast of the inside of an entire room exhibited as a mummified object. *Ghost* has since travelled the world, and at 30 Whiteread is the rising star in the English art firmament — currently on a German government scholarship to Berlin and short-listed a second time for the Turner Prize.

Now she has mummified a whole house. Teams of workers first made a concrete cast of the inside and then, having ensured the stability of this new structure, removed the original bricks to leave it exposed. What it amounts to is a house replaced by a negative of itself: not so much recorded as reinvented.

We discussed the implications of this transformation as it took place, standing in the concreted and cavernous dark of what was once the front parlour. A fine dust was palpable and the din of machinery deafening; but Rachel Whiteread remained undaunted, a slight figure, hair ponytailed out of the way, readily amused but totally focused on the worrying amount of work still to be done. After two and half months she felt "spent", though her energy seemed unbounded.

"*Ghost* was more personal, more about my family — a specific room like the one I had as a child and as a student. Here I am making a monument to a house, to a home, but it's much more generalised; more to do with the state of housing in England; the ludicrous policy of knocking down homes like this and building badly designed tower blocks which themselves have to be knocked down after 20 years."

"So it's a 'political statement'?"

"In part, yeah, but I hope that will be obvious from the piece. I'm not going to stand on the street corner saying: 'This is a political statement.' It's just a typical Victorian house most people in England have lived in at some time or other. And the context is important. It's site-specific and outside, I chose the location very carefully. Just about everything is there."

The site, which has been kept a closely guarded secret in the art world, can here be revealed as the corner of Roman Road and Grove Road, London E3. It does represent a peculiarly abundant historical and architectural meeting-place. Standing beside the old Roman road which still dictates the ground plan after 2,000 years, one can see a rare factory chimney; the traditional C of E parish church of St Barnabas alongside the Jehovah's Witnesses and the Victoria Park Baptist Church; grim 1960s high-rises and tarted-up 1980s ones; four of the snug 1880s terraced family homes of which *House* is an example, and, like everywhere else in London, the 21st-century megastructure of Canary Wharf.

"When I say I'm calling it *House* people laugh and say, 'How original!' But actually it took me a long time to think of it because it's such a particular word and there were so many other titles and thoughts I came up with. But *House* seems just right."

ON THE first floor I checked the reaction of one of the concrete sprayers, Rob King. The technique is usually employed to build relatively indestructible things like sea walls and bridges; but the initial agreement with the council is that *House* will be knocked down and the site cleared by the end of November. Another inversion. King is supportive. They are concreting the interior from the bottom or what's known in the trade as "slab level" up, the last one out coming through the roof and sealing it behind him.

The job of stripping off the original walls — a delicate task "more like an archaeological dig" — was not his concern. "I look forward to seeing it when it's finished. Why? because it's different." Like the bold title this statement neatly seemed to sum it up.

Away from the din and darkness, I tried to find from what recesses of her past the idea to take casts of the improbable, often the intangible, had come. One clue emerged. As a girl in Muswell Hill she used to have fun working on the restoration of old Highgate Cemetery. "There was an incredible atmosphere to that place. We were basically ["basically" is a word she uses a lot] clearing a way for paths so people could walk around it. We found these little offerings on the tombs from people doing witchcraft. It was actually quite spooky."

The first casts she made were in wax, impressions of the cavities formed by objects like sea-shells, "the other side of things; of the space created. Sarcophagi have always interested me. Some of the early pieces I made of the space under tables and in bath-tubs were very much like tombs. You had this sense there was something inside."

Last week I returned. An eye-infection resulting from the work meant she could not be present, but James Lingwood, co-director of Artangel, showed me around. Artangel is an organisation which commissions site-specific art projects. It has done the negotiations and fund-raising for *House*. As the builders cleared away the final bricks and mortar like shell from an egg, the spectral concrete effigy could be glimpsed behind the scaffolding and net.

"It's the end of the movie," said Lingwood, as we studied details left in the concrete mould. True, there was a sad finality about this last mute rite in the life of that particular hive of London life that had been 193 Grove Road; and something valiant too. "Like with all art, it makes you think but it doesn't tell you wh
to think."

Later I rang Rachel Whitere
for her latest reflections. She w
pleased by local interest. One
resident told her *House* alm
marked the spot where the fi
V2 rocket had landed, a f
which added more spice to t
historical brew. And she had be
surprised by the sensation
standing on the finished roof.

"It felt quite profound.
seemed so small, 14ft by 14ft
whatever, and with noth
around. Like being on top o
plinth." 14ft by 14ft — so th
are the dimensions with wh
most of us bound the greater p
of our lives. Not much, basica
but the mathematical limits o
monumental metaphor, for wh
she should surely win the Tur
Prize.

☐ 'House' can be seen at the junctio
Roman Road and Grove Road, E3 (n
est tube Mile End) throughout Nov
ber. It has been commissioned
Artangel with Beck's, co-sponsored
Tarmac Structural Repairs.

The 1993 Turner Prize shortlist exh
tion is at the Tate Gallery from Nov
ber 3 to 28.

JUSTIN LEIGHTO

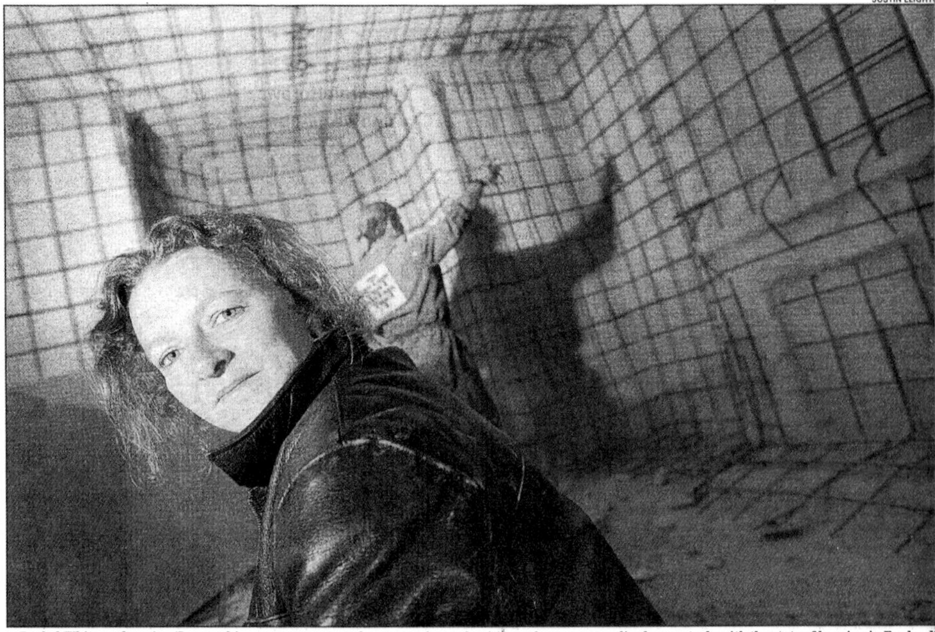

Rachel Whiteread on site: 'I am making a monument to a house, to a home, but it's much more generalised; more to do with the state of housing in England

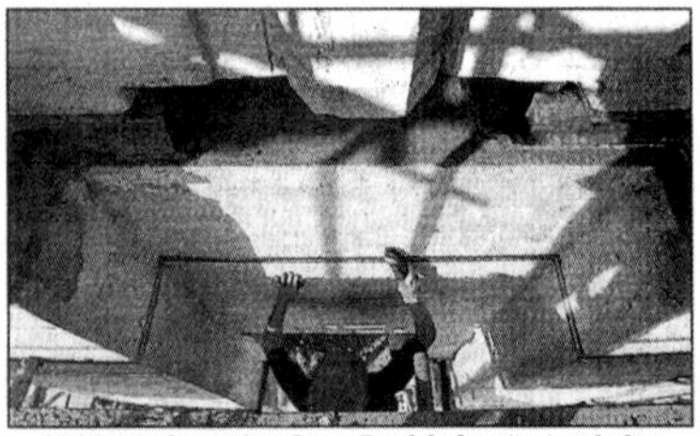

Positive and negative: Grove Road, before (top) and after

Independent on Sunday, 31 Oct 93

OPINIONS

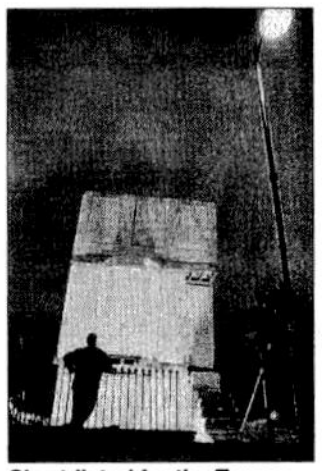

Short-listed for the Turner Prize – Rachel Whiteread's concrete sculpture

Is this art?

TOBIAS MEYER, Head of Contemporary Art, Sotheby's: Absolutely. She's completely, utterly brilliant. The sculpture is beautiful. The idea is interesting, the location is controversial — which is always important for contemporary art — the surface of it is like a painting. She's a complete star, she's wonderful. I would like nothing more than to own a work by her.

JOHN SHARLAND, foreman of the house's construction: I'm just the mug that did what the artist told me to. I worked on this for two months and it was soul destroying. I met the artist once and to be quite frank she was a pain in the arse. It's not original — if I stood in the middle of the road and took my trousers down, I'd attract the same attention and I'd only charge a tenner. Artists — they're all crackpots aren't they, no wonder they go cutting their ears off.

EDUARDO PAOLOZZI, sculptor: Why not? Anything goes; after Duchamp anything's possible.

AL MALTBY, builder: It's an amazing piece; a real achievement. What I want to know is how she filled it up. The whole house could've fallen apart. Concrete is warm and can explode. It's a great feat of engineering.

LES BOYD, director, housing charity: Well, I think it's a bit ridiculous. I'm not very interested in art — I'm not that kind of person. If I had £50,000 I wouldn't waste it on a concrete block like that. I'd go to Spain.

ROBIN SIMON, editor, *Apollo* magazine: It's utterly depressing. I haven't even the energy to discuss it.

PETER BLAKE, artist: I have mixed feelings. In principle, I don't approve of her art. It's too simple to take a mould from something which already exists. Also, it depends where the money's coming from; but if it's been *completely* sponsored by Tarmac then I approve.

MRS PENN, housewife: It's a monstrosity, an eyesore. I've lived here all my life and I've never seen anything like it. I hope it's coming down soon.

VANESSA LINDLEY BLUNT, designer: I call it a political statement more than a work of art and I think it works very well. As far as I know, the artist bought out the sitting tenant, who was being compulsory purchased by the council. So this is a statement about housing and homelessness. Look at it! They might have budged him, but it's going to be a hard job budging that!

STEVE HARDING, National Gallery warder: Filling a house with concrete is not art, it's not a work of artistic creativity. All contemporary art is pretentious, there's no formal structure, no story. Some of the best artists in Britain have come from the Pre-Raphaelites, even though it isn't cool to say that at art school. I suppose I'm just a traditionalist.

Independent on Sunday, 7 Nov 93

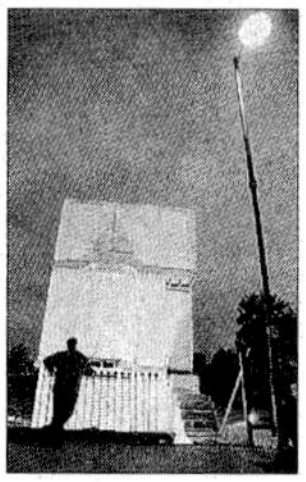

Rachel Whiteread: an apology

LAST Sunday's Opinions column included a quote from a Mr John Sharland about the construction of the sculpture "House" by Rachel Whiteread. We now understand that Mr Sharland was not the foreman of the house's construction as was stated, had no involvement with the realisation of the work at any stage and had never met the artist. We regret the distress which this has caused Rachel Whiteread, Artangel and the contractors involved in the work.

Sculptor could scoop award for her concrete capers

There's a stoney house!

BEFORE and...

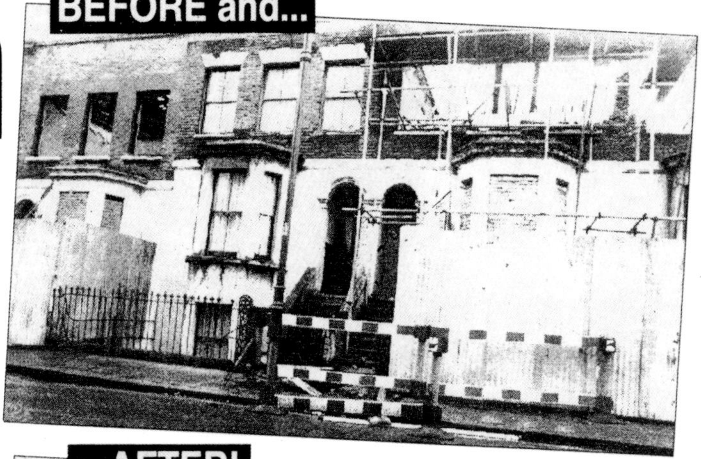

...AFTER!

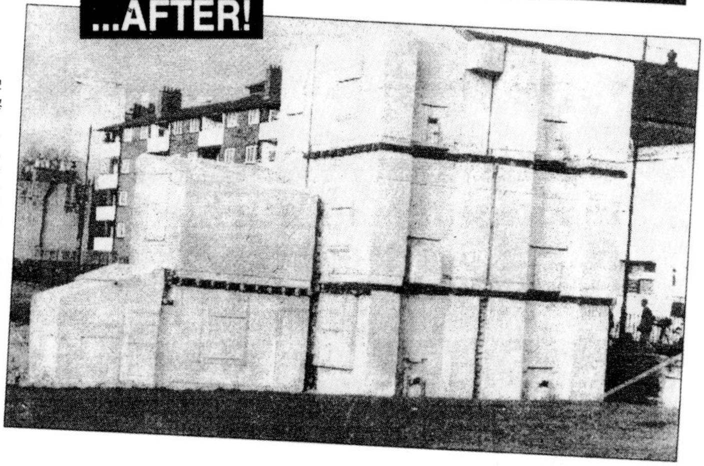

THE arts world flocked to the East End this week when a top sculptor unveiled a cast of a Victorian house.

BY ULLA KLOSTER

The three-storey lump of concrete could win Hackney-based artist Rachel Whiteread a top national prize.

Bow Neighbourhood, which had bulldozed a string of houses to add to Mile End Park, struck a deal with the 30-year-old artist earlier this year.

Rachel would tear down the house - 193 Grove Road - after she had filled it with concrete and turned it into a memorial to a home.

The piece, only feet from where the first V2 rocket landed, is named 'house' and made with a £50,000 sponsorship.

But ex-tenant and war-hero Sidney Gale, who was ordered out of his childhood home by the neighbourhood, was not impressed by the 'house'.

He said: "That money would be better spent on buying a new house.

WEE WEE

"They've taken the wee wee out of me."

The white sculpture, finished on Tuesday, will be razed to the ground by the end of November. So far it has got mixed reactions from East Enders.

Bow nanny, Harriet Wyborn, 22, said: "You must be joking! I thought it was an old building waiting to be knocked down."

Retired bus driver Jim Champness, 62, of Roman Road, Bow, said: "I've got my memories of growing up in Whitechapel during the War already without this. I think it's a waste of money."

But Palmer's Road based designer, Dick Stringer, 40, said: "I think it's brilliant. I like the inside-out quality. It's a new way of looking at traditional things."

Rachel, hailed the rising star in the English art establishment, has been shortlisted for the Turner Prize. Some of her other work can be seen at the Tate Gallery.

■ OFFTHE CUFF P24

East London Advertiser, 28 October 93

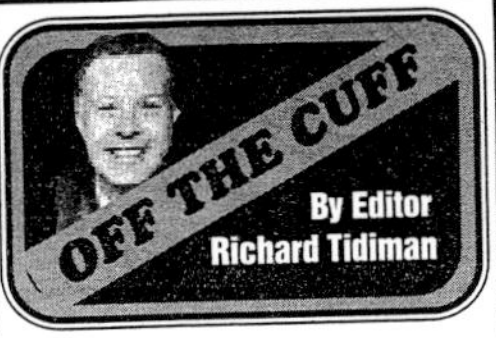

OFF THE CUFF

By Editor Richard Tidiman

When a house is not a home

IT'S a waste of money, it doesn't do anything and it doesn't look particularly lovely. Of course, I'm talking about the new concrete 'house' in Grove Road, Bow.

It was unveiled this week to what is commonly called 'a mixed reception' from East Enders.

But the £50,000 it cost was never destined to be spent on something 'more worthwhile' for the benefit of East Enders.

And, even if it isn't the greatest bit of art since the Venus de Milo lost her arms, it's still a nice little bit of English eccentricity.

And when people sometimes find life a little on the grim side, I'm all for that.

This is the house that Rachel built

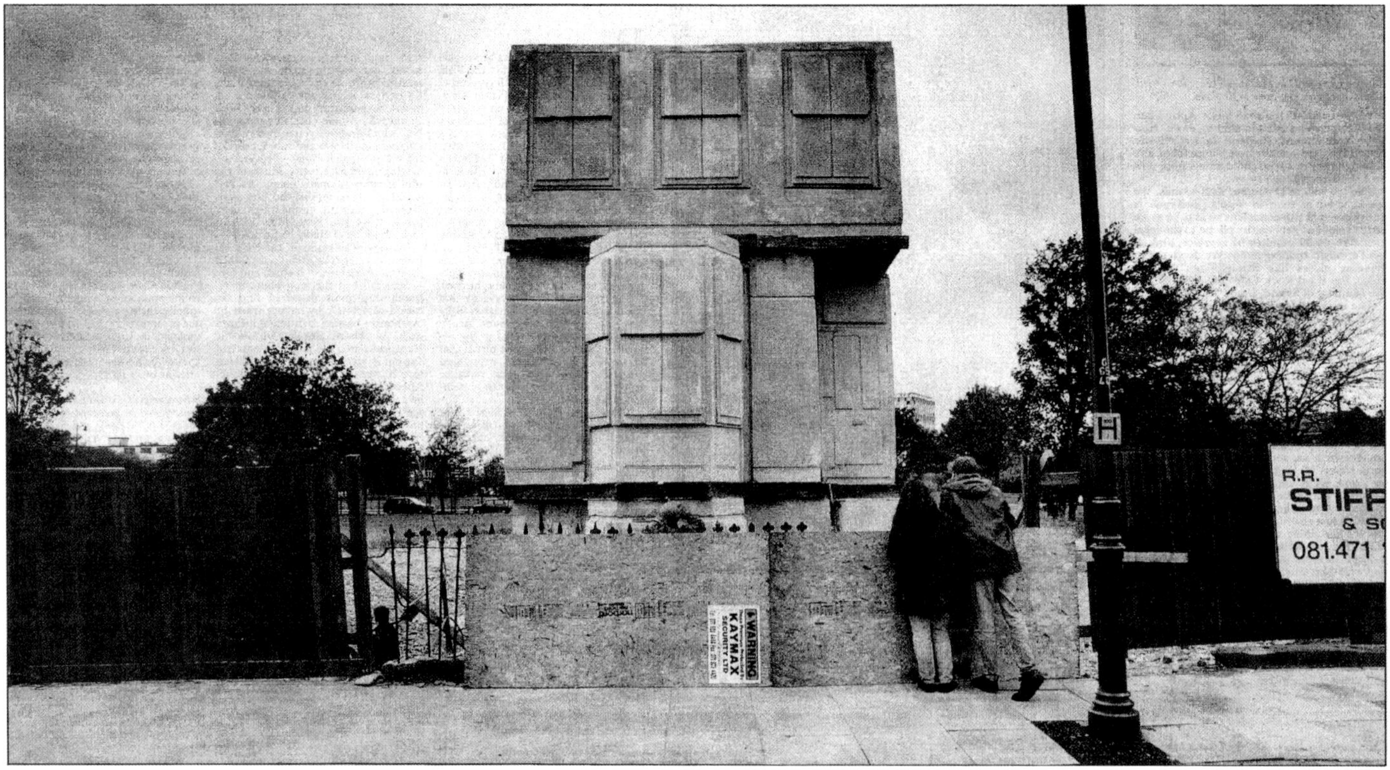

Rachel Whiteread's *House* is one of the most extraordinary public sculptures to have been created by any English artist working this century, says **Andrew Graham-Dixon**. Here he examines the work *(pictured by Nicholas Turpin)*, and, below, Whiteread and three other artists nominated for the Turner Prize describe their work

Number 193 Grove Road used to be an unexceptional Victorian house in the East End of London. "Mile End, E3 — 3 storey end of terrace Victorian house, 4 beds 2 receps, original features," an estate agent might have described it. Extensively remodelled, improved beyond habitability, it has become both monument and memorial. It has become Rachel Whiteread's *House*: a strange and fantastical object which also amounts to one of the most extraordinary and imaginative public sculptures created by an English artist this century.

193 Grove Road is no longer a home but the ghost of one perpetuated in art. It has no doors, no windows, no walls and no roof. It was made, simply (although the process was complicated, the idea itself was simple) by filling a house with liquid concrete and then stripping the mould — that is, the house itself, roof tiles, bricks and mortar, doors and windows and all — away from it. The result could be described as the opposite of a house, since what it consists of is a cast of the spaces once contained by one.

Facing *House*, on the other side of Grove Road, stands the Kingdom Hall of Jehovah's Witnesses. Now the Witnesses can knock on the door of number 193 until kingdom come but there will be no one home. Rooms that were once lived in have become solid blocks of stone, megaliths piled one on top of another like an infant giant's building bricks. Foursquare sash windows that once looked out on to the world have become blind, heavy, cruciform reliefs. Doors that once opened have become sealed panels of rock. The house has, itself, become a giant sarcophagus, a mausoleum containing (but also concealing, as mausoleums do) the lives and memories of all the people who once lived there.

Whiteread's *House* (1993) expands on Whiteread's *Ghost* (1990), which was an exact plaster cast of a bedsitting room in an abandoned house on the Archway Road, cut into blocks and reconstituted in the Chisenhale Gallery, London. *Ghost*, a monument to cramped living conditions in N6, was bought by Charles Saatchi but *House*, being the size of a house and heavier than one, will be going nowhere. The terrace that 193 Grove Road once occupied has been demolished, and *House* itself is scheduled for demolition at the end of this month. Whatever happens to it, it will live a long time in the memory.

To visit *House* or (as many will do) simply to come across it, isolated in a scrubby patch of parkland at the corner of Roman Road and Grove Road, is to be suddenly and disconcertingly transported elsewhere. It is to be taken to another world, like and yet completely unlike this one: the world of the photographic negative, with its phantom-like reversals of known fact; the world that Alice enters through her looking glass; the world that lurks behind the molten silver mirror in Cocteau's *Orphée*, where normal relations between objects have been summarily suspended. Denatured by transformation, things turn strange here. Fireplaces bulge outwards from the walls of *House*, doorknobs are rounded hollows. Architraves have become chiselled incisions running around the monument, forms as mysterious as the hieroglyphs on Egyptian tombs.

House may seem perverse to those who persist in the belief that a work of art does not really count, as art, unless it looks like an easel painting or hand-carved sculpture. But it is in many respects an extremely traditional work. The artist has taken something very ordinary (but no more ordinary than the traditional painter's oil and ground pigment, or the traditional sculptor's piece of wood or stone) and made of it something extraordinary. The artist has asserted her right to construct her own world out of the materials of this one, to make a fantasy real and palpable. Like much of the most compelling traditional art, *House* has the quality of a thing that had to be made to exorcise the compulsions of its maker.

Looking at *House* is temporally as well as spatially distorting. It is like looking at an object from the present that has suddenly been pitched far into the future or far into the past. An English terraced house has been remade as an archaeological find, and what an oddly simple thing it turns out to be. Just a squat arrangement of spaces to inhabit, a stack of caves honeycombed together. *House* contains the traces of late 20th-century living habits and technology, which survive in odd details like the impressed patterns of a fossil caught in its surface: the zigzags of a wooden staircase running up one of its walls, the indented relics of plug sockets. But the overall effect is one of extreme, primitive simplicity.

To solidify the interiors of a house may be to conceal them, to seal them off, but it is also to reveal how basic our needs and our lives have remained down the centuries. There is a kind of pathos in the revelation. Our houses tend to be places that we like to think of as containing the evidence of our own unique sensibilities, repositories where we store the evidence of our sophistication and impeccable tastefulness. *House*, being a house without furniture, a house reduced to the shape of the air that a house contains, serves as a reminder that we are all, on one level at least, utterly and primally the same: creatures that have always sought shelter, a roof over our heads.

House is a sculpture that memorialises, in its transfiguration of an ordinary person's home, the ordinary lives of ordinary people (ordinariness, it suggests, is one thing we all have in common). Unlike other kinds of monumental statuary — Nelson's Column, say — which suggests that history is made by the great and merely lived by the rest of us, *House* is stubbornly unheroic and democratic. Whiteread has made an image of how we all live, caught between solitude and sociability, out of the separate but abutting cells of the rooms in a house in London E3.

House is a paradox made concrete since it is a monument made out of void space, a thing constructed out of the absence of things. Being a dwelling in which it is not possible to dwell, a building that you cannot enter, it has the character of a tantalus. It is both a relic and a prompt to the imagination (Who lived here? What did they do? What did they feel?) as well as a sculpture that is charged with a deep sense of loss.

All houses (and many works of art, too) are tombs of a kind: most of the people whose memories th
contain have gone, have surr
dered their tenancy of the wor
House is about the past and it is a
about the unrecoverability of
past, about the fact that what
gone cannot be revived. Death,
nally, is its theme. The sculpt
has a peculiar, almost anthropom
phic quality, or at least the traces
humanity that it bears are so stro
that it ends up feeling oddly hum
for such an evidently non-figurat
work of art. Something that v
once full of life, open to light a
sound and movement, has been t
minally stilled, made dumb a
blind and inert. *House* is mon
ment, memorial, and *memento m*

□ Rachel Whiteread's *House* v
commissioned by Artangel a
sponsored by Beck's Beer and T
mac Structural Repairs. It is at
junction of Roman Road and Gr
Road in London E3.

□ To complement the Turner Pri
the Tate Gallery is hosting a deb
on contemporary art on 10 Nov
8.30pm). Speakers will include H
ton Kramer, the art critic and
thor, and Michael Craig Martin,
artist. Tickets £7.50/£5 (0
887 8000).

□ *Turner Prize show details below*

A concrete idea well worth preserving

THERE it stands on a scruffy patch of parkland in Bow, east London, the concrete ghost of a Victorian terrace house, opposite the Kingdom Hall of Jehovah's Witnesses in Grove Road. But those who bear witness, Bible in hand, will knock on the concrete door of No 193 in vain. This is a house inhabited only by solidified particles of sand and concrete.

Rachel Whiteread, who created this remarkable artefact, is one of the four artists shortlisted for the much-criticised Turner Prize. Three years ago she gave the world *Ghost*, a plaster cast of a bedsitting room in an abandoned house in the Archway Road, London. It was bought by Charles Saatchi, and one of its offspring, *Untitled Room*, is among the works by the shortlisted artists on view from today at the Tate Gallery on Millbank, London. *House*, as the creation in Grove Road is called, is a logical development of those smaller works.

Whiteread's inspired idea was to use the derelict house that stood on the same spot as a mould, a traditional method of making bronze sculptures. Room by room, floor by floor, the house was filled with concrete. Then the brick walls and windows that formed the mould were delicately removed. The result is unexpectedly moving. Sightless, solid windows indented by vanished transoms and mullions gaze out unseeing. A departed staircase zigzags up a wall. The hole that was once a fireplace protrudes like some primitive adornment. For a sculpture, the bulk is impressive, yet the overall effect is strangely spectral.

Whiteread's was in many ways a wacky as well as a brilliantly original idea: just the sort of thing that people who dislike much contemporary art, and especially abstract art, tend to hate. Yet the artist has, in the most traditional way possible, taken an everyday object — albeit a very large one — and transformed it into a work of art. Being literally a concrete image of a dwelling, *House* could not be further removed from the abstract.

Bow Neighbourhood Council, which generously lent the site to the sponsoring organisation, Artangel, had requested that *House* be demolished at the end of this month. It would be performing a service to art if it were to extend its presence there not just for a month or two more, but until it has lost its pulling power. That is likely to be a long time hence.

The Independent, (letters page), 17 Nov 93

'House' should be demolished

From Mr Peter Merry

Sir: I spent an hour with Rachel Whiteread's *House* in Bow the other day, and found it every bit as impressive as press coverage had led me to expect. The campaign for its preservation is understandable, but perhaps I may contribute a dissenting note.

Much of its impact, its ability to move and provoke, comes from the very fact of its transitory nature: a heroic idea made real for a brief instant to challenge values and perceptions. Were it to be "saved" its nature would change completely, both psychologically and physically.

House has probably not been built to last and would need strengthening and continual conservation. It would have to be protected against vandals and graffiti-artists. Considerations of public safety and civic aesthetics would lead to the manicuring of the site, the erection of a substantial surrounding fence, the posting of special bye-laws. Before long, all that would be left would be a bizarre, dated, pointless, rather charming artefact.

Rachel Whiteread's masterpiece should survive in documentation and in the memories of those who saw it in its short physical life — as, for example, is the case with Christo's projects. Wouldn't it be nice were the demolition of *House* to be used as an excuse for fireworks and a party in the little park for the kids of the neighbourhood; perhaps the generous sponsors of the project might consider signing off their involvement in this way?

Yours sincerely,
PETER MERRY
Merstham,
Surrey,
15 November

The Independent, 15 Nov 93

Sculpture brings good luck to Bow

From Mr Tim Neilson

Sir: It is to be hoped that Bow Neighbourhood Council is beginning to realise, from the enormous amount of interest that has been generated by Rachel Whiteread's sculpture "House", what an extraordinary piece of good luck has befallen it.

Without commission, without cost and without a team of town planners, one of the most significant public sculptures of recent years has simply emerged in the council's brand new park. It is a once-in-a-lifetime gift that a thousand towns and cities across Europe would seize readily.

Yet, with undisguised relish, the chair of the Parks Board (Letters, 5 November) has indicated that the decision to demolish "House" will go ahead.

It hardly needs to be repeated that this is a major work — probably a masterpiece — by a young British artist (and Turner Prize nominee) with an impressive body of work behind her and a brilliant future ahead.

Bow Parks Board, with its excellent rejuvenation of Victoria Park, has already shown what it can do. Now, if it is bold, it has the chance to give the East End a landmark which would undoubtedly become a "must see" in every guidebook to London.

Yours sincerely,
TIM NEILSON
London, E9
12 November

From Cllr Eric Flounders

Sir: We will be brave, Mr Neilson (letter, 16 November), we will be brave! We will be brave enough to ignore the fusillade of froth from the arts lobby and remove the monstrosity as soon as the contract allows.

We have enough concrete in Bow already, and what we need is not more of it, but trees and grass. Those we will have.

As far as I am concerned, any of the "thousands of towns and cities across Europe" that Mr Neilson feels would love to have *House* are welcome to it.

Yours faithfully,
ERIC FLOUNDERS
Chair
Bow Parks Board
Bow Neighbourhood Council
London, E3
16 November

The Independent, 25 Nov 93

Timetable for Bow sculpture

From Cllr Eric Flounders

Sir: I take strong exception to Nigel Glendinning's suggestion (in his letter about Rachel Whiteread's *House*, 20 November) that I have abused my local authority office. The award of the Turner Prize to Ms Whiteread does not change any of the facts.

In March, the Bow Neighbourhood Committee, of which I am chair, endorsed the decision of the Bow Parks Board, of which I am also chair, to allow the Artangel Trust to take over the property in Grove Road so that Rachel Whiteread's "sculpture" could be created. At the same time it laid down a timetable by which the sculpture had to be removed and the site cleared. This timetable was adopted unanimously by the committee with no dissent of any kind, was accepted by Artangel, and was supported by the Neighbourhood's officers.

What I have done publicly ever since is promote and defend that evidently sensible decision by my committee with which I entirely agree. If defending committee decisions is abusing my local authority office, then, on reflection, I have been doing it for years.

For the record, the agreement Artangel signed stipulates that the structure should be removed by 31 October and the site completely cleared by 30 November. They are already in default of that agreement, so it is hardly surprising if I am being resolute about the final date.

Surely those like Mr Glendinning should not be whining about a local authority wishing to stick to a universally agreed contract, but should be grateful that this piece of experimental nonsense which they love so much was permitted to exist in the first place.

The antics of Artangel in failing to abide by the agreement, of course, will make this and other councils wary of such agreements in future.

Yours faithfully,
ERIC FLOUNDERS
Chair
Bow Standing Neighbourhood Committee
London, E3
24 November

Value of a house set in concrete

From Mr John Stathatos

Sir: Your leading article "A concrete idea well worth preserving" (3 November) urging the preservation of Rachel Whiteread's *House* was perceptive, for it has taken very few days for a consensus of informed opinion to emerge that *House* is perhaps the most impressive work of public art to appear in this country for many years.

I spent two hours or so on the site last Tuesday, and can testify to a steady stream of fascinated viewers, including a couple from Birmingham and a man who had travelled specially from Lyme Regis. Nor is support coming only from specialist visitors; about half the locals I spoke to were in favour of the work.

Bow council is to be commended for its imaginative support of Artangel; now that it finds itself with what is rapidly becoming a nationally famous monument on its hands, it should consider maintaining it in perpetuity. We tend to think of any public art not made of bronze or marble as essentially ephemeral, but the demolition of *House* after a mere four weeks would be a tragedy.

Perhaps not surprisingly, even those I spoke to who disliked the piece finished by commenting on the waste of money implicit in its destruction.

It would be nice if what began as a short-term project ended up, almost as it were accidentally, providing London with its first contemporary monument of lasting value.

Yours sincerely,
JOHN STATHATOS
London, N4
3 November

From Cllr Eric Flounders

Sir: Those poor, unsophisticated readers who share my view that Rachel Whiteread's concoction *House* is utter rubbish can rest assured that, despite the pleas of the *Independent*, the monstrosity will not remain in place beyond the end of November.

The Bow Neighbourhood Committee decided on a date for removal even before work began, in order that we can continue laying out a new park. This half-constructed park is, naturally, littered with bricks, bulldozers and half-demolished roads as work goes on. Your dismissal of it as merely "scruffy" leads me to wonder what sort of standards you have in municipal parks as well as in art.

Yours faithfully,
ERIC FLOUNDERS
Chair, Parks Board
Bow Neighbourhood Council
London, E3
4 November

The Independent, Various (letters page) 20 Nov 93

'House' fits the neighbourhood

From Mr David Coombs

Sir: In the perspective of the past, Rachel Whiteread's *House* has many of the characteristics of the best examples of public sculpture (Letters; "'House' should be demolished", 17 November). It is large, noticeable and controversial. In the particular context of a famous London residential neighbourhood, it is relevant, memorable and an uninhibited political statement.

The very attractive series of green parks now bounding much of the western edge of Grove Road, Bow, contain at least one other contemporary monument — the series of large wood carvings on Haverfield Green commemorating the great storm of 1987.

Whether *House* on the edge of Wennington Green is entirely appropriate for that site is arguable. While, for example, it cannot match the fine intrinsic quality of the metal railings that bound it, *House* is in its own way just as self-confident a statement as "Driftway", the splendid 19th-century historic building opposite.

However, I believe that the key to the present argument is much more basic in so far as, unlike the great public sculptures of the past, *House* may not be made to last; witness for example the many exposed wooden joists. Has anyone thought to ask the artist or her patrons?

Yours faithfully,
David Coombs
Editor
The Antique Collector
London, W1
18 November

From Mr Nigel Glendinning and others

Sir: Councillor Flounders has every right to express his personal dislike for Rachel Whiteread's *House* in your columns, but it seems an abuse of his local authority office for him to imply in his correspondence (Letters, 5 and 17 November) that he speaks for the Bow [parks] committees he chairs in this matter, and that he represents the views of the electors he is meant to serve. Mr Flounders refuses to allow appeals for a stay of execution on *House* to be formally discussed by the relevant neighbourhood bodies, showing scant regard for normal democratic procedures and the legitimate concerns of local residents.

Nobody knows exactly what the balance of local feeling is towards *House* at this juncture. Opinion is divided in Bow as it is nationally. But the response to the work's challenging presence is strong, and its power and validity are hotly debated.

We believe that our neighbourhood committees should recognise the considerable swell of public interest in Rachel Whiteread's work, in Bow as elsewhere, and delay demolition — originally set for the end of this month — for the time being.

Yours sincerely,
NIGEL GLENDINNING, ELTON BASH, JOHN BESFORD, SONJA BESFORD, JAMES BOWEN, JOAN GRIFFITHS, PATRICK HALL, MARIAN HOBSON JEANNERET, ELAINE KOWALSKY, LIZ MAUDSLAY, CAROL MORRIS, MONTY NELSON, LINDA PEARCE, VICTORIA POLAND, ALICE SIELLE, SANDRA SUDI, JEANNE WISEMAN
Bow
London, E3
19 November

Art house in a cul-de-sac

The judges of the Turner prize have ceased to appreciate the craft of creation

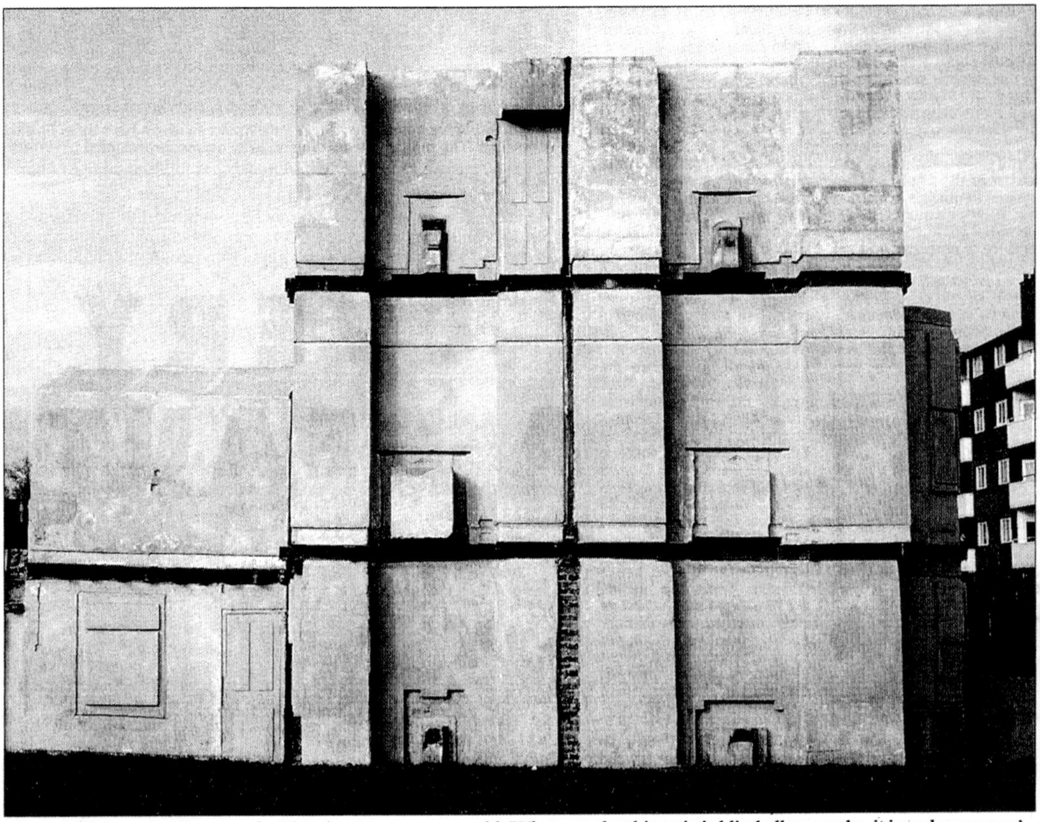

Rachel Whiteread's *House* used a Victorian terrace as a mould: 'Whatever else this artistic blind alley may be, it is no longer new'

Simon Jenkins

Go see it for yourself, cried the *Financial Times*. "Go to the junction of Grove Road and Roman Road in E 8", where stands "one of the only successful pieces of contemporary monumental sculpture" in London. Who could resist the call (even if the sculpture is really in E 3)? For this is November and Turner prize time. The winner is to be announced next Tuesday and work by the four shortlisted candidates is on show at the Tate.

Each year I go, I see, I yearn to be conquered. Here allegedly is the cream of new British art, chosen under the aegis of the Tate's austerely modernist director, Nicholas Serota. The prize entries, he declares, offer "new insights into the society and culture in which we live and share". Booker's novels, Swet's plays, Bafta's films make no such grandiloquent claims. Why, I wonder, does art have to talk so big? Can it not speak for itself? But even the loudest mouth deserves a hearing. So each year I make the effort. I try.

I fail. I feel a numbing sensation that what is on trial is me, not art. This year's shortlist comprises Sean Scully's abstract paintings, Hannah Collins's photographs, Vong Phaophanit's strips of neon light covered in rice, and Rachel Whiteread's structures, including the one in E 3. Of these, only Scully is a painter, albeit of coloured stripes. Collins is a photographer. Phaophanit and Whiteread are young people who have hit on simple ideas — putting neon in odd places and spraying concrete inside rooms — and executed them with some panache.

If there is talent, let alone genius, in all this then it must lie in the conception rather than the execution. The skills prized by the Turner judges are neither painterly nor plastic. The judges themselves are called art "professionals". Their chairman, Mr Serota himself, is clearly an opponent of the present revival of representational styles and subjects. While he is supported by a small group of critics, such as this paper's Richard Cork, others such as Giles Auty of *The Spectator* are out for his blood, not least for demeaning the name of Turner. The row is longstanding, if rather anaemic.

But back to east London. Whiteread's house is certainly worth a visit before its demolition next month. It is a memorial to a Victorian terrace that was inexplicably destroyed to create a small, fenced park. Whiteread secured a stay of execution on one property, sprayed its interior with concrete and knocked away the surrounding roof and walls. She has previously done this with cupboards, baths and a whole room, but this is her first house. The work is variously alleged to be "a statement about Thatcherism" and a "ghostly negative of reality".

We used to do such negatives at school. We called them not statements but moulds. This one is big and, illuminated at night, undeniably impressive. As requested, I pondered "the quiet, spiritual, poetic" qualities of the concrete as, in the *FT*'s words, it "exposed in a way no one has ever quite done before the spaces which shape our lives". Putting all thought of Vermeer and Cezanne out of mind, I concentrated hard on the concrete shape. With the best will in the world, its message was facile and fleeting.

Whiteread's house is what most would term a folly, a brutalist version of the picturesque structures that Pope and Walpole erected in their Twickenham gardens. It must have taken her time and effort, but then so does a grotto. By all means let it stay where it is, a cenotaph not to Thatcherism, but to the destructiveness of municipal socialism. But clothing it in the jargon of art criticism does it no service. Nor are Phaophanit's piles of neon-lit rice elevated by the claim that they "typify the meeting of east and west". The same could be said of a Toyota crashing into a Ford.

We must tread softly here, because we tread on strange dreams. A new novel or play can be discussed in an agreed language. They use English grammar to bid me marvel at their art. I can go into the street and argue whether Booker has picked the right winner or compare a Pinter with a Stoppard. When a writer says his work reflects Conrad and Faulkner, I understand what he means. When Sean Scully invokes the same inspiration for his stripes, as he does, I am defeated. Did the Turner judges nod sagely and say to each other, "Ah yes, Conrad and Faulkner"? Phaophanit's mounds of rice require no more artistry than my doodling in a sugar bowl. How can putting them in the Tate render them "an extraordinarily satisfactory marriage, rich and complex in both material effects and possibilities of meanings"? The obscurantism suggests a collapse of critical faculty. No other art form abuses language this way.

I sense that the Turner judges have forgotten what it is they are rebelling against, what they are supposed to be hating. They have adopted Duchamp's silly phrase "I do not believe in art, only artists", and assumed that it lets them off the hook of judgment. At the Tate, visitors giggle, embarrassed, in front of the works, like tourists accosted by a three-card trickster. They then cluster with relief round the video of the artists at work. The video is the art. A work has no meaning except when its creator, or a friendly critic, talks about it — and precious little then.

The Turner sponsor, Channel Four's Waldemar Januszczak, asks that we take the prize "properly and seriously". He complains that we have all "grown afraid of change". The implied challenge is reasonable. But the existence of a prize suggests judgment refined by competition. By sticking, year in year out, to the same conceptual coterie, the Turner judges protect their favourites from radical comparison. They also defeat their objective, which is supposedly to seek out the new. Whatever else this blind alley may be, it is no longer new.

Mr Serota presumably believes I have a brain lobe missing, that I suffer from a retarded aesthetic sensibility and cannot receive the subtle vibrations put out by his artists. I am Ruskin to his Whistler, gormless atavist to his innovator. When Whistler offered up his sublime creations, I would have dismissed them as so much thrown paint. What can I say, except I think not? I am a passionate Whistlerian: "Art should be independent of all claptrap, should stand alone and appeal to the artistic sense of eye or ear without confounding this with emotions entirely foreign to it."

I acknowledge this philosophy in Mr Serota's brilliant rehanging of the British pictures at the Tate. The longer I stand before these works, the more I love them. Yet I stand before his Turner prizewinners and am bored and irritated. Welling up within me is a conviction that while they may be sincere, they are massively banal. A mistake has been made. History will see the selectors not as neo-Whistlers but as neo-Dadaists, sponsoring a salon art that has lost all originality or charisma. They have simply walked away from the struggle.

Modernism should be hard. It should be taxing. I long for the Tate's new modern gallery to find a home and wish God-speed to its fundraisers. But something has gone terribly wrong with the Turner prize. An article in the Tate's own magazine discusses whether Turner in his own day would have won it, and concludes that he would have been pipped at the post by Lawrence. Neither would be on the Tate shortlist today: wrong style, wrong subject matter, wrong politics. George Eliot would win the Booker and Wordsworth would make Poet Laureate. But on Tuesday Britain's premier art prize will go to a folly.

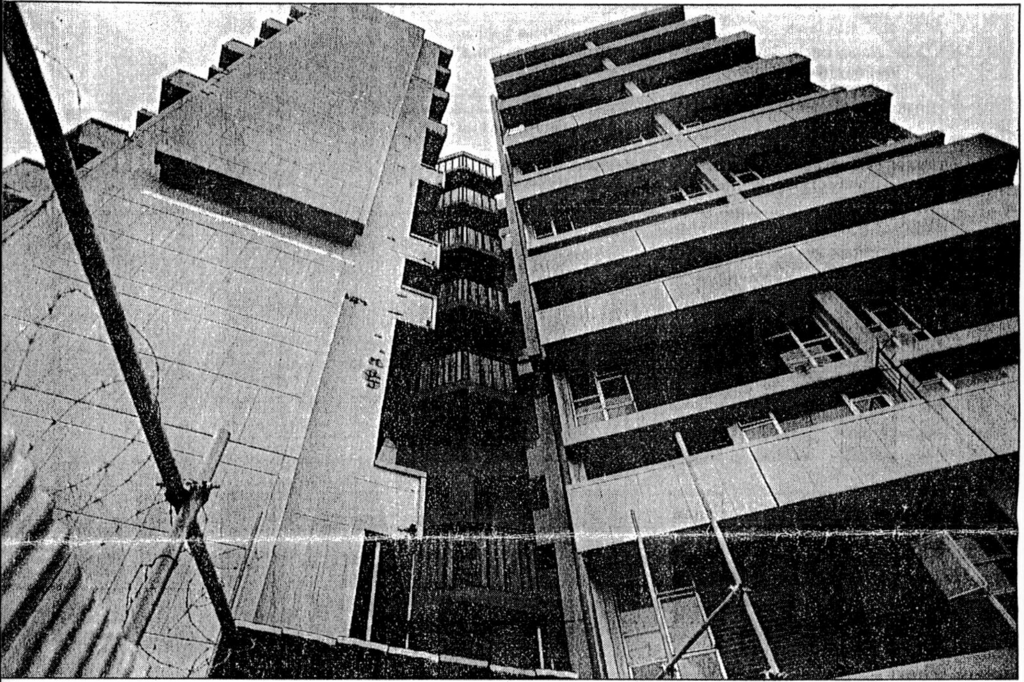

Worth saving? Keeling House, a derelict East End tower block

PHOTOGRAPH: FRANK MARTIN

Art
attack

be arts establishment found itself on e defensive this week when it gave the urner Prize to a concrete casting of a ouse (below). But who cares what the undits think? ***Deyan Sudjic reports***

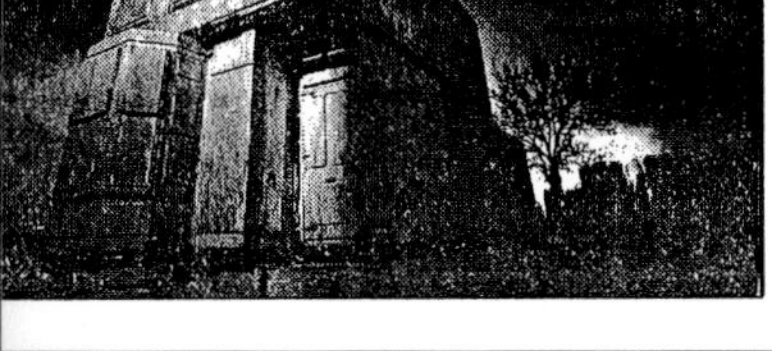

THE ABIDING image of this year's Turner Prize will not be the poignant, graffiti-scarred hulk of Rachel Whiteread's House, marooned in the swirling dereliction of the East End, nor even Vong Phaophanit's gently undulating rice dunes inside the Tate.

The picture that really grabbed hold of the zeitgeist, and which will stay in the memory long after the dust of demolition settles, was the grim sight of Peter Palumbo, handing Whiteread her cheque at the Tate on Tuesday night. His face white and sweaty, vainly trying to appear martial, he looked for all the world like the late Salvador Allende in his tin helmet, clutching his assault rifle on the steps of the presidential palace as Pinochet's tanks swept him from power. Here was a man who looked to be in the grip of a palpable sense of paranoia, his eyes rolling and haunted as he addressed the Turner Prize audience that clearly felt, like him, that it was trapped in a bunker surrounded by hostile forces.

"Don't let the dunces have their day," he said in an attempt to clinch his defence of avant-garde art but with a scarcely credible lack of judgment. This was not a speech of triumph, nor the celebration of a young artist's achievements, but the grim realisation that the barbarians were at the gate. In the case of Tower Hamlets, where the bulldozers are revving up to flatten House, literally so.

Slow and ponderous, Palumbo seemed to know even as he spoke that he was looking failure in the face. His words were ostensibly an attempt to rally the troops, but he looked more as if he was leading the rush for the fall-out shelter. He had allowed himself to be forced lamely on to the defensive. The dunces were dictating the terms of the discussion.

Yet it is perfectly obvious that there are other ways to make art than through the use of representational paint on canvas. And that emotional responses to mute concrete or tricksy image manipulation are just as possible as they are to what is now accepted as mainstream art, but which was — from Giotto to Cezanne — equally challenging, disturbing and disruptive in its own day.

Perhaps the Turner Prize could handle routine local authority philistinism, but the heavy-handed Magic Christian mockery of the KLF, the group of rock biz pranksters who doubled the prize money with an award for what they called the worst artist of the four on the shortlist, seemed to be too much for the Prize's fragile sense of purpose. The equilibrium of its greatest defender had cracked.

As if to underscore the message that avant-garde culture in Britain is an elitist plot aimed at taking the country for a ride, it became known with perfect timing on the same night that officials from Peter Brooke's heritage department had stepped in to list Keeling House, a derelict 1950s tower block in the East End, the work of Sir Denys Lasdun, architect of the National Theatre. The move was greeted with carefully orchestrated howls of derision that were curiously reminiscent of those that accompanied the unveiling of Rachel Whiteread's House. Assuming that the kind of people who see virtues in austere architecture from the middle period of the career of a heavyweight architect, and those who are prepared to take on art that refuses to limit itself to three-point perspective, have something in common, what seemed to be unravelling was a whole cultural consensus. The comfortable domination of the definition of what constitutes good and bad in art and architecture that people like Palumbo have effortlessly enjoyed for two generations seemed as if it was coming apart over the dinner tables at the Tate. Modern art was incomprehensible, modern architecture uninhabitable.

For one moment, this really looked as if it might be a genuine turning point, a watershed in which nerves finally cracked and what might be called the Prince of Wales view of culture swept triumphantly on from the beach-head it had established in architecture into other areas too. It was nonsense of course. Palumbo's speech was the product of a very particular, and somewhat overheated, set of circumstances. A moment's reflection makes it perfectly clear that to get something out of art, as much as to make sense of darts, or cricket, at least a fleeting grip on the rules of the game is required. To put this across, there is no need for the defenders of the avant-garde to lapse into paranoia and abuse.

Nor is the Turner Prize the benchmark of the avant-garde. Rather it is one particular view of what art can be.

In one sense, the reactions to the attacks on the Turner Prize are not a little hysterical: the point of avant-garde art since the 19th century has been in part to provoke, to upset, and to twist the tail of the establishment. Now the roles seem to have been reversed: what was once the avant-garde has turned into the establishment consensus, and it was having its tail twisted. To judge by the look on Palumbo's face, it didn't like it one little bit.

But if art really is meant to provide a sense of otherness in a materialistic culture, then why should artists and their champions feel as if something has gone wrong when they succeed in their complacency-shaking activities?

In fact this division between high culture, and low, or between avant-garde and popular taste is by no means as clear cut as the propagandists for traditionalism would have us believe. Despite the Alf Garnett performances of Tower Hamlets Liberal Democrats, spitting bile and venom, who persist in seeing House as a slap in the face for their constituents, Whiteread's work has already transformed the way a lot of people who have never set foot in a gallery see the mundane street in which it stands. They may not know exactly what it means — and Whiteread probably doesn't either. But it does have a presence, it does seem to suggest that there are other aspects to life than the everyday struggle for survival.

House has in fact already entered the everyday visual currency that shapes the way we see the world, just as much as the famous Carl Andre bricks, or Boy George or Punk — all once the subject of horrified outrage, and all quickly co-opted into mainstream sensibility, to be recycled as knowing, sly jokes, to appear as the inspiration for the imagery of advertising, to be used as seasonings to the blandness of everyday life.

Magritte, Duchamp, Fontana and many others have already provided the starting points for cigarette advertising campaigns. Their apparently enigmatic images clearly do have a power to reach people outside the elite.

And, as the less than convincing experience of the Prince of Wales's attempt to harness militant architectural populism has shown, it is by no means safe to assume that the remarkably visually literate British do not know when they are being patronised by those who assume that they are incapable of getting the point of culture that is challenging.

By the standards of art that sets out deliberately to offend, Whiteread's House is pretty tame stuff. This is not Jeff Koons caught in flagrante, or a Serrano-style hymn to bodily fluids.

The idea that people confronted with it might not begin to understand that the point is to produce some sort of emotional response that might have something to do with the sense of absence, of sadness, of transience and that this cannot be understood by large numbers of people, is as insulting as the idea that anybody will fail to feel the emotional pull of, say, Le Corbusier.

In fact, the avant-garde has shown a remarkable robustness and longevity. Given the chance, a surprising range of people do indeed get to understand that there is a wider range of flavours to savour than the instant gratification of saccharine sweetness. People do, given the chance, get to understand that difficult things can be worthwhile. Remember the much-publicised disgust which greeted the arrival of Impressionism in the National Gallery in the 1960s with the purchase of a Cezanne that was denounced as obscene and a crude daub. Or, for that matter, the howl of protest that greeted the Eiffel Tower.

Of course the idea of the artist as a critic of society, providing an outsider's view, is a relatively recent one: based on a romantic 19th century idea. It was a deliberate attempt to create an elevated sense of status, to present artists not as the quattrocento tradesmen who had happily contracted to paint specified numbers of figures, who had set up semi-industrialised production lines, calling in specialists to work on hands, and collars, but as a quite different breed who would see their artistic integrity compromised by the slightest truck with the preferences of their customers. And in a curious way, it is perhaps Whiteread's most impressive achievement that she has managed to put art back into the street.

Daily Telegraph, Garland, 25 Nov 93

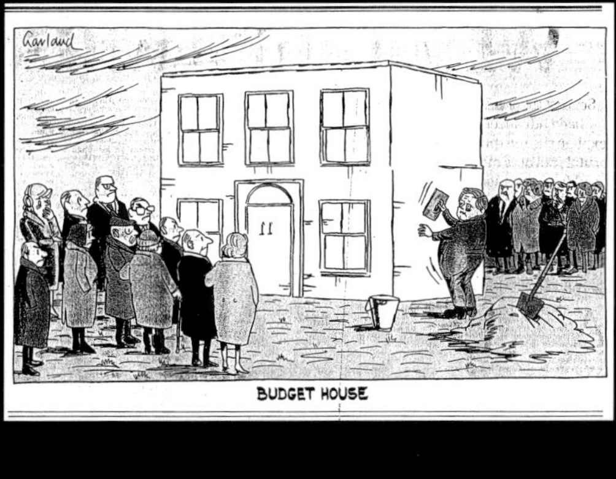

The Independent, 27 Nov 93

More time for 'House'

From Mr Tim Dickenson

Sir: Cllr Eric Flounders' decision to enforce the deadline for the removal of Rachel Whiteread's sculpture may be within the law, but his comments (Letters, 25 November) typify how inflexible the committee he chairs can be.

Under regular planning law, what is to prevent an extension of the deadline set by the original agreement so that more people can view this innovative work? Perhaps Cllr Flounders should remember that the Eiffel Tower was supposed to have been pulled down. It's hardly done Paris any harm.

Yours faithfully,
TIM DICKENSON
Bow and Poplar
Conservative Association
London, E14

The Times, *Editorial*, 22 Nov 93

REWARDING ART

Modern art is meant to open new windows not close old minds

Tomorrow Lord Palumbo, the chairman of the Arts Council, will announce the winner of this year's Turner Prize. Channel 4 will show a film illustrating the work of the four artists on the short list. And a hubbub of incomprehension, ridicule, rage and envy will break out from campaigning zealots of the art world. Phone-in pundits and headline-writers of the "Is it art, or is it rubbish?" school of journalism, who have not always taken the trouble to look for long at the works on view, will add their pennyworths. And so, as usual, the prize will have achieved its purpose of promoting discussion of developments in contemporary British art.

Rachel Whiteread, on this year's short-list, has one of her building sculptures standing for a few more days in the East End of London. Her cast of the inside of a Victorian terrace house has since had its outer shell demolished around it, leaving a haunting ghost of domestic past frozen in time — or a load of old concrete, according to taste. Taste as well as technique and tradition define a work of art; and there is no legislating for tastes. Splashes of pale green and yellow on the walls of Whiteread's *House* are spectral reminders of the wallpaper that used to decorate the rooms before they were translated into conceptual art.

As the most famous critic of the day wrote: "Wallpaper in its embryonic state is more finished than that seascape." But that was in 1874, and he was referring to *Impression: Sunrise* by Claude Monet. For years Monet and his friends had to put on their own exhibitions in an unfashionable studio because they were rejected by the Paris Salon, the arbiter of established taste. They too were savaged with incomprehension and ridicule. But they opened the public's eyes to new ways of looking at the world: Monet's rejected painting eventually gave its name as eponym to the Impressionists.

Turner's name is taken in vain by critics of the prize named after him. But when he was elected the youngest Royal Academician in 1803, his unconventional modern art was dismissed by many as decadent and unrealistic. And 40 years later some temperamentally blindfold critics were still suggesting that he had gone mad, because of the violence of his colour and the increasing vagueness of his form. Traditionalists complained when the Dutch started painting realistic bourgeoisie instead of stylised saints. No doubt vested interests were complaining a hundred centuries ago about the modernist switch from conformist representation of animals hieroglyphs.

A safe and uncontentious prize for contemporary art is an oxymoron. Artists, who must work with imagination as well as traditional skills, are the visionary scouts and dangerous vanguards for the rest of mankind. Their work is too important to be defined by the past or shanghaied by any gang of temporarily correct critics. It must be seen and judged by their contemporaries — and the future.

The Independent, 29 Nov 93

Private prejudice, public interest and Bow's 'House'

From Mr James Lingwood

Sir: Once more, Eric Flounders conflates private prejudice with public interest (Letters, 25 November). The decision by the Bow Neighbourhood Committee, on his casting vote, not to allow Rachel Whiteread's *House* a briefly longer life takes no account of the prodigious interest this sculpture has generated. Only last weekend more than 3,000 people signed a petition on site in only 12 hours. Many of these were not representatives of the "chattering classes" whom Mr Flounders acknowledges may be interested, but people who live and work locally.

We do not deny that Artangel agreed that the site should be cleared by today. However, our agreement also implied that the work would be visible for a period of about three months. We had hoped to begin work at the beginning of June. For reasons beyond both Artangel's and Rachel Whiteread's control, we did not gain access to the vacated property until August. Given the several false starts we had suffered, our specialist contractors could not begin until September.

All that Artangel had requested from Bow Neighbourhood Committee was an extension to compensate for the loss of time at the beginning. Then the sculpture would come down. We believe that this was, and remains, an extremely modest request. To turn it down places iconoclasm and intolerance before genuine local and national interest.

Yours faithfully,
JAMES LINGWOOD
Co-Director
Artangel
London, W1
29 November

From Mr Richard Shone

Sir: Eric Flounders' letter (25 November) shows a Gradgrindian adherence to the facts of the commission and a Pecksniffian attitude to the spirit of its execution. The supposedly objective tenor of his letter is called into question by his expressed dislike of the work itself. He calls it "this piece of experimental nonsense": *House* could not be further from an experiment.

As with all her work, Rachel Whiteread's initial conception was carried through to its foreseen conclusion and shows no signs of trial or uncertainty. Nor can I see how it could be called "nonsense" when it is so potent in its allusions to public and private life, to memory and materiality, fact and poetic evocation, embodied in a form that is immediately accessible. It is an oustanding work of our time.

If there is anything experimental about *House*, it was the Bow Parks Board's decision (admirable in itself) to allow it to be erected. But it appears, from the evidence of the vote for demolition taken on 23 November, that the board is unable to deduce the right conclusion from its experiment: that it has worked triumphantly.

Yours faithfully,
RICHARD SHONE
Associate Editor
The Burlington Magazine
London, WC1

The Guardian, 22 Nov 93

Home truths

ANNA BLUNDY asks passers-by what they think of that House:

MR GAMMER, a retired computer programmer from Hampshire: **I'd say it was worth the prize money she won. I'd tip in a penny of my Council Tax any day. I don't think it's social comment, it's an abstract puzzle. I like the positive and negative relief of it. I wouldn't say everyone agrees with me though — a lorry driver just shouted at me, 'It's the biggest piece of shit I've ever seen.' Definitely worth the trip I think: it's fascinating.**

BEN, a cleaner on a nearby council estate: **You'd have to be a really lonely person to sit around and bother to think up something like that. It's an eyesore. All that time and money . . .**

DAVID, a local resident: **It's crap, isn't it? Give me £20,000 and I'll show you some art. When they pull it down I reckon I'll come along and give them a hand.**

PHILIP JOSEPH, a bus driver, who lives opposite: **It's very impressive, a lovely piece of art. A good thought. I hope they don't take it down — we could set up a stall selling tea and everything.**

HENRY DALY, a local builder: **It reminds me of when we were kids. It's a statement of how things used to be. I grew up in a house like that. I expect she [Whiteread] has a different interpretation, but it's how you see it isn't it? It's like going to the moon.**

The Guardian,, 25 Nov 93

Politicians who give no House room to art

Commentary

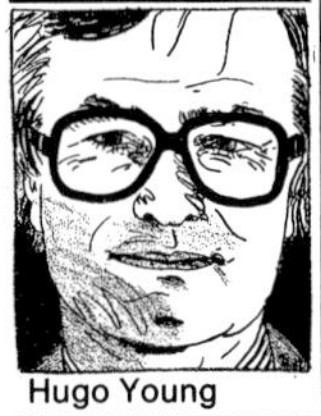

Hugo Young

MOST artists in this country scorn politicians. Few politicians have any serious time for art, or even the arts. It is a relationship shot through with derision, and sometimes hatred. Now this attitude finds its policy, and its emblem.

In the East End of London, Rachel Whiteread's architectural sculpture, House, has been voted into destruction. House is a modern masterpiece. In it an ingenious idea is realised with great evocative power. Taking a derelict dwelling, Whiteread has turned it inside out by casting the interior in liquid concrete then removing the bricks. What is left is a monument to past domesticity, a coarse yet intricate edifice, alone in the space it once occupied with a hundred similar residences. It satisfies contemplative as well as aesthetic taste. Once seen, it makes you look at all houses in a new way.

On Tuesday night the Bow standing neighbourhood committee voted to pull House down. Six politicians, all Liberal Democrats, took the decision on the casting vote of the chairman, Cllr Eric Flounders. As an artefact of modern art, House, although puzzling, is among the most accessible. It arrests the eye and the mind. But Cllr Flounders, a man apparently not without the outward signs of education, called it "excrescent", and "a monstrosity", from the moment it was unveiled last month. He was determined to expunge it from Tower Hamlets at the earliest moment.

More telling than the vote, however, was the extremely modest request which it overrode. This was not that House should stand for ever. The limited life of the excrescence was contractually prescribed from the start. What disappeared this week was merely a stay of demolition until January. It seems to have been inconceivable to either the artist, or her sponsor, Artangel, that this structure, once created, might deserve indefinite preservation. They were just pathetically grateful for their chance. The notion that House might improve Mile End Park, or that, once emerging from experimental darkness into the light of widespread acclamation, its fate might be reviewed, was beyond the imagination of anyone in the art world, let alone the political. "A park is a park", the Lib Dems said, and the work just disappears.

Such routine philistinism, however, does not belong to Tower Hamlets alone, or the Liberal Democrats. Cllr Flounders speaks from the heart of the body politic in all its grim bipartisanship. The massive cut in next year's national arts budget comes straight out of the Whitehall school that believes in equality of misery for all, with the caveat that some are less equal than others. At the bottom of this is an attitude to culture of which the vandalism in Tower Hamlets, unremarked as far as I know by a single politician high or low, is but a congruent instance.

This attitude begins with the personal. Not everything in politics is determined by the personal. A great deal of the next public spending round is more mechanical than discretionary, though this time the proposed assault on welfare digs up ministers' personal prejudices more than usual. But as to arts spending, the questions are essentially personal. How central do you believe culture is to the health of the country? How much more willing are you to see massive overspending on rip-off motorway contractors than minimal public sustenance for the arts? How hard will your personal commitment induce you to fight for a vibrant cultural life?

We know rather little about the cultural predispositions of the present Cabinet, but I will attempt a synthesis. They begin, I think, with an infirm belief in the place of public culture at all. The right would like to eliminate public subsidy altogether, the rest would like to feel the heritage is being preserved at the lowest possible expense. Neither group likes a fuss, but if the fussing can be stigmatised as an emanation of the chattering classes then its serious purpose can be politically neutralised. If culture can be fitted into the matrix of the economic ideology — as a tourist-booster, a customer-maximiser, a bottom-line-in-the-black exemplar — it may make a more acceptable call on public funds, although in the current assault even the passing of those tests is no guarantee of survival. Culture is vaguely good for national prestige. The Tories wouldn't like to preside over a wasteland. But the more this can be kept at bay by private money the better.

The personal cultural habits of ministers start with the absence of time to take any culture seriously. Mr Portillo, like Mr Major's wife, is known to be keen on opera. Mr Hurd plainly has time to read, as well as write, some books. Mr Heseltine has his trees and Mr Gummer goes to church. Mr Brooke reveals the traces of a classical education. There have been ministers recognisably possessed of cultural passion. But the names of Stevas, Gowrie, Patten (C) and Ridley have long since gone missing. Far better represented are overworked political obsessives who are unlikely to make space to go to a movie, let alone visit a challenging exhibition. As a serious follower of modern painting, Richard Ryder, the chief whip, is wholly eccentric.

So the median cultural stance of the people in charge of the cultural budget would appear, on all available evidence, to veer between negligent and hostile. They think they're doing us a favour by allocating any money at all. As for promoting an open-minded attitude to the nature of art, almost no politician in any party can be relied on. The idea that art must innovate, still less that it might dare to offend, is one that most politicians, if they ever address the question, are incapable of accepting. To the always urgent problem of distinguishing between pretentious trash and real creative excitement, they make no contribution. And yet they have great influence, which goes beyond the budgetary. They make room for the Queen Elizabeth Gate, a tinselly kitsch embarrassment nailed for ever into the heart of London, but see House destroyed without a blink, righteously declaring, if asked, that green spaces must be saved from artistic defilement.

"We must let the artist fail", said Lord Palumbo, in an eloquent little speech before awarding Rachel Whiteread the Turner Prize. More, the artist must surely be let to live when she has succeeded. In Britain, philistine revelling underpins niggardly public provision. It wouldn't happen in France, where politics has fathered great cultural boldness. It doesn't happen in Germany, where the political class has a secure hold on the connection between money for the arts and contentment for the nation. Only in Britain do politicians, as a conscious act, while resentfully putting up with artists, actually disdain the purpose of art.

From Bauhaus to that House: G2.

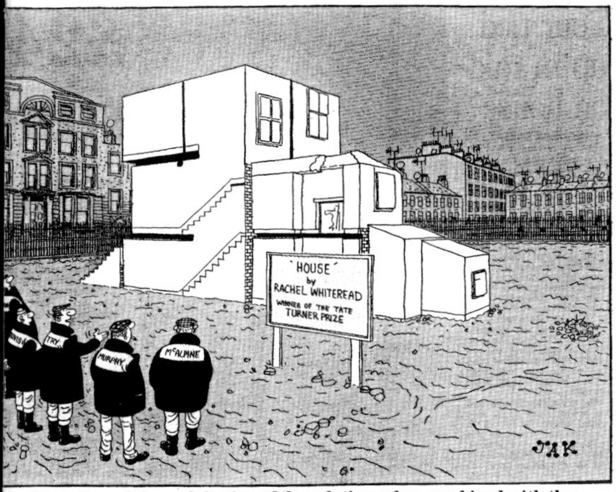

"Note the subtle exploitation of the relative value, combined with the juxtaposition of pure form in relation to. . . !"

Jak's Year 1993 is now available from all good bookshops, priced £3.99

Sunday Times, 5 Dec 93

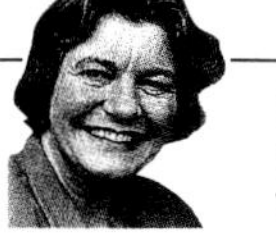

LYNN BARBER'S WEEK

House calls

Have spent the week living in a weird and wonderful fantasy — being Lord Goodman. I had visions of myself as a fixer in the corridors of power, quietly "putting in a word" here and calling in old favours there. I would do it all discreetly, and for the best of all causes — the cause of Art.

It all started last Sunday morning when I went to see Rachel Whiteread's House, in Bow, east London. It was a staggeringly cold day; the Bomb could have dropped, so deserted were the streets. And then I came to Grove Road and the scrubby open space with the strange concrete house which speaks so eloquently of the preciousness of private lives. Someone had graffito-ed on the house Wot for? to which someone else had graffito-ed Why Not? But the main point was that on this freezing glum Sunday morning, the house was surrounded by a field full of folk, all chatting, arguing, laughing, and urging one another to sign the petition. This was to stop Tower Hamlets demolishing the house on Wednesday and to get a six weeks' stay of execution. Well, why not?

Then — this is where my personal Lord Goodman fantasy started — I noticed that the petition was addressed to Eric Flounders, leader of the Bow Neighbourhood Committee. Now it happens that Eric is a friend. We met on a press trip to Brazil a few years ago, and have lunched regularly ever since. So I thought I'd just ring him in a Lord Goodman-ish way and say, "Look here, old bean, I know you don't care for this arty-farty rubbish," — Eric is a Yorkshireman — "but you mustn't demolish that house." And then Eric would say "Fine" and I'd have done my bit for Art. So I rang him and started my spiel and he said, "Oh, not you, too. Bugger off."

What would Lord Goodman do? He would not give up. It occurred to me that it was time to remind Eric of at least one favour I had done him (the soft approach) and if necessary move on to the hard approach of reminding him that I had photographs of him in Brazil that he might not care to see in the public prints. I would butter him up with a good lunch first, then ply him with brandy and raise the matter of the House. This scheme foundered when (a) Eric said he didn't drink at lunchtime and (b) launched into a great tirade about how he wished the council had never agreed to let Artangel (Whiteread's sponsors) use the site, and how unfair it was of them to renege on their agreement to clear it by November 30. Also, he said, he was thoroughly sick of busybodies like me who'd never even been to Bow sticking their noses in local affairs. At this, I became heated and used words such as "Philistine", "pig ignorant" and "fascist", which I suspect are not in Lord Goodman's vocabulary. We ended the lunch on thoroughly bad terms and stomped off our separate ways.

On Tuesday, I decided to switch tacks and rang Karsten Schubert, Rachel Whiteread's agent. He said they were very upset about the council's attitude because people were coming from all over the world to see the house. Artangel had offered to pay the council £7,500 to rent the site for a further six weeks (the council has no plans for it beyond planting a shrubbery), but had not yet had a reply. Although Milton Keynes had offered to take the House, Whiteread didn't want to move it because it was "site-specific", but, on the other hand, nor did she want to leave it up for ever because "contemporary sculptors are quite wary of permanent structures — the curse of Henry Moore and all that".

On Wednesday, I rang Eric to ask what time the bulldozers were moving in. "Oh, not today," he said, sunny as a gambolling lamb. "We'll let it stay till Christmas at least." But — what happened? "The Artangel people are not being as unreasonable as I thought. I've had a charming letter from Mrs Saatchi, a woman who really knows how to approach these matters. It's so nice to know that someone appreciates our local problems — not like you high-handed media types, who just barge in getting up everyone's noses." Another fantasy bites the dust.

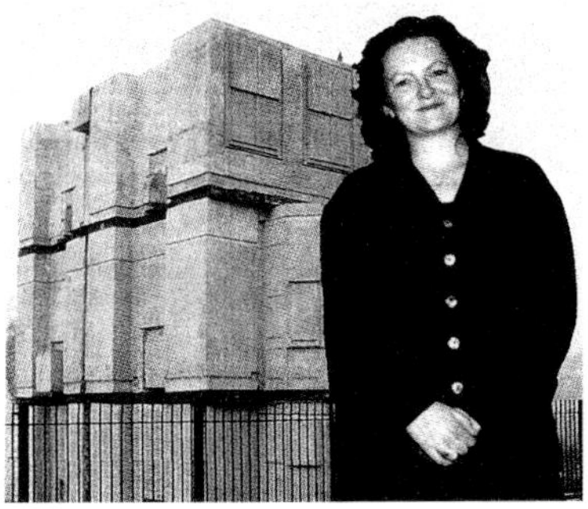

Whiteread: a Turner for the books

OBSERVER

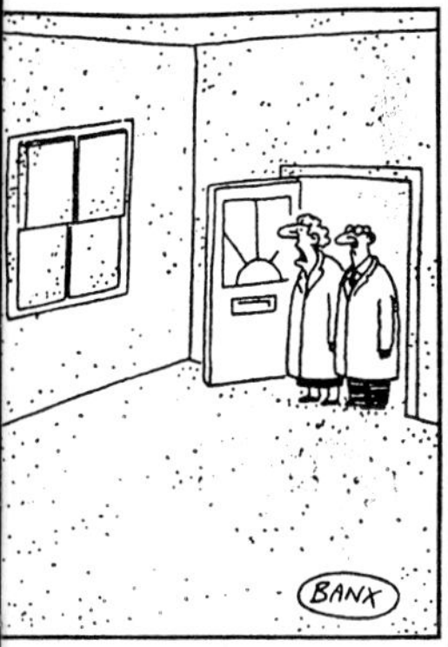

'Oh no! We've had artists'

The Independent, 29 Nov 93

Monumental art

From Ms Marjorie Allthorpe-Guyton

Sir: Rachel Whiteread's *House* has captured the imagination of 500-800 visitors daily. They leave with the image of a work of art they will not forget. It was indeed generous of Bow Standing Neighbourhood Committee to allow *House* to be made (Letters, 25 November). It would be even more public-spirited for members to allow it to remain a few weeks so that others could see it.

House was not intended to be a monument but it has become *monumental*. Relatively few people outside the art world see much work by Turner Prizewinners. We owe it to them and to the artist to persuade Councillor Flounders and his colleagues to reconsider their decision. They have nothing to lose, perhaps everything to gain.

Yours faithfully,
M. ALLTHORPE-GUYTON
Director of Visual Arts
The Arts Council of Great Britain
London, SW1
26 November

East London Advertiser, 13 Jan 94

Rachel Whiteread's controversial sculpture finally bites the dust

Bringing the House down

THE controversial House sculpture finally bowed out this week as it was razed to the ground.

Artist Rachel Whiteread grimaced as a bulldozer ploughed through her Turner Award-winning sculpture on Tuesday.

The concrete cast in Grove Road, Bow, which was unveiled on October 25 last year, had become the talk of the East End.

And reactions were mixed as House finally bit the dust.

Asked if it was a sad day for her, Rachel Whiteread said: "I'm not sure really. Yes, I suppose it's sad."

But it was happy days for two people living opposite the sculpture who are fed up with the crowds eager to see the sculpture every weekend.

Theatre producer Robert Warner said: "I find the sculpture interesting, but it's in the wrong place.

"Every weekend we have had arrogant people taking photos and blocking the road."

Joe Cullen, charged with demolishing House with a mechanical digger, was also unimpressed. "It's just a block of concrete really," he said. Scores

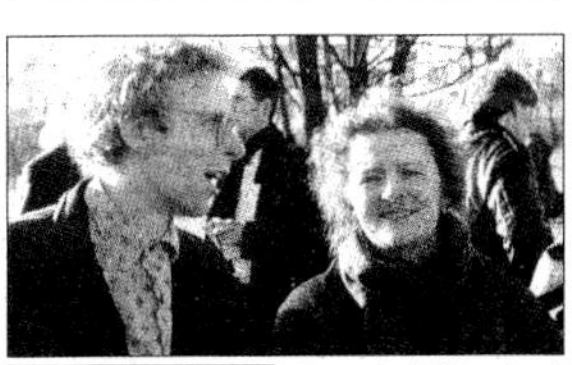

BY ULLA KLOSTER

of papparazzi trained their cameras on Joe started work at 10am.

The cast of the outside loo was first to give in.

He then worked his way through the kitchen and the spare bedroom till the front room of pensioner Sid Gale's former home was destroyed.

In less than two hours one of the most controversial pieces of art in Britain in years was reduced to a pile of rubbish.

The piece had attracted thousands of visitors since it went up in October.

Even Heritage Secretary Peter Brooke made a one-minute visit in his chauffeur driven Rover during a private visit to the East End recently.

The site will be grassed over as part of a government plan to extend Mile End Park.

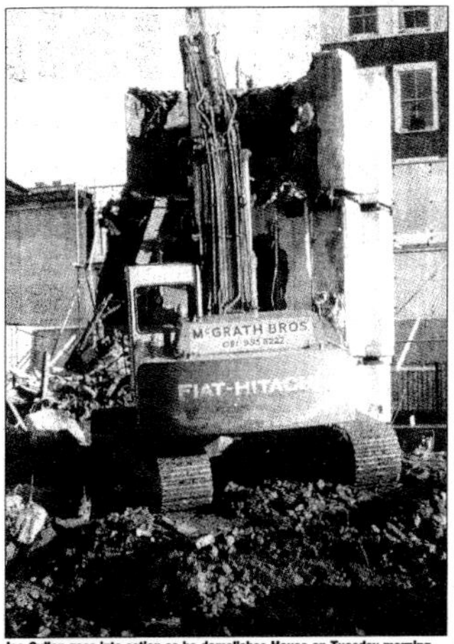

Joe Cullen goes into action as he demolishes House on Tuesday morning

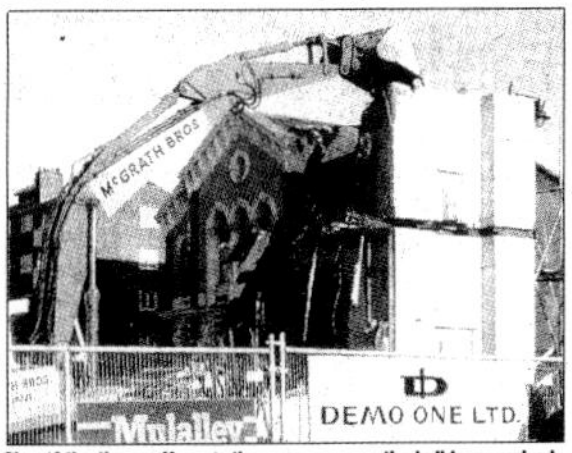

Sign of the times - House's time was up once the bulldozer arrived

I used to live there, but it's all over now

AS the House sculpture came crashing this week so did the celebrity status of East End war hero Sid Gale.

The ex-docker has been the main critic of the controversial 'inside out' cast of his childhood home in Grove Road, Bow.

Sid, who has moved to Kenilworth Road, has appeared in newspapers and on television here and abroad.

Strangers have stopped him in the street and pointed to him when he was out shopping.

The 71-year-old first appeared in the Advertiser in January last year as he fought Bow Neighbourhood's plans to turn his terraced home into park land.

Sid refused to leave even though bulldozers were knocking down neighbouring homes.

Since then fellow bus travellers turned their thumbs up and gave him encouraging winks.

But he shot to fame after the Advertiser revealed his home was to be turned into a concrete cast by a Hackney artist. In a fury he said: "They are taking the wee wee out of me."

And when the piece helped artist Rachel Whiteread win the top Turner Prize of £20,000 and a booby prize worth £40,000, journalists from all over the world wanted him to talk to him.

He said: "Oh it definitely does something to you. People in the paper shop were pointing to me, it's nice. I could have made a fortune this morning giving interviews."

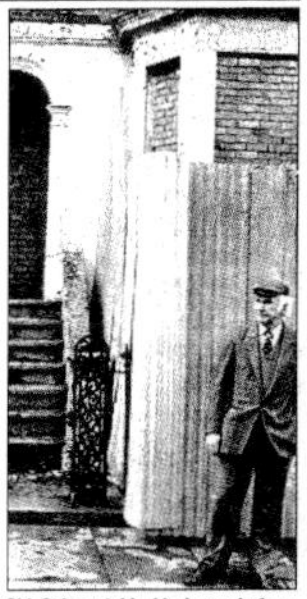

Sid Gale outside his home before it was demolished

'House' raises questions of art

From Sir Anthony Caro

Sir: I delayed writing in support of Rachel Whiteread's *House* because I felt sure that Bow council would finally have the sense to let it stay. This work is one of the best forward-looking pieces of monumental sculpture that I have seen in years, and to my delight it has been recognised as something special by large numbers of visitors.

For the council to be determined to pull it down is philistine. Not only philistine but short-sighted. This sculpture puts the new park at Bow on the map. How sad that the councillors cannot realise the advantages — practical as well as spiritual — of having such an example of living culture right on their doorstep.

Yours faithfully,
ANTHONY CARO
London, NW3
30 November

From Mr Peter Forster

Sir: Rachel Whiteread's *House* is one of those rare works of art that unexpectedly touches the nerve of the public. It could be described as a cenotaph commemorating ordinary working-class lives and deaths; and its situation, in a new east London green space, is infinitely more appropriate than, say, the superior neighbourhood of the Tate Gallery.

If *House* is demolished, not all will be lost. Some enterprising public or private body (my money is on Scotland) will surely offer Ms Whiteread another similar house as the matrix for a permanent memorial. The demolition of the sculpture may be only a local tragedy, felt deeply by people, like myself, who live and work in the district; but it may have wider implications. Councillor Flounders' exultantly philistine bravado is, as your recent leading article ("Putting public gain above private prejudice", 26 November) reminds us, "illiberal".

Would it be only a minor local tragedy if the fate of Ms Whiteread's *House* at the hands of a Liberal Democrat council, two of its fingers raised in the face of public opinion (so soon after those Tower Hamlets Liberal Democrat election leaflets), persuades people like me, whose Liberal Democrat vote in a two-party system is essentially "a curse on both your houses", to shrug our shoulders and not vote at all in the spirit of "a curse on all your houses"?

Yours faithfully,
PETER FORSTER
London, N4

house press
July 1993-April 1994

September 93

2-16 **Tower Hamlet News**, *Sculptor's new lease of life for old house*

Art and Design, James Hall, *British Art Now*

October 93

Tatler, Celia Lyttelton, *Ghost Story*

24 **Independent on Sunday**, Jan Dalley, *The World Turned Inside Out*

24 **Sunday Telegraph**, John McEwen, *The house that Rachel unbuilt*

24 **The Independent**, Dalya Alberge, *House of Ghostly Memory*

27 **Time Out**, Sarah Kent, *Home Work*

28 **East London Advertiser**, Ulla Kloster, *There's a stoney house!*

28 **Evening Standard**, Jeff Postlewaite, *Inside-out 'art' turned my home into freak show*

28 **East London Advertiser**, Richard Tidiman, *When a house is not a home*

29 **Building Design**, Kester Rattenbury, *Internal Affairs .....*

29 **New Builder**, Helena Russell, *Reverse Images*

31 **The Observer**, William Feaver, *Tired Turner needs a Tonic*

31 **Sunday Telegraph**, Catherine Milner, *Turn Off Turner*

31 **Independent on Sunday**, Varied, *Is this art?*

November 93

2 **The Independent**, Andrew Graham-Dixon, *This is the house that Rachel built*

2 **Financial Times**, Antony Thorncroft, *Down but not out*

3 **The Independent**, *A concrete idea well worth preserving*

3 **The Architects' Journal**, *Astragal*

3 **The Independent**, Colin Wheeler *(cartoon)*

3-10 **Time Out**, Kipper Williams, *The Lady & The Wimp (cartoon)*

4 **The Guardian**, James Hall, *I can't go on, but ...*

4 **Evening Standard**, Brian Sewell, *Ballyhoo and the glittering Prize*

4 **East London Advertiser**, Ulla Kloster, *'If that is art then I'm Leonardo da Vinci!'*

4 **East London Advertiser**, Various (letter), *Concrete Art is Hard going*

5 **The Scotsman**, William Cook, *Prize opportunity to learn a new language*

5 **The Independent**, John Stathatos, Eric Flounders (letters), *Value of a House Set in Concrete*

5 **The Times**, Richard Cork, *Monuments to a great adventure*

5 **Daily Express**, *Bringing the House down*

6-7 **Financial Times**, Lynn MacRitchie, *House that Rachel built*

7 **Sunday Telegraph**, *How not to prize art*

7 **Financial Times**, Christian Tyler, *Shedding light on the paddy fields of art*

7 **Independent on Sunday**, *Rachel Whiteread: an apology*

7 **Independent on Sunday**, Cal McCrystal, *Is This Worth all the Sneers*

8 **Newsline**, A guest reviewer, *The Turner Prize 1993*

8 **Sunday Times**, Waldemar Januszczak

10 **Daily Telegraph**, Stephen Pile, *Are the old masters really any better?*

10 **The Independent**, Gordon Burn, *Why so hard to swallow?*

10 **Inside Housing**, *Art Class*
10-17 **Time Out**, David Lillington, *Turner overdrive*
10-17 **Time Out**, *Concrete bungle*
11-24 **Tower Hamlets News and East End Life**
11 **The Independent**, Dr Virginia Button, *Right of Reply*
12 **New Statesman & Society**, Sue Hubbard, *The colour of memory*
13-14 **Financial Times**, William Packer, *An open race for also-rans*
13 **The Spectator**, Giles Auty, *Whiff of Paint*
14 **Sunday Times Magazine**, Louisa Buck, *Rachel Whiteread*
15 **The Independent**, Tim Neilson (letter), *Sculpture brings good luck to Bow*
17 **The Weekly Telegraph**, Stephen Pile, *Are the old masters really any better?*
17 **The Guardian**, Robin Hunt, *The House that Rachel built*
17 **The Independent**, Peter Merry/Eric Flounders (letters), *'House' should be demolished*
20 **The Independent**, Various (letters), *'House' fits the neighbourhood*
20 **The Times**, Richard Morrison, *Good taste art?*
20 **The Spectator**, Giles Auty, *Prized apart*
20 **The Spectator**, Simon Jenkins, *Art house in a cul-de-sac*
20-26 **The Economist**, *Rice v paint*
21 **Sunday Telegraph**, *Decision day looms for the best and worst of the Turner Prize*
21 **Sunday Independent**, *A Critical Guide*
21 **Sunday Express**, Brian Sewell/Simon Wilson, *Tate and bile*
21 **Sunday Express**, Brigit Grant, *State of the art*
21 **Sunday Times Magazine**, *Without walls: The Turner Prize*
21 **Independent on Sunday**
22 **The Times**, *Rewarding Art*
22 **The Guardian**, *Home Truths*
23 **Eastern Daily Press**, *Turner's odd legacy*
23 **The Independent**, Heath *(cartoon)*
23 **Sunday Times**, Sally Payne, *Critic's Choice*
23 **Daily Telegraph**, Richard Dorment, *Turner: most radical of the lot*
23 **The Times**, Richard Cork, *Paintpots flung in the face of apathy*
23 **The Guardian**, *Pass Notes: Nicholas Serota*
23 **Evening Standard**, *Channel 4 Listings*
24 **The Times**, Alison Roberts, *Turner's best equals the worst*
24 **Daily Express**, Margaret Hussey, *This building won a £20,000 art prize ...*
24 **Daily Telegraph**, Susannah Herbert/Victoria Combe, *Balaclava bonus for Turner winner*
24 **Financial Times**, *News: UK*
24 **Daily Mail**, Bill Mouland, *Disaster in plaster*
24 **The Guardian**, Mike Ellison/Lawrence Donegan, *Cadillac terrorists carve up sculptor*
24 **The Guardian**, *Front page*
24 **The Independent**, David Lister, *Turner Prize won by the 'worst' artist in Britain*
24 **Evening Standard**, Tim Cooper, *The Turner winner and my night with the art 'terrorists'*
24 **Evening Standard**, Robin Stringer, *Bizarre night as £60,000 sculptor is the best and worst*
24 **Evening Standard**, Tim Cooper, *My mystery tour with the masked 'terrorists' of art*
24 **Construction News**, *Rachel casts an image of how the East End lives*
24 **San Francisco Chronicle**, *Sculptor Wins Prize for Rooms of Concrete*
24 **The Independent**, Andrew Graham-Dixon, *I don't know much about art, but I know what I hate...*
24 **Yorkshire Post**, *Sculpture takes prize*
24 **The Yorkshire Evening Post**, *Rachel's House floors critics*
24 **Manchester Evening News**, *Rachel puts cash where her art is*
24 **Kent Today**, *Bad mix for concrete*
24 **The Northampton Chronicle & Echo**, *Sculptress in casting conundrum*
24 **Evening Echo**, *'Worst artist' wins prize*
24 **The Nottingham Evening Post**, *The art of success - and failure*
24 **The Birmingham Evening Mail**, *'Double prize' for Rachel*
24 **Eastern Daily Press (Norwich)**, *£20,000 for an inside view of sculpture*
24 **The Birmingham Evening Mail**, *Best artist is 'worst'*
24 **Evening News**, *Top sculptress lands contrasting awards*
24 **Evening Courier**, *Sculptress shows her best and worst side*
24 **The Echo Southampton**, *'Worst' wins top award*
24 **The Huddersfield Daily**, *Worst award for top sculptress*
24 **The Wigan Evening Post**, *Rachel best and worst*
24 **The Birmingham Post**, *Concrete interior design is a winner*
24 **Shropshire Star**, *Artist Rachel takes the good with the bad*
24 **The Nottingham Evening Post**, *Art of success ... and failure*
25 **The Times**, Peter Brookes *(cartoon)*
25 **The Guardian**, Hugo Young, *Politicians who give no House room to art*
25 **The Independent**, Eric Flounders (letter), *Timetable for Bow sculpture*
25 **East London Advertiser**, Richard Tidiman, *Quite a Turn Up*
25 **The Guardian**, Deyan Sudjic, *Art attack*
25 **The Guardian**, Mike Ellison, *Ups and downs for art House*
25 **Financial Times**, Banx *(cartoon)*
25 **The Guardian**, Steve Bell, *Belfast Turner Prize sensation (cartoon)*
25 **Evening Standard**, Tim Cooper, *Who failed the £1,600 art test?*
25 **East London Advertiser**, Ulla Kloster, *Rachel's joy falls flat as well as her House*
25 **Evening Standard**, Jak *(cartoon)*
25 **Daily Telegraph**, Garland *(cartoon)*
25 **Western Morning News - East Devon**, *£40,000 gesture by artist Rachel*
25 **The Press and Journal**, *Worst artist*
25 **Yorkshire Post**, *Sculptor's £40,000 cast-off*

25 **Hannoversche Allgemeine Zeitung**, Peter Fischer, *Die Totenmaske eines Einfamilienhauses*

25 **Frankfurter Rundschau**, Peter Fischer, *Monstrum oder Meisterwerk?*

26 **The Herald**, Clare Henry, *No room for House?*

26 **Daily Telegraph**, Susannah Herbert, *A man with muscle for Palumbo's post*

26 **Daily Mail**, Andrew Alexander, *An art to being daft*

26 **Daily Express**, Frances Hubbard, *Has taking us for a cultural ride become a new art form?*

26 **The Independent**, *Putting public gain above private prejudice*

26 **The Echo**

26 **Rotherham Advertiser**, Tony Cape

26 **Frankfurter Allgemeine Zeitung**, *Ist es Kunst?*

26 **Shropshire Star**, *For pity's sake, Rachel, you don't call this art?*

26 **The Hull Daily Mail**, *Drinks are on the House*

27 **Financial Times**, Antony Thorncroft, *Prize bed of nails*

27 **The Times**, Andrew Pierce, *MP urges public to save 'monstrosity'*

27 **The Times**, James Lingwood, *Our house is a very nice house*

27 **The Independent**, Tim Dickenson (letter), *More time for 'House'*

27 **Nürnberger Zeitung**, Peter Fischer, *Monstrum oder Meisterwerk?*

27 **Kultur**, Freidrich Meschede, *Die Bauform der Erinnerung*

27 **Neue Bürcher Zeitung Feuilleton**, George Waser, *Beste und schlechteste Künsterlin*

28 **Sunday Independent**, Colm Toibin, *Spoofers, chancers ... and artists*

28 **Sunday Independent**, Jim Cogan *(cartoon)*

28 **Sunday Independent (Ireland)**, Patrick Gallagher, *The rice of Vong*

28 **Planning Week**, *A Statement carved in concrete*

28 **Mail On Sunday**, Daniel Farson, *A Turner for the worse*

28 **Sunday Times**, David Mills, *A conspiracy of theorists*

28 **Sunday Telegraph**, John McEwen, *Just who are the real dunces?*

28 **The Observer**, Peter Hillmore, *Is this death of the artist or wot?*

28 **The Observer**, Richard Ingrams

28 **The Independent**, Rachel Whiteread, *Overheard*

28 **Radio 2**, *Hayes on Sunday*

29 **The Independent**, James Lingwood, Richard Shone (letters), *Private prejudice, public interest and Bow's 'House'*

29 **The Times**, Various (letters), *Modern: but is it 'new' and is it art?*

29 **The Independent**, Marjorie Allthorpe-Guyton (letter), *Monumental Art*

30 **The New York Times**, Roberta Smith, *The Best of Sculptors, the Worst of Sculptors*

30 **The Independent**, Jonathan Glancey, *Not rubbish, and perhaps tomorrow's masterpiece*

Nov/Dec 93

Flash Art, James Lingwood, *We are trying to invert the iceberg*

Parkett 38, Adrian Searle, *Cumulus*

December 93

The Art Newspaper, *Rachel Whiteread a popular choice*

1 **Weekly Telegraph**, *'Bonus' for Turner Prize winner*

1 **Der Tagesspiegel**, Peter Fischer, *Das Meisterwerk wird abgerissen*

1 **The Independent**, Sir Anthony Caro/Peter Forster/Michael Daley (letters), *'House' raises questions of art*

1 **The Guardian**, Eric Flounders (letter), *House room*

1 **The Guardian**, Maev Kennedy, *Huff, puff, but they can't blow it down*

2 **The Independent**, *Sculpture reprieve*

2 **East London Advertiser**, Various (letters), *Make a home for Rachel's House*

2 **East London Advertiser**, Ulla Kloster, *Have an 'art Bow!*

3 **The Times**

3 **The Daily Telegraph**, Prof. Alastair Flattely (letter), *How to change Turner rules*

4 **The Times**, Tom Husband *(cartoon)*

4 **The Guardian**, Peter Lennon, *Home truths for a street fighter*

5 **Guardian Weekly**, Mike Ellison, *Ups and downs for art House*

5 **Sunday Telegraph**, Peter Simple, *House of War*

5 **Sunday Times**, Lynn Barber, *House calls*

6 **Daily Telegraph**, *The joke continues*

6 **Daily Telegraph**, Susannah Herbert, *Wanted: 150 abseiling window-cleaners*

7 **The Times**, Alan Brewer, *But is it art?*

9 **East London Advertiser**, Various (letters), *The Little House of Horrors*

9 **East London Advertiser**, Ulla Kloster, *I quit!*

11 **The Times**, Prof. H.C.Higgins, *But is it art?*

11 **The Spectator**, Giles Auty, *Temporary truce*

13 **Time magazine**, Margot Hornblower, *Wot For? Why Not?*

13 **The Guardian**, Various (letters), *Perils of switching off life-support for the arts*

15 **The Times**, Alison Roberts, *Art house propped up by benefactor*

15 **The Huddersfield Daily Examiner**, Bethany Atkinson, *Hope in our art*

15 **University College London Newsletter**, Janine Ogier, *Whiteread wins Turner Prize*

15 **The Independent**, *'House' reprieved*

16 **The Guardian**, James Lingwood (letter), *House room*

17 **Evening Standard Magazine**, Lucinda Bredin, *Artist: Rachel Whiteread*

17 **The Daily Telegraph**

18 **The Guardian**, Mike Ellison, *Cuts hit small art groups*

21 **The Independent**, *I know about art and I know what I like*

21 **The Big Issue**, Alex, Finchley Rd, *The beauty of a House*

21 **Time Out**, Steve Grant, *Christmas Quiz*

23 **East London Advertiser**, *Santa says: 'Hey, where's the chimney?'*

24 **The Guardian**, *Pictures*

26 **The Observer**, William Feaver, *Exit to the crash of broken paving stones*

26 **The Observer**, *The Arts in 1993 - a quiz for Boxing Day (Question 1. - Art)*

26 **The Observer**, *Quiz of the Year (Maids-a Milking: Question 7)*

31 **The Independent**, Alex Renton/Helen Birch, *Our brilliant year*

31 **The Guardian**, Ian Mayes, *In the house of philistines*

31 **The Guardian**, Suzanne Moore, *She-devils, saints and single mums*

Winter 93/94

Untitled, Tom Lubbock/David Thorp, *Two responses to Rachel Whiteread's House*

Winter 93

The Royal Academy, *Etcetera*

January 94

London Psychogeographical Association Newsletter, *Housey! Housey!*

2 **Sunday Independent**, Jack Hughes, *Cries and Whispers*

2 **The Observer**, Keith Watson, *The go-between set to run and run*

2 **Independent on Sunday**, Charles Nevin, *93 not wanted in '94*

4 **The Independent**, Ian Gale, *Choice*

6 **Evening Standard**, Various including Rachel Whiteread, *Enough of Sewell's off-the-wall remarks*

6 **Evening Standard**, Martin Delgado, *Evening Standard critic stirs up a storm in art world*

7 **The Guardian**, *Pass Notes: Brian Sewell*

7 **The Guardian**, Mike Ellison, *Attack backfires on critic's critic*

8 **The Independent**, Sandra Barwick, *Art's unlikely man in the street*

10 **The Times**, Andrew Pierce, *Concrete house bites the dust*

10 **Evening Standard**, Various (letters), *Why Sewell is such a good art critic*

10 **Evening Chronicle - Bath**, Derek Stollar, *It's controversial, yes: but is this really art?*

11 **Evening Standard**, Jeff Postlewaite, *Coming down, that infamous work of art*

11 **The Huddersfield Daily Examiner**, *'Eyesore' coming down*

11-17 **The Big Issue**, Mark Abraham (letter), *Bringing the House down*

11-19 **Time Out**, Brian Sewell (Quote), *Fast and loose*

12 **The Independent**, Andrew Graham-Dixon, *Artless earthmover finally brings 'House' down*

12 **Daily Telegraph**, Ben Fenton, *Demolition man breaks prize-winner's art*

12 **Daily Mail**, Bill Mouland, *Art house collapses as digger breaks the mould*

12 **The Guardian**, Mike Ellison, *Digger's quick work brings the House down*

12 **The Times**, Alison Roberts, *Best and worst of art bites the dust*

12 **The Times**, *People in the Times*

12 **Docklands Recorder**, *Sculpture finally bites dust*

13 **East London Advertiser**, Ulla Kloster, *Bringing the House down*

13 **Evening Standard**, Francis Joseph (letter), *Hostility House*

14 **The Independent**, Various (letters), *Final farewell to 'House' of mixed repute*

14 **Hackney Gazette**, *'House' crashes to earth*

15 **Financial Times**, Lynn MacRitchie, *The end of the house that Rachel built*

15 **The Independent**, *Brooke's turn in the park*

15 **The Independent Magazine**, The Weasel, *Up & Down The City Road*

16 **The Sunday Times**, Tim Rayment, *The art of confusion: a pile of toilet rolls and chocolate walls*

16 **Sunday Independent**, Rachel Whiteread (Quote), *Overheard*

16 **Sunday Independent**, Joe Cullen (Quote), *Quotes of the week*

22 **The Independent Magazine**, Len Clarke (letter), *House room in America*

24 **The Guardian**, James Hall, *The brickslayers*

24 **Evening Chronicle - Bath**, Derek Stollar, *Museum art is better than no art at all*

Jan/Feb 94

Frieze, Adrian Searle, *Rachel doesn't live here any more*

Kunst-Bulletin, Friedrich Meschede, *London: Rachel Whiteread in der Grove Road*

February 94

The Art Newspaper, Martin Bailey, *Seriously Subversive Art: real banknotes*

21 **Asahi Shimbun Weekly**, *Aera*

Feb/Mar 94

Galeries Magazine, *The News*

Art & Text, Andrew Renton, *A Song from under the Floorboards*

March 94

Art Monthly, Eric Troncy, *Dis engagement*

Mar/Apr 94

Sculpture, David Cohen, *Reviews*

April 94

Art & Antiques, Angela Choon, *Rebels of the Realm*

May 94

The Face, Ekow Eshun, *British Art Special*

Contemporary Art, David Thistlewood, *Reflections on the demolition of House*

house: a chronology 1991-1994

1991
Autumn First discussions between Rachel Whiteread and James Lingwood of Artangel

1992
February Whiteread makes first preparatory drawings

Spring Research into possible locations in East and North London
Beck's agrees to commission project with Artangel

Summer Unsuccessful approaches made to secure permission to use properties in Islington and Hackney

October Rachel Wyndham identifies Grove Road as a potential location. At this stage, a large proportion of the terrace is still standing. The tenant of 193 Grove Road, Sydney Gale, is approached about Whiteread's idea.
Neil Thomas of Atelier One agrees to draw up structural plans

1993
March 11 Public Meeting of Bow Parks Board to consider Artangel's request for a temporary lease on 193 Grove Road. Councillors vote in favour by a majority of 4 to 3 in the absence of the Chair, Cllr Eric Flounders

March 12 Chair of Bow Parks Board requests that the decision is reconsidered

March 18 Public Meeting of Bow Standing Neighbourhood Committee confirms the original decision with a guaranteed timetable. Artangel is advised that Mr Gale will move in May

May The remaining terraced houses apart from 193 Grove Road and the two houses on either side are knocked down by demolition companies working on Bow Neighbourhood's behalf

June 17 Contracts are exchanged between Artangel and Bow Neighbourhood for lease of 193 Grove Road until October 31 at a peppercorn rent. Artangel agrees to have the site restored as parkland by November 30. Dissatisfied with the alternatives offered by the Council, Mr Gale and his family do not move out

July 30 Council advises Artangel that Mr Gale is about to leave

August 2 Artangel take possession of vacated property. Whiteread and her team begin to clear the interior and prepare walls for casting

August 30 New foundations laid to support the cast

September 5 Tarmac Structural Repairs begin gunnite spraying process. Continue for 5 weeks

October 12 Scaffolding is put up around the house and the process of removing the exterior walls and roof begins

October 24 First national press appears

October 25 The making of *House* is complete. Small opening reception in Victoria Park
For newspaper response over the following weeks, refer to list on pp.140–143

Informal discussions begin with Bow councillors about extending the lease of *House*, and are initially encouraging

November 8 Cllr. Flounders refuses to table any request for an extension. Later agrees to discuss it at special closed meeting called for 23 November

November 23
14.00 pm Whiteread is awarded the K Foundation prize of £40,000 for 'worst' artist in Britain

19.30 pm Bow Neighbourhood refuse to grant an extension of the lease on 193 Grove Road and demand the immediate demolition of *House*

21.30 pm Whiteread is awarded the 1993 Turner Prize at the Tate Gallery live on Channel 4 Television. Makes short acceptance speech and condemns Bow's decision

November 24 Explosion of media interest. Bow Neighbourhood Centre besieged by calls and faxes

November 26 Early day motion tabled by Mildred Gordon MP and Hugh Bayley MP, calling for Tower Hamlets to allow *House* to remain for three months so that local people can properly be consulted. Motion eventually collects over 50 signatures. Karsten Schubert puts together a consortium of organizations and individuals including Channel 4 and Beck's who offer to lease the site from Bow

November 26 Petition calling for *House* to stay collects over 3500 signatures on site in 12 hours. A counter petition urging its demolition collects 800 signatures over the coming weeks from local residents

December 10 Bow Neighbourhood agrees in principle to lease the site until January 12, 1994

December 22 Extension to lease is finally agreed by Cllr. Flounders

1994
January 11 *House* is demolished

March 10 Site of *House* turfed over